MW00624363

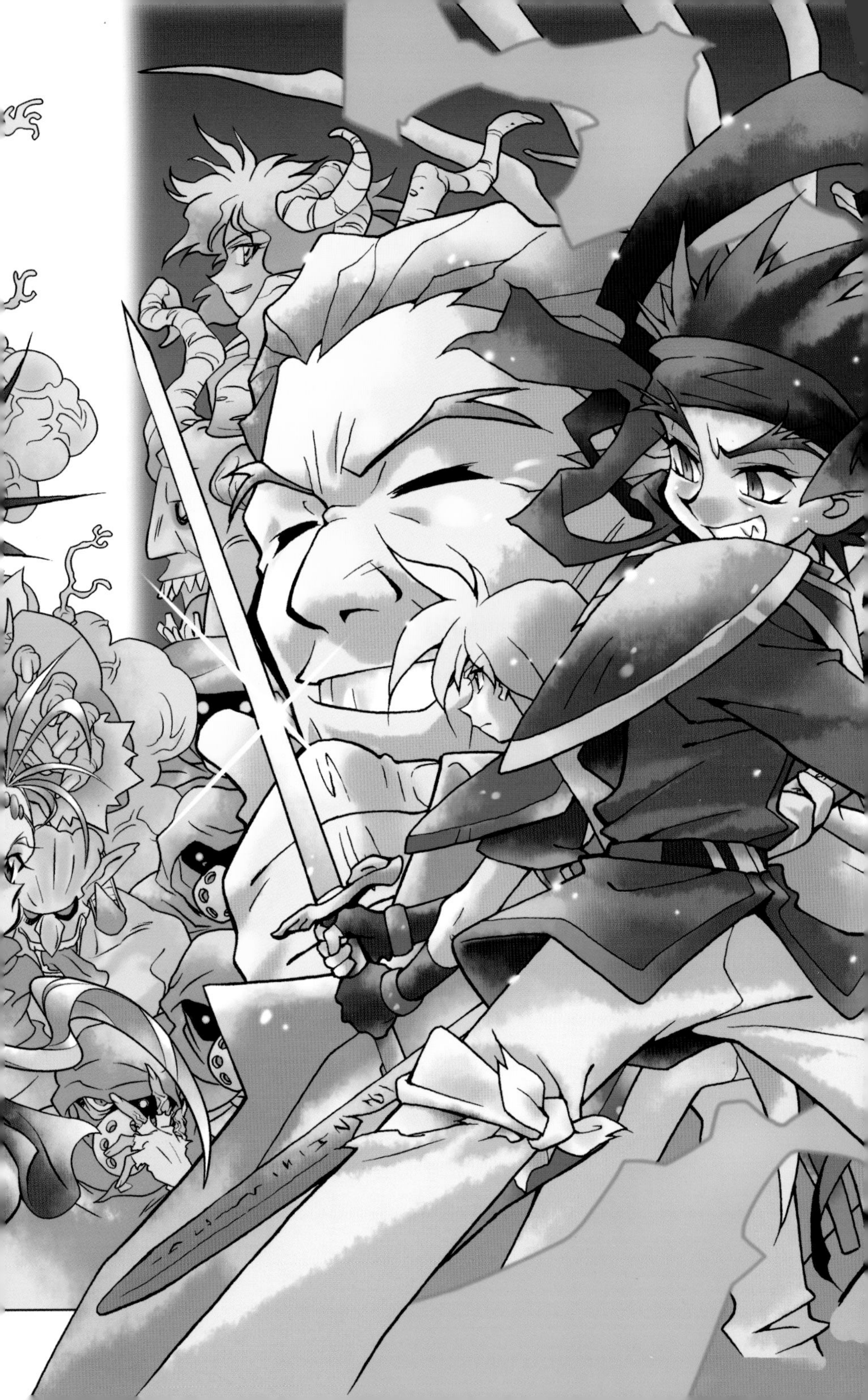

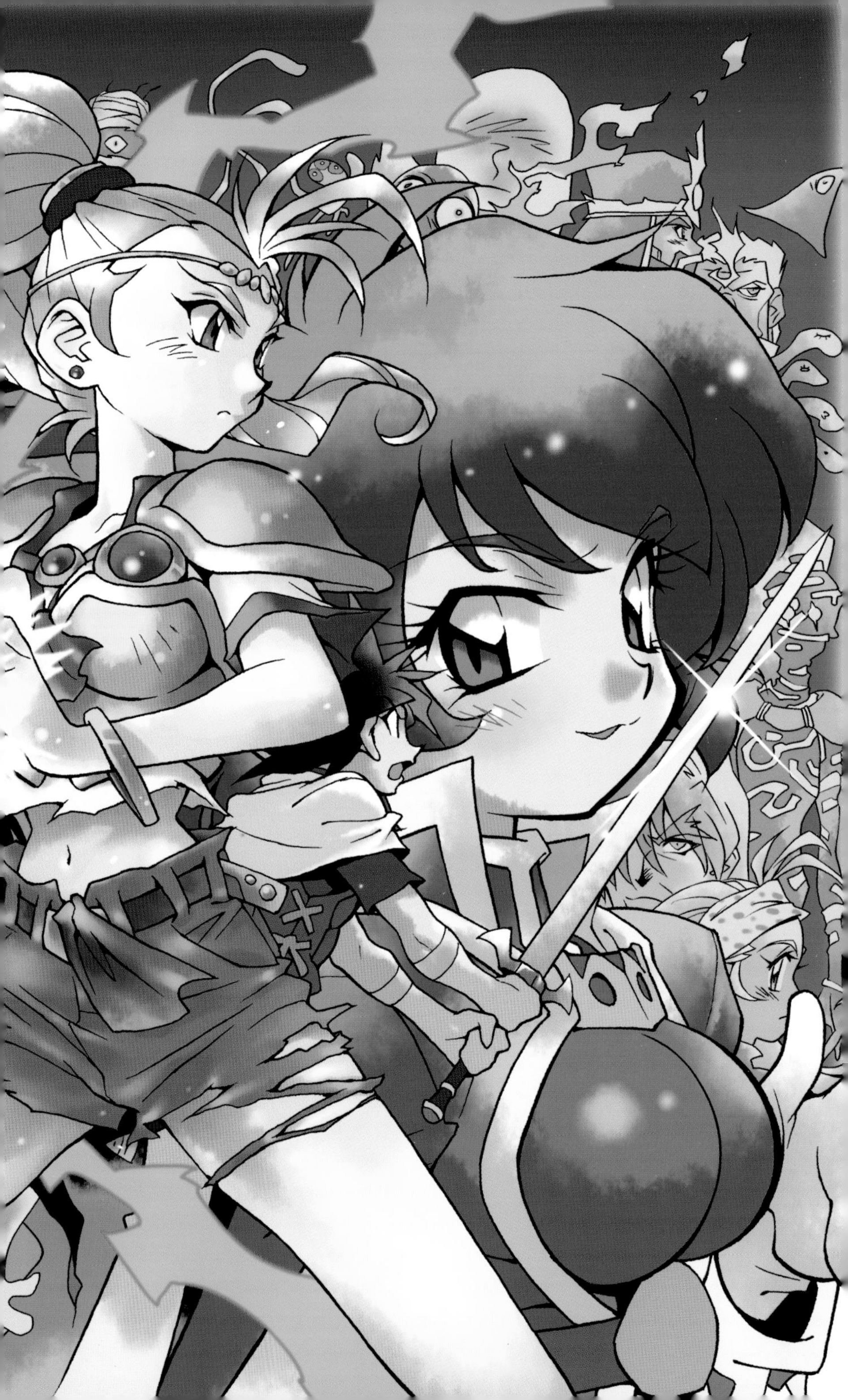

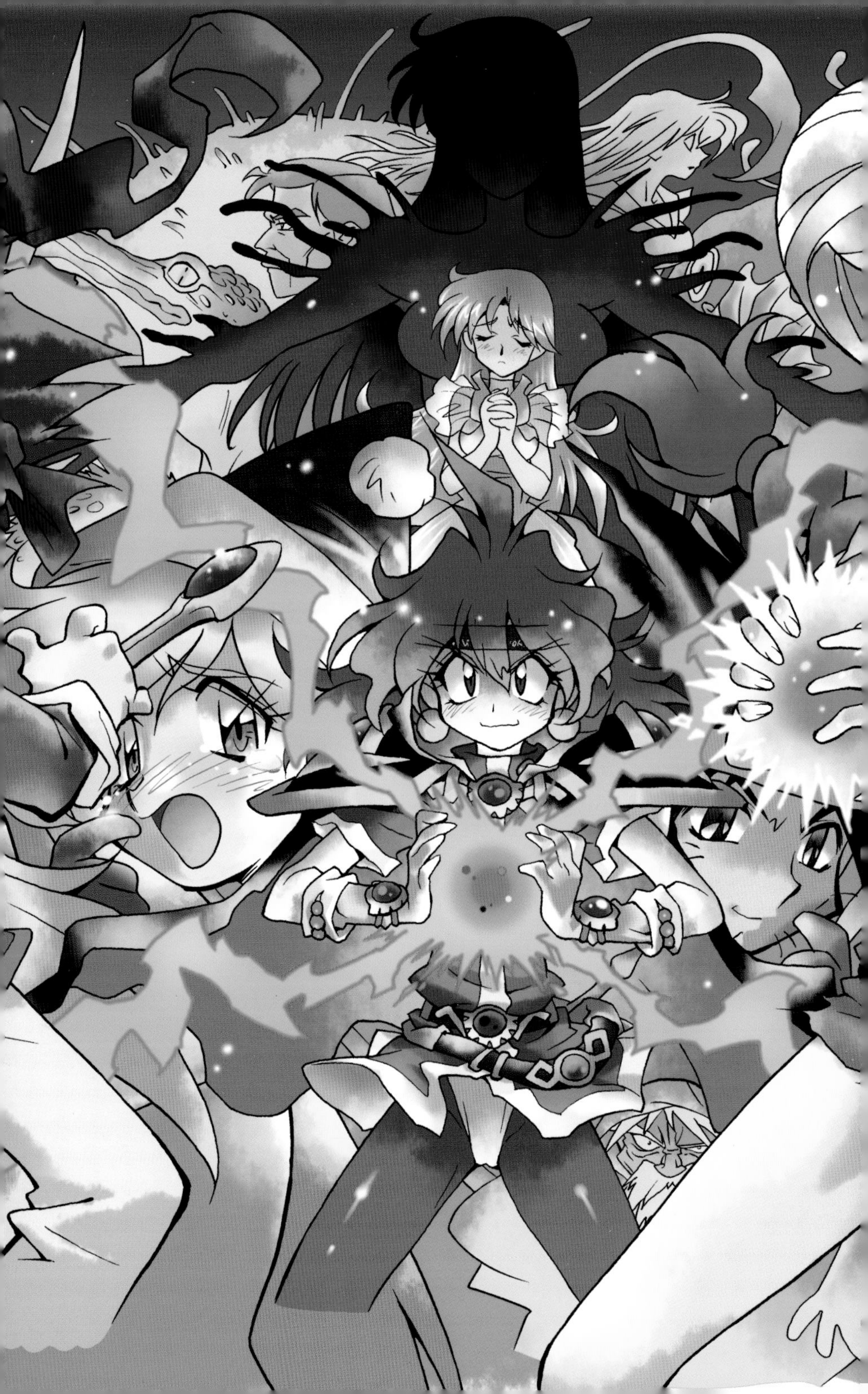

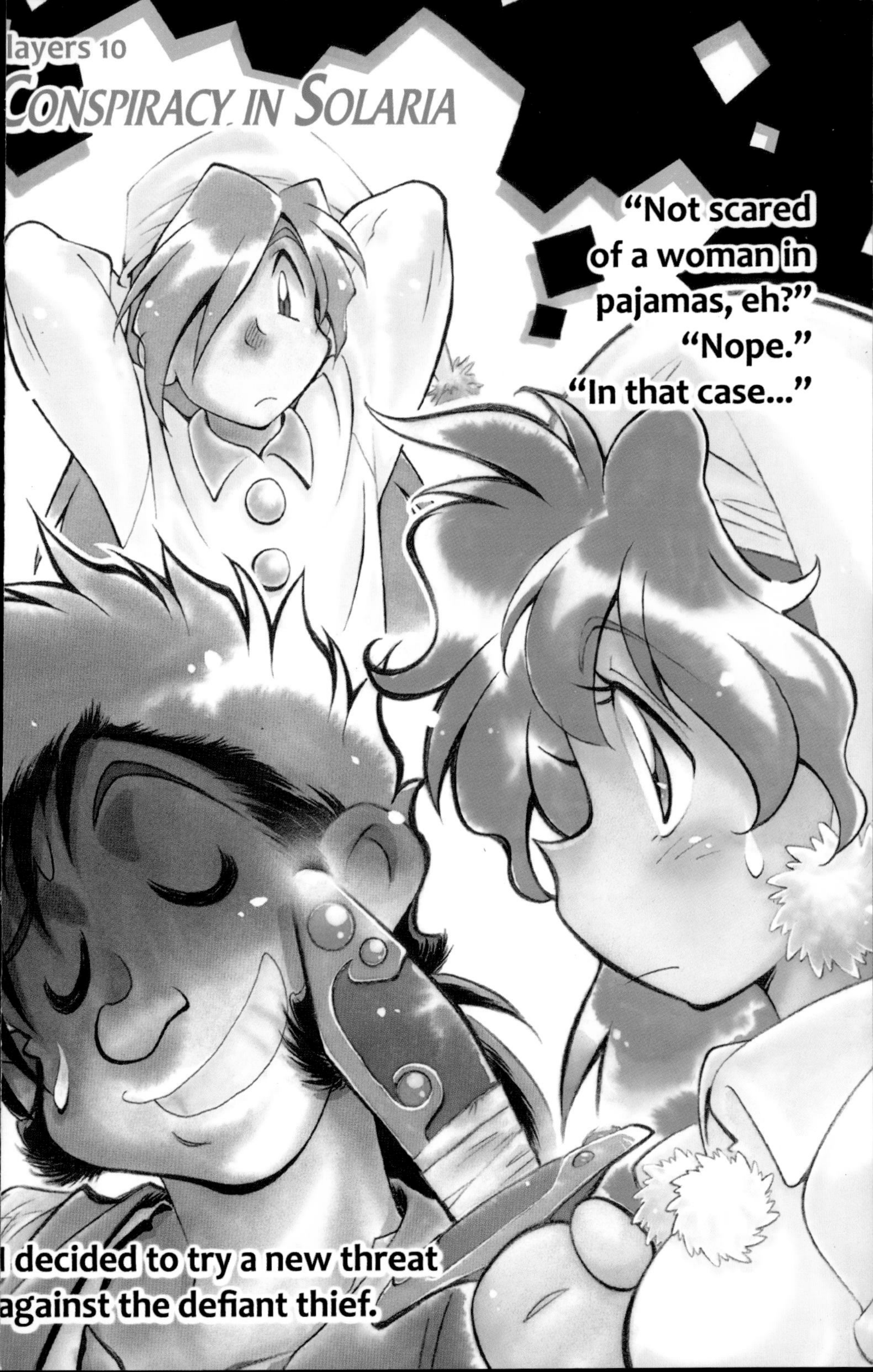

layers 10
CONSPIRACY IN SOLARIA
"Not scared of a woman in pajamas, eh?"
"Nope."
"In that case..."
I decided to try a new threat against the defiant thief.

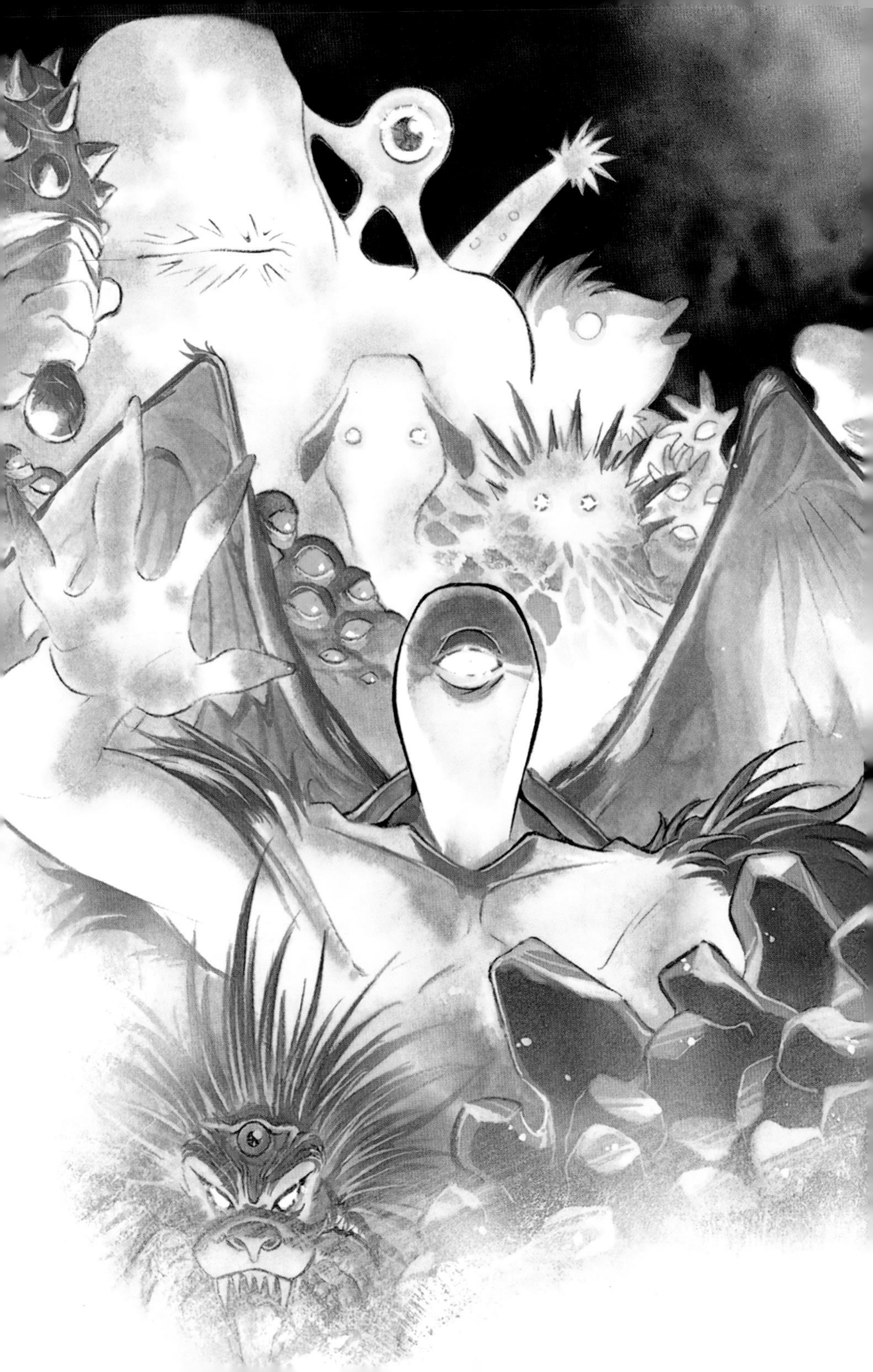

The sealed chimeras flooded out from the broken tubes!

With a magnificently timed sweep,
Luke cut deep into Zord's side.
But then.

DELUSION IN CRIMSON

"Huh... Guess something's up."

We were about to enter the town when I spotted something displayed on the stone gatepost...

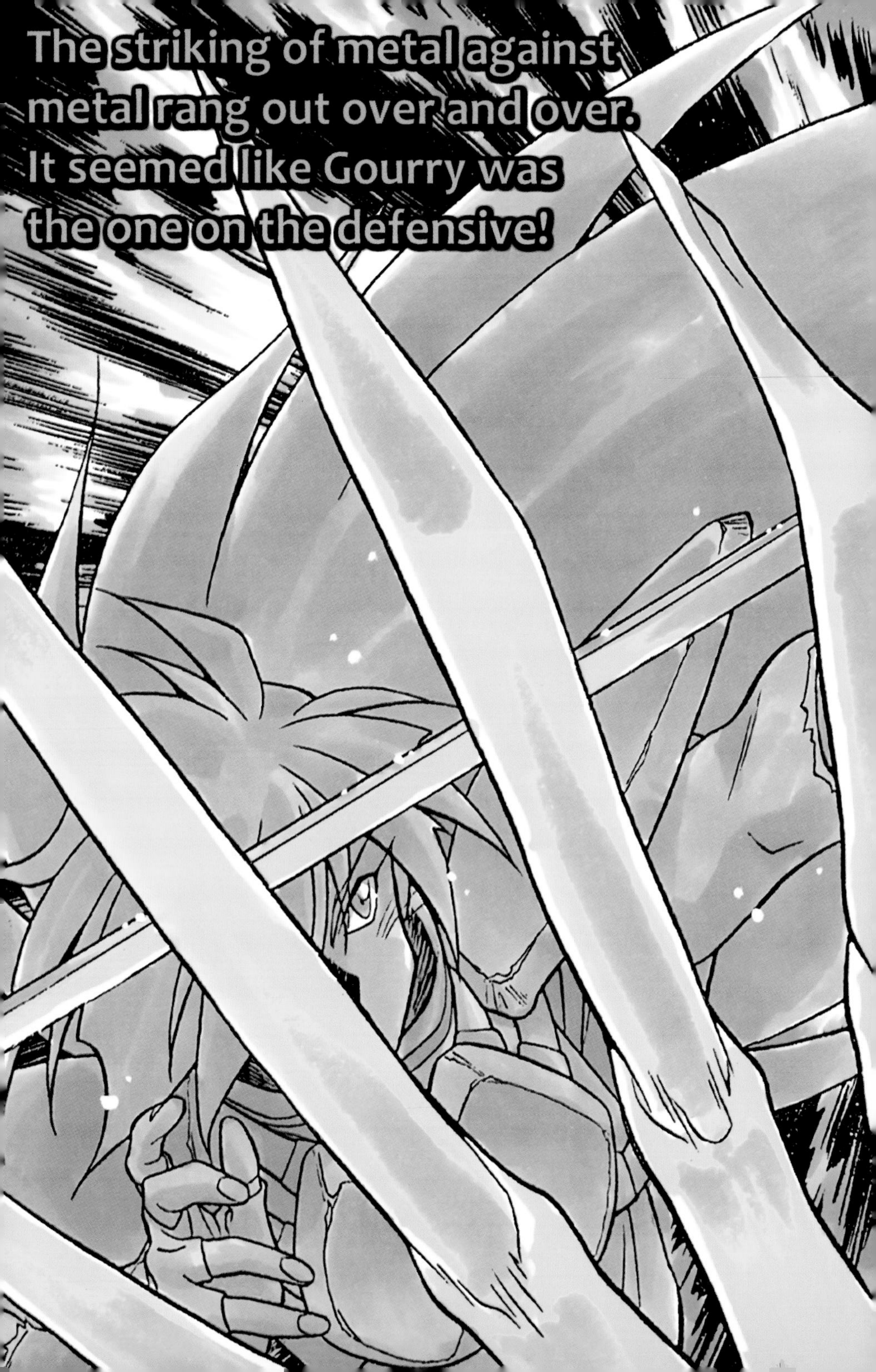
The striking of metal against metal rang out over and over. It seemed like Gourry was the one on the defensive!

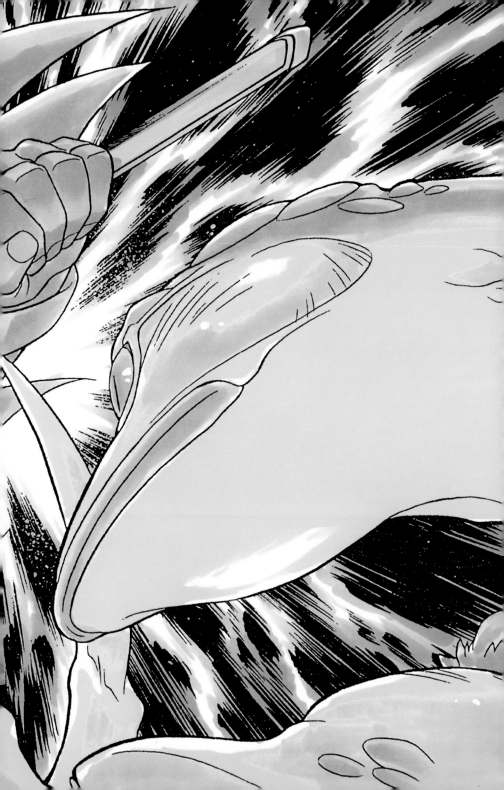

I could already
feel the warmth
leaving his body.
I knew what it felt
like when someone
was dying.

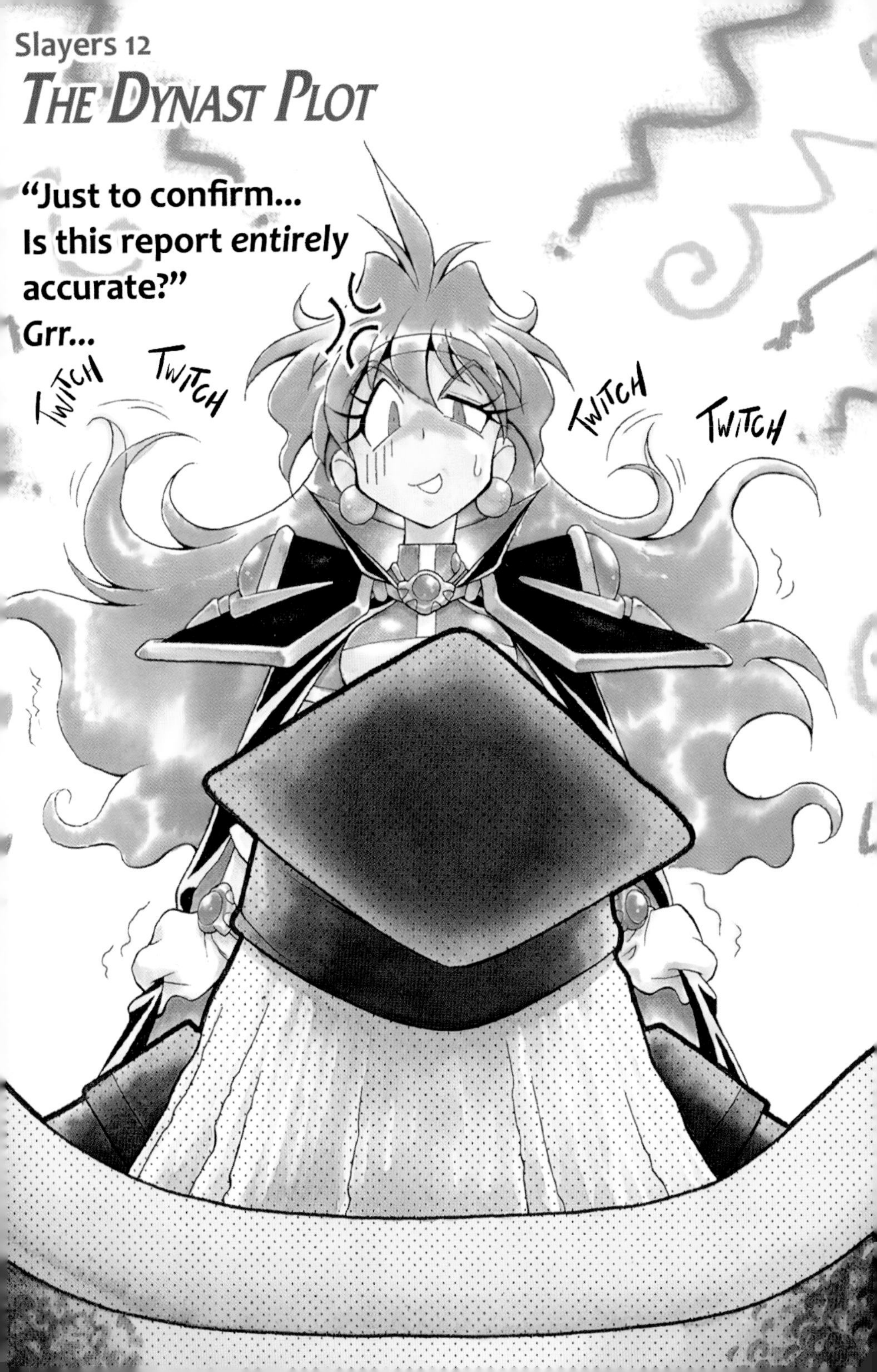
Slayers 12
THE DYNAST PLOT
"Just to confirm... Is this report *entirely* accurate?"
Grr...
TWITCH
TWITCH
TWITCH
TWITCH

"Looks like you got wrapped up in more weird crap...
So how long are you two gonna play piggyback?"

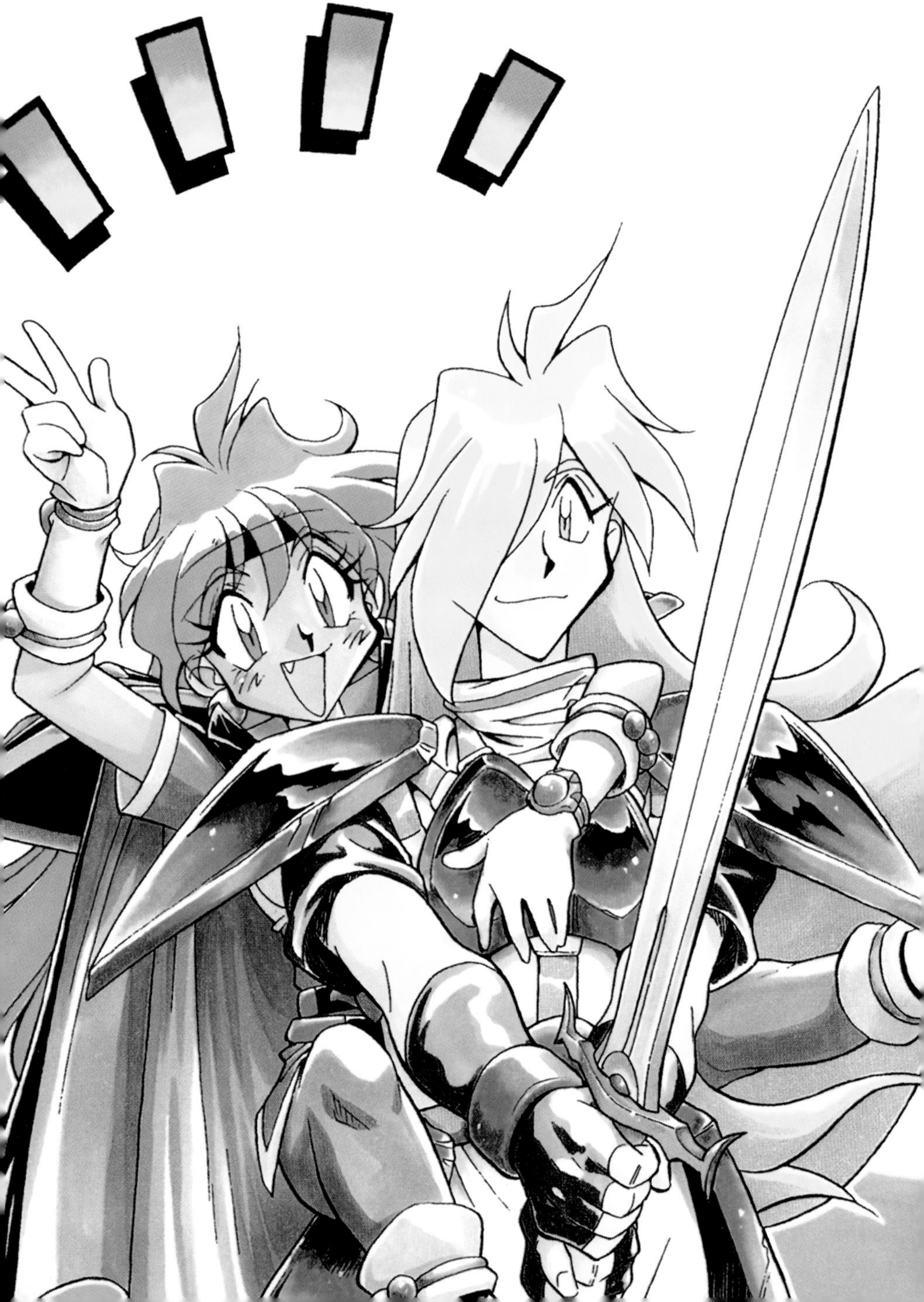

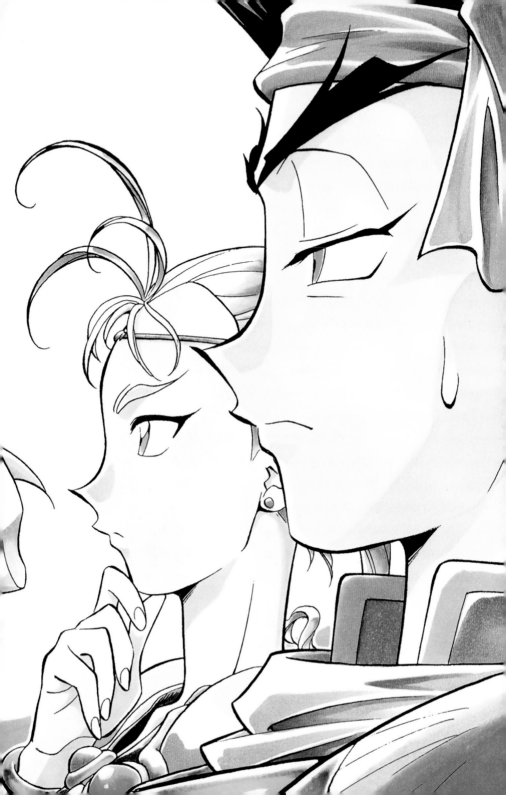

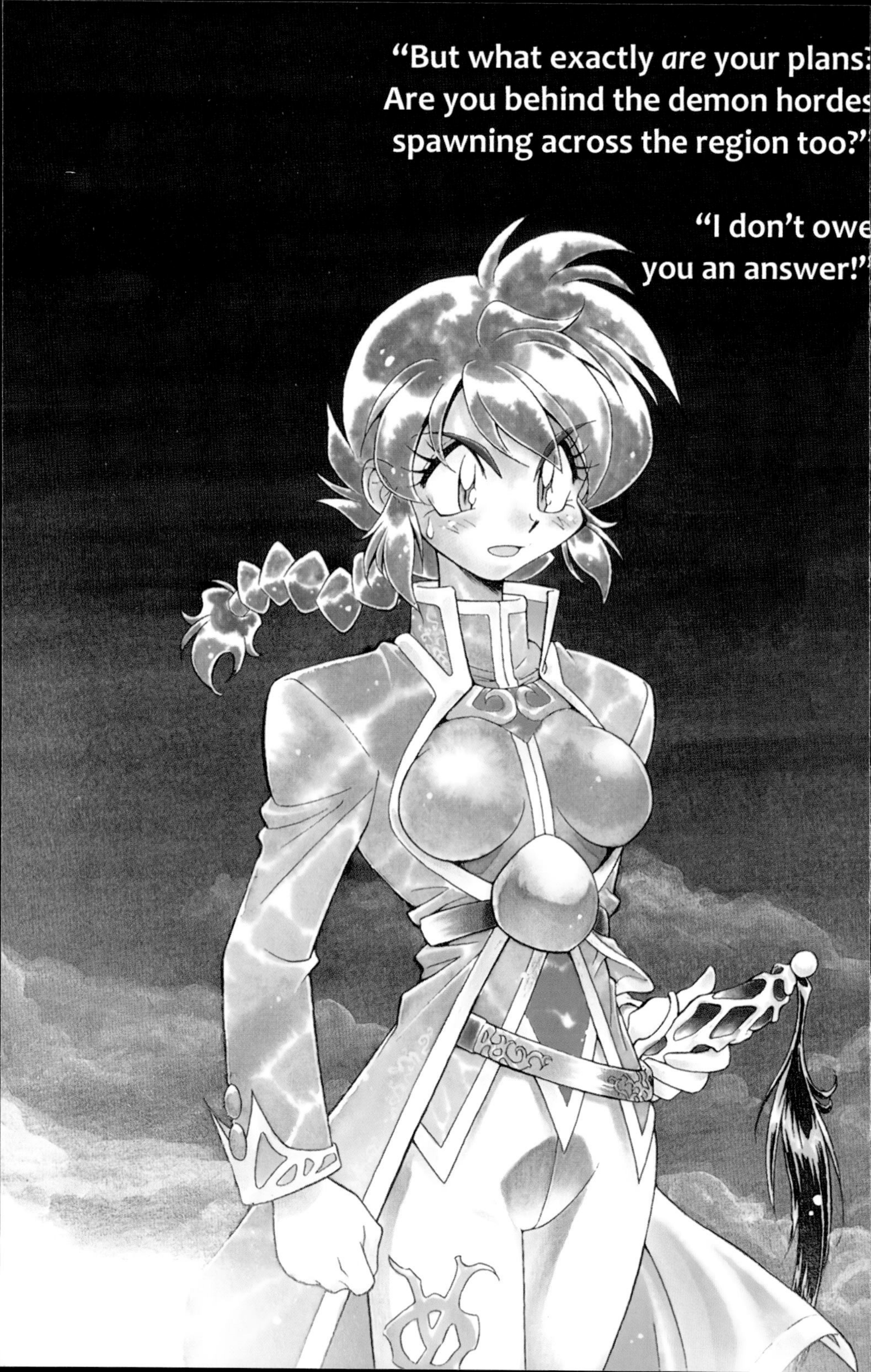
“But what exactly *are* your plans?
Are you behind the demon hordes
spawning across the region too?”
“I don’t owe
you an answer!”

Collector's Edition 4

By Hajime Kanzaka
Illustrations by Rui Araizumi

Slayers: Collector's Edition Volume 4
by Hajime Kanzaka

Translated by Elizabeth Ellis
Edited by Megan Denton
Layout by Cheree Smith
English Logo by Pekka "Vodoka" Luhtala
English Print Cover by Kelsey Denton

Copyright ©Hajime Kanzaka, Rui Araizumi 2008
Illustrations by Rui Araizumi

SLAYERS Vol. 10
SLAYERS Vol. 11
SLAYERS Vol. 12
First published in Japan in 2008 by KADOKAWA CORPORATION, Tokyo
English translation rights arranged with KADOKAWA CORPORATION, Tokyo

Find more books like this one at https://j-novel.club!

Managing Director: Samuel Pinansky
Light Novel Line Manager: Kristine Johnson
Managing Translator: Kristi Iwashiro
Managing Editor: Regan Durand
QA Manager: Hannah N. Carter
Marketing Manager: Stephanie Hii
Project Manager: Nikki Lapshinoff

ISBN: 978-1-7183-7513-0
Printed in Korea
First Printing: September 2023
10 9 8 7 6 5 4 3 2 1

CONTENTS

By Hajime Kanzaka

Illustrations by Rui Araizumi

CONTENTS

Chapter 1:   Another Day, Another Magic Sword Search

The desolate ruins were steeped in darkness. Gourry and I held our breath, searching for any sign of movement. Dim light radiated from the glowing magical orb over our heads as silent moment after silent moment passed. There came a shadowy flicker in the light. And then, after an instant that felt both all too short and dreadfully long... it appeared.

Gourry! I wanted to shout, but before I could, he turned to face the presence emerging from the wall.

"Hyah!" With a cry of effort, he took a great slash with his sword!

I could hear the hum of a collapsing vacuum as he cut through the thing coming out of the wall—the ghost. *Greeeee!* It let out an ear-splitting squeal as it disappeared in a puff of white mist.

"Did I... do it?" Gourry asked, keeping his fighting posture.

I nodded firmly in response.

"All rrright! I did it!" Gourry beamed, raising his sword triumphantly.

I stood there at something of a loss for how to react to Gourry's revelry. I mean... it was just a ghost, man. Nothing *that* exciting.

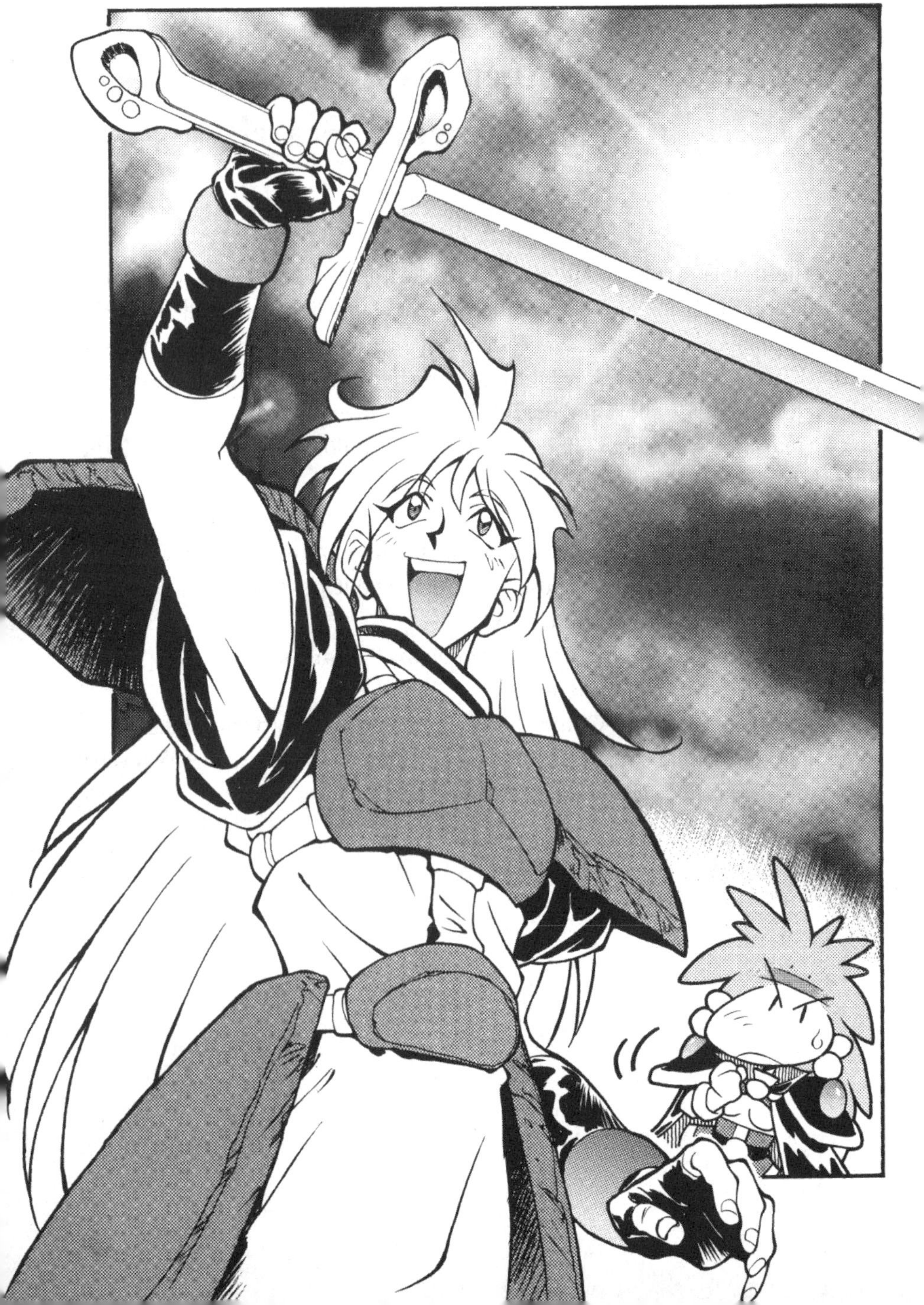

"Seriously, cutting down one dang ghost isn't anything to write home about," I was still muttering to myself as we sat eating dinner in a small establishment.

"But I've never had a sword that could hurt ghosts before... so I think it's pretty great, personally," Gourry responded lightly as he shoveled down some fried sardines.

I replied with a deep sigh, "What about the Sword of Light before, man?! Don't tell me you forgot that already!"

"Why would I forget?" Gourry asked, completely unfazed.

Darn it...

The Sword of Light was one of the most legendary magic weapons known to man. It appeared in many a minstrel's saga, and there wasn't a sorcerer out there who hadn't heard its name. Said incredible magic sword was formerly in the possession of Gourry Numbnuts here... but he'd lost it as the result of a particular series of events. So here we were, off on a long, meandering journey to find him a replacement magic sword.

Now, you might be thinking, "What, can't he make do with a normal sword?" And if so, the joke's on you, buddy. There are baddies in this world that a regular ol' sword can't even scratch—and I mean that literally. The weakest are your ghost-type creepies; the strongest are your pure demons. Now, if ghosts were our biggest worry, then sure, Gourry could just kick back while I dished out the old attack spell buffet. But demons? They required, let's say, a more layered approach.

In truth, we'd had to fight a demon recently, and I gotta say... Gourry with a mundane sword just hadn't cut it. That whole encounter lit a fire under my ass about getting him a magic sword—any magic sword at all—so I'd picked up a stopgap at a magic shop in town the other day. Pretty much the only reason we'd taken the crummy banish-the-ghost-from-the-creepy-old-ruins-for-chump-change job was to give his new blade a test run.

"Okay, Gourry. Listen up," I said, waving my fork around meaninglessly. "That sword can slay a ghost, true, but it's still just a standard silver-plated blade inlaid with a couple of jeweled talismans. It ain't gonna do squat against a sorcerer's Flare Arrows, much less a pure demon. Also, this might go without saying, but it *will* break if you put enough force into it."

"Aha…" Gourry paused in his eating and stared keenly at the sword leaning against the table. He then grumbled, "So it's cheap."

"It's cheap, huh?! Just who do you think paid for that thing?! I mean, sure, as magic swords go, it is more on the budget-friendly side… But it was still ten times more expensive than any normal sword!"

"Oh, so it's expensive?"

"Yes! So be careful with it, okay? You should probably treat it mostly like you would a normal sword. Got it?"

Gourry just hummed and scratched his head in confusion.

"For your information… if you're about to say 'I wasn't listening' or 'I was listening but I already forgot what you said,' I'm gonna lay you out flat, so don't even think about it."

"No, I was listening, and I remember what you said. It can't cut through magic or demons, and it'll break if I'm too rough with it, right?"

Wow! The big lug actually listened for once! "Then what's with the hemming and hawing?"

"Well… I can remember all that now. I'm just wondering if I'll still remember when it comes time to use it."

"Don't be so self-defeating! Make a commitment to remember!" I shouted, skewering some chicken teriyaki, which I immediately shoved into my mouth and gulped down. "That sword is gonna have to last you until we find a better one, so freaking be careful with it already!"

"R-Right…" Gourry nodded firmly, perhaps too cowed to argue, as he snagged a fried shrimp with the fork in his other hand.

Don't accuse me of nagging, okay? That thing cost me a fortune! Even at the cheapest price possible as a secondhand article, a sword with talismans means a through-the-nose surcharge.

"But Lina, do you really think we're going to find a powerful magic sword? We've been searching for a few months now, and all the rumors we hear turn out to be frauds and fakes."

"I admit finding one won't be easy, but we'll do it someday. I believe it. There's always a chance," I said, echoing wisdom a golden dragon elder had once shared with me. I followed up with a sip of hot black tea to wash down my meal.

Later that night, I was awoken—*Thump*—by some kind of sound.

Hmm? I listened hard for a while, still lying in bed in my room at the inn. Nothing reached my ears but the rustle of the wind and insects buzzing outside my window.

Just my imagination? I wondered. But then...

Thump. Whomp-omp!

This time, I could clearly hear the noise coming from the next room— Gourry's. It didn't sound like someone rolling out of bed either. It almost sounded like a scuffle...

Fwsh! I silently threw off my blanket, grabbed just my shortsword, and strode out of my room in my pajamas. I stood on guard outside of Gourry's door.

"Gourry? What's up?!" I called.

"Oh, hey, Lina. Got a visitor is all," Gourry responded in his usual laid-back way.

A visitor?!

"Come on in," he offered. "It's open."

Curious, I pushed the door inward. Gourry's rather small room was illuminated by the dim orange glow of a single lamp, accompanied by the distinctive smell of burning animal fat. Gourry stood in the middle of the place... over an unfamiliar man who lay unconscious on the floor.

"Hiya, Lina," Gourry said lightly, holding up a hand in greeting.

"What in the world...?" I nudged the head of the unconscious man with my sheathed sword. "Would this so-called 'visitor' actually be a burglar?"

"Hey, good guess!"

"It seems pretty obvious, given his current state..."

I took the opportunity to root through the guy's pockets, find some rope, and tie his hands behind his back with it. He'd probably thought he'd be the one tying someone up tonight. Rotten luck that he'd chosen Gourry's room to infiltrate... My dude had animallike senses, so it would take more than your average intruder to break into his room undetected.

"There we go!" I said as I pulled the knot tight with gusto.

"Geh..." Just as I finished up, the man opened up his eyes with a groan. "Ah! Crap!"

Realizing the situation he was in, he instantly began to struggle. I'd tied him too tightly for that to work though (natch).

"You can't wriggle your way out of this one, pal," I informed him. "Give it a rest already."

"Ngh!" The man glared at me but ceased his resistance.

"Now... how's about we ask a few questions? What were you planning to steal out of this room?"

No answer. The man just gave me the silent treatment.

Why interrogate him instead of just taking him to the authorities, you ask? Ha! Amateurs! Cities rife with petty burglaries are frequently home to a fence operation or two. If I got him to point us to their home base, I could raid it and net myself a double- or triple-dip of profits.

"We've got a few other ways of making you talk, y'know," I said, pressing the tip of my sheathed sword against him.

But the man, cool as a cucumber, replied, "You think I'm scared of a little girl in her pajamas?"

Oh, right... I *was* still in my pajamas. Not exactly my most intimidating moment, huh? *Okay, then let's try this!*

"Not scared of a woman in pajamas, eh?"

"Nope."

"In that case..." I pointed over at Gourry. "How'd you like being propositioned by a man in *his* pajamas?!"

"Whaaaaat?!" The man let out a scream, apparently appalled by the thought.

Gourry didn't seem fond of the idea either, but I ignored his plaintive expression.

"D-Don't tell me... he's..." the man faltered with a fearful glance at Gourry. "He's into *that?!*"

"You bet he is," I responded unflinchingly.

"Hey..." Gourry finally spoke up, but I kept ignoring him.

"F-Fine! I'll talk, I'll talk! Just spare me, please!" This threat induced the man to struggle and cry.

Wait... did this guy have bad memories or something? Dang... But questions about his past aside, it looked like he was willing to talk now.

"First, why come after us? And don't try to tell me it was a coincidence, okay?" I pressed.

"Yeeeeek! I won't, I won't!" The man shot another uneasy glance at Gourry. "I… I overheard you… in the restaurant… You were saying you had a magic sword, yeah? I thought I could sell it for some good money."

"I see… So you know someone who's paying top coin for magic swords, eh?"

"W-Well… sort of, I think…" the man responded vaguely.

"And? Who is it?"

The man sank into silence for a moment before imploring, "I can tell you, but… do me a favor in exchange. Please?"

"What kind of favor?"

"If I tell you, I'll be selling out my partners. That means I'm basically dead to them. In fact, I could end up *literally* dead… If I get arrested and there's suddenly a crackdown, they'll know I sold them out. So please… I'll tell you, but in exchange, don't turn me over to the authorities, okay?"

"So you want us to let you go?"

"W-Well… that's one way to put it, yes… Oh, I know! If you let me go, I'll give you all the money I have!" he whispered weakly, watching for my reaction.

Hmm… I wasn't a fan of letting criminals loose out of the goodness of my heart. Still, I didn't want to flat-out say no and have him get cold feet about spilling the beans. *Wait, I know!*

"Fine. I'll think about it," I compromised.

"You mean it?!"

"Hey now!" Gourry objected. (I was still ignoring him, of course.)

"Well? Who's your connection?" I asked, encouraging the would-be burglar to continue.

"So, there's a guy I know who's always hurting for money. Then recently, out of nowhere, he buys us all a round of drinks. I ask him what's up, and he says he happened to get his hands on a magical sword, which he then sold to a certain buyer who filled his purse for the favor."

"A certain buyer?"

"Yeah… You know Solaria, a little ways to the west?"

"Sure. It's the largest city in the area." I didn't know too much about it, but I'd at least heard its name.

"It's a pretty big castle town, and the castle at the center belongs to the local lord, Lord Langmeier."

"This is gonna take a while, huh?" I said dryly.

"No, I'm almost done," the man insisted, shaking his head hastily. "He said that Lord Langmeier will pay a premium for magic swords."

"The lord himself is making the offer?"

"Apparently. It's what my friend said, anyway... See? That didn't take long at all, did it?!"

Hmm... It had the ring of plausibility, at least. People who collected swords were typically either filthy rich or filthy thieves. Local lords, generals, and people with great political power were particularly inclined to the hobby. And if someone like *that* was the one hoarding magic swords 'round here, I couldn't just waltz in and use my standard smack-'em-around-and-take-the-loot trick. That's how you end up a wanted woman, after all! I'd need a different plan.

"So... if you believe me, then please untie me!" the man begged.

I folded my arms and cocked my head. "Hmm... but if I let you get away, you might do the same thing to someone else, or you might come after us again. I'm gonna turn you in after all."

"W-Wait, please!" The man's face turned bright red. "You promised! You said you'd let me go!"

"You should've listened better," I said, wagging my finger at him. "I said I'd *think* about it. So I did, and I've decided to turn you in after all!"

"Damn you! You tricked me!"

"Didn't, tho!" I said with a big grin.

"You swindler! Devil! Hag! Bitch!" the man cried, glaring at me.

"You think childish insults like that are gonna hurt me? You're just revealing your own ignorance."

"Wh-What'd you say?! In that case... Child! Pipsqueak! Washboard!"

Grrrrr! Th-Those ones... did sting a little...

Still, if I socked him one, it'd be like admitting he'd won. The best thing to do at times like this is just grin and bear it. Keeping your cool always gets someone's goat way better than any outburst. So I fought back the urge to start cooking up a Fireball, and said, calmly, "I commend your effort, but those are still lowbrow insults."

"Urgh! Nrgh!" The man purpled and fell silent.

Ha! Got 'im. But just as I was basking in my victory...

"Fine." The man gave me a strained smile. "If you want real trash talk, I'll lay it on you. This is the worst insult in history. One I haven't used since it ruined a lifelong friendship..."

"Yeah? Sounds interesting. Give it a try, then."

"You're..." he began, glaring up at me as I smirked. "You're more disgusting than Lina Inverse!"

Snap!

"What the hell is that supposed to mean?!"

"See?! Ha! I got you mad!"

"Agh! Calm down, Lina! Please don't use a Dragon Slave!"

The cries of the three of us—me, the burglar, and Gourry—echoed through the inn in the still of the night.

"Hmm... not much of a haul, was it?" I whispered with a sigh as I checked the money in the small leather pouch. We'd gotten it as a reward for handing the burglar over to the authorities.

Turned out the guy was a repeat offender, but he was only worth a mere five silvers. I mean, sure, he wasn't an especially pernicious criminal—and I'd come to expect stinginess from the local authorities by now—but still, five silvers?

"This just confirms it's way more profitable to bully bandits and loot their bases like a normal person," I muttered as we walked on.

"But it's better than nothing, right?"

"Well... I guess. Anyhoo! Off to Solaria City to bust up a local lord and swipe a magic sword or three!"

"W-Wait a minute, Lina!" Gourry said, quickly dousing my excitement.

"What?"

"What do you mean, what? You can't do that! He's a lord, remember? If you blast him and steal his treasure, we'll end up on wanted posters for sure!"

"Hahhhhhhhh..." Gourry's words drove me to an exhausted sigh. "Dude... you really think I'd be that reckless?"

"You really think I think you *wouldn't* be that reckless? Er, I mean, never mind... Of course you wouldn't! Please continue!" Perhaps noticing the rage building in my eyes, Gourry quickly withdrew his complaint.

"I don't wanna end up on the lam for this either. I figured we'd do the diplomatic thing and make him an offer: 'Give us a couple of magic swords and we won't tell the king that you're buying stolen goods!'"

"You call that diplomacy?"

"Where I'm from."

"What the heck goes on where you're from?"

"Never you mind! It's also possible our burglar was lying to us, of course, so we should investigate before all else. In other words... on to Solaria City!"

The bigger a city gets, the more lively it becomes... and the more twisted. Solaria was a prime example of such ongoing distortion. I'm not saying it was unsafe or anything. I'm saying the place was laid out like a maze.

It was common enough for a castle town to be totally surrounded by defensive walls, and this one was no exception. Except when a city grows, its population and needs can quickly fill the place up and then some. So you end up building residences and facilities outside the wall. Then you have to build a new wall around *those*, and when *that* space fills up... rinse, repeat. This process had resulted in Solaria City becoming a disorderly mess of snaking walls cordoning off each of the various city blocks. It was easy to get disoriented if you hadn't lived there all your life.

A hypothetical outsider, then, might find themselves walking toward the castle's spires and suddenly find their path blocked by a wall. They might then decide to follow said wall until they happened upon a way through, but without knowing the shortest route there... they might end up wandering through city blocks in a completely hopeless detour.

Long story short, Gourry and I were lost.

"Hey, that inn we passed a while back..." Gourry piped up.

"What about it?" I replied sullenly as we soldiered on through the darkening city.

"I feel like we passed a place with the same name just now..."

"We did."

Gourry considered my answer for a moment, then asked, "Is it a chain?"

"We're lost, okay?! Dead lost!"

"Oh, okay!" Gourry clapped his hands in understanding. "That explains it."

"S-Sure it does…" I muttered limply, having lost the will to yell.

We'd arrived in the city some time after noon, found an eatery for a light lunch, and then set out to find an inn nearer to the castle… but we still weren't anywhere close.

"Couldn't we have just asked for directions at the restaurant in the first place, Lina?"

"Sure… I just didn't expect navigating the city to be *quite* this annoying…" I whispered in exhaustion as we continued our aimless wandering.

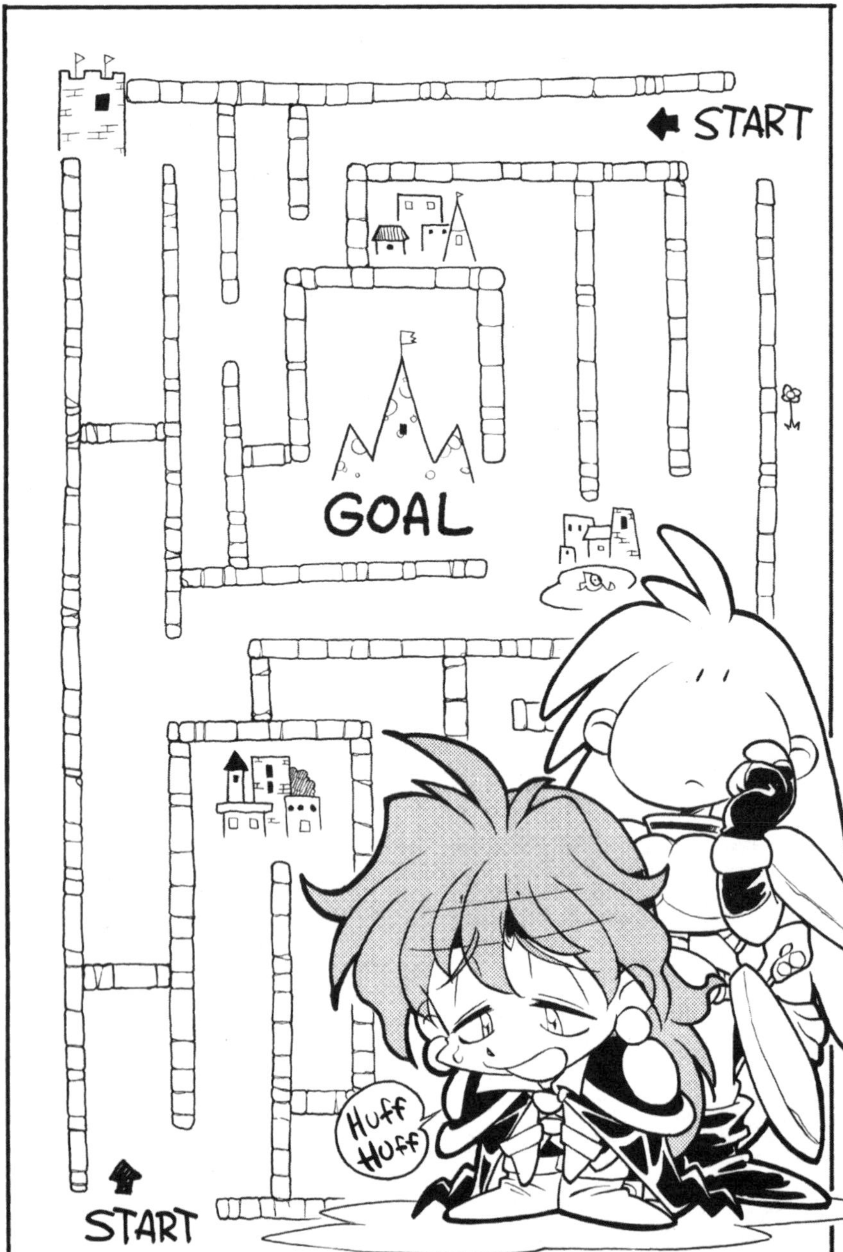
START
GOAL
Huff Huff
START

The smells of dinner began to drift from the houses around us. I caught a whiff of vegetables in broth—probably stew. Then there was the heavenly aroma of fatty fish frying from the nearest house. The irresistible smell of seared meat emanated from a few other residences as well.

I'm so hungry...

I stopped, let out a deep sigh, and said, "I guess we'll just call it a night at the closest inn and try again in force tomorrow."

"Yeah. That's a good idea. Uh-huh," Gourry said in immediate, thought-free agreement.

The sky above the city was already turning indigo.

"Wow, there sure are a lot of big buildings around here," I remarked as we wandered the blocks encircling the castle.

It was the next day now. We'd stayed the night at an inn and asked the old innkeeper for directions before setting out again.

In terms of scale, Lord Langmeier's castle was neither especially large nor especially small. Its architecture wasn't anything remarkable either. It was made of light-gray stone, and its decorations were perfectly modest. To be frank, it was pretty much your archetypal castle. But there was one point of interest: the various facilities *around* the castle.

As a city grew, its central district usually came to replace ordinary residences with government offices and temples. But the sheer quantity of newly built structures in the heart of Solaria seemed mighty fishy to my eye. At a glance, they looked normal enough... except they were all walled off for some reason, with guards posted at all times. Any attempted visitors got turned away on obvious pretexts. According to the innkeeper, quite a few of these had popped up recently.

"Say, Lina, what are we supposed to learn by walking around like this?"

"Nothing," I responded.

"C'mon..." Gourry whined, his primary objection seeming to be to all the walking.

"But we can do plenty of speculating."

"What do you mean?"

"Do you see all these places? What the innkeep described as 'unusual buildings built to look usual'? All these well-guarded, walled-off structures?"

"Matter of fact, I did notice a whole lot of stone-faced types around 'em…"

"Right? They're probably all military facilities."

"Military?!"

"Hush! Keep your voice down! You don't know who might be listening!"

"O-Okay… But what exactly are you getting at?"

"Military facilities springing up, plus rumors that the lord's buying up magic swords… Makes you think someone's getting ready for war, doesn't it?"

Gourry gasped and fell silent in shock.

"These are all signs of someone preparing for a fight. But I doubt a lone lord would attack another country out of nowhere. It's far more likely that this is a domestic affair… In other words, he's going after the king."

"I see… So it's insurrection."

"I'll admit there are plenty of other explanations. Maybe they're researching new weapons, or selling them to other countries…"

"B-But… doesn't that mean your plan to steal a sword is pretty dangerous?"

"Yeah. Probably."

Going up to someone plotting a rebellion and blackmailing them for buying stolen goods was basically like asking to be permanently silenced. Of course, Gourry and I weren't gonna just sit back and let that happen, but there was no need to push our luck.

"But on the other hand… if we can find proof of insurrection and report it to the king, he might give us a magic sword as a reward!"

"You're a nasty lady, you know that?"

"What are you talking about? An insurrection would put lots of innocent people in danger! And we'd deserve a reward for saving them all! Or are you saying we should just sit on our hands when we know a rebellion is brewing?"

"Oh… Well, when you put it that way…"

"See? So we'd better hurry! Let's sneak into one of these babies tonight and find us some proof!"

The only sound in town that night was the wind. If there were bars nearby, we would have been able to hear their raucous din, but they were absent here in the city center. Street lamps aglow with Lighting spells stood here and there, offering halfhearted illumination against the oppressive darkness.

When the half-moon above dipped behind the clouds, everything apart from the city lights was drenched in black. And blending into that blackness...

Gourry and I darted down the road, heading for a building we'd scouted out earlier. We were hiding our faces with black masks and headwraps in case anybody spotted us, and we had swapped our usual outfits for nondescript dark clothing.

Our target was the facility that had seemed to have the strictest security during the day. It looked like an ordinary temple on the outside, but the high wall around it and the security at the gate even at this hour told a different tale.

Why'd we choose this spot? It was obvious: the strict security was a sign of the building's importance. I mean, what would be the point of breaking into an easier place if it didn't have what we needed inside?

"Levitation!" I released a hushed incantation, and Gourry and I lifted off into the dark sky.

"Dang... Lots of guards, huh?" Gourry whispered, clinging to my collar.

The overhead view was pretty revealing. Inside the wall was a lone temple-like structure with a domed roof. It was surrounded by ornamental trees and stone garden pillars, behind which were countless guards keeping a vigilant eye on the lawn.

"Lina, look at all these guards. They'll see us right away if we aren't careful."

"Yeah. I guess we'd better be careful then, huh? I'm taking us in, so zip your lips for a bit, capisce?"

I directed my spell to take us right over the building, then lower us down slowly onto the central roof. The guards were only watching the ground, after all. We should go completely unnoticed coming from above.

I pulled a thin rope from a bag I'd brought with me, tied it to the large stone idol at the apex of the dome, and used it to slide down. The rope was magically reinforced, of course. It appeared thin, but it was strong enough to hold a dragon... er, at least a small one.

When I hit the edge of the roof, I first confirmed that no guards were looking, then peered down below. I scanned left and right until I spotted what looked like a small door a little ways away. I signaled to Gourry with my eyes and then adjusted my position, still holding the rope. Once we were over the door, I observed the patrol patterns of the guards in the area, and...

Okay! Now! I judged my timing, hit the ground, and checked the door. There wasn't just any lock on it... It seemed to be sealed shut with a Lock spell.

I began a quiet chant, then tapped the doorknob with my right index finger. "Unlock," I incanted, unleashing a lockpicking spell I'd learned recently.

Clack. The sound from the knob suggested the spell had worked. I signaled to Gourry, who jumped off the roof after me. We then swiftly entered the building through our newly opened door.

"Dark in here," I muttered softly enough that only Gourry could hear.

Even with the moon behind the clouds, we'd still had ambient starlight outside. But there wasn't a single lamp on in here. It was as close to pitch black as you could get. Nevertheless, through the... atmosphere, let's say, or the flow of the air around us... I could tell we were in a rather cavernous space. I didn't sense anyone present other than Gourry.

"Seems kinda... empty," he remarked.

"Can you make out anything, Gourry?"

"Kinda, yeah."

Wow. He really does have exceptional eyesight... But while I was appreciating his eyes, my own were gradually growing accustomed to the darkness as well with the help of a faint moonbeam straying in through the stained glass window in the roof. The first thing I noticed was that, as I'd guessed, we were in a big, open room. The second point of note was rows of something boxy lined up before us.

"They're just seats, I think," Gourry said, gesturing toward one.

I walked up to touch one, and he was right. The rows of boxy shapes were wooden pews, like you'd find in any place of worship.

"Huh..."

We wandered around with hushed footsteps for a while, but in all respects, the place seemed like a run-of-the-mill church.

"Just an ordinary cathedral, huh?" Gourry observed for himself.

"By all appearances, sure. But remember there's a wall around this building and a dozen guards outside. The door was also magically locked. You think they'd put security like that on an ordinary cathedral?"

"Maybe they're paranoid."

"Get real. You know how much a detail like that costs?"

"Then what's going on here?"

"I suspect the real facility is down below. They designed it this way so that if anyone did manage to break in, they'd *think* it was just an ordinary cathedral. And even if someone figured out it wasn't, they'd have a heck of a time finding a hidden door or switch in a room of this size."

Let's assume there's a switch on one of the kneelers or the feet of one of the pews. It'd take long enough to find it in the daylight, but trying to uncover it now is nigh impossible...

And while I was thinking about that... *Tug!*

"Wugh?!"

Gourry had suddenly grabbed my hand and pulled. A second later...

Vwomm!

A bolt of light streaked past my head! It continued to sail through the darkness, then broke apart against the floor.

"Pretty sharp for a little rat," echoed a hoarse, deep male voice from all around us.

"You're pretty impressive yourself. I didn't sense you at all," Gourry responded.

I followed his eyeline to the stained-glass panes... Aha! There was a person just in front of them—floating in the air. But just as I spotted him, he dropped down into the darkness below.

"He's coming!" Gourry called.

"On it!"

We both drew our swords and stood at the ready. In that moment, I sensed movement in my peripheral vision.

Whoosh! I quickly whipped out of the way, but something grazed by me—probably a throwing knife of some kind.

This wasn't a great position to be in. Our opponent didn't seem to have any trouble in the dark, which put me, at least, at a severe disadvantage. That being the case...

I chanted a quiet spell and incanted, "Lighting!"

This produced a reduced-luminosity ball of magical light, which I threw over my head. It was dim, but it flooded the room with just enough light to see by if your eyes were already adjusted. Now that the enemy knew we were here, there was no point in playing around in the dark. I was hoping this might distract my opponent while allowing me to see what was going on.

My light illuminated white walls and a long row of wooden pews... with a dark figure amongst them.

"Huh?!"

He looked familiar to me... at least, his clothes did. He was dressed in all black, with even his face covered so that only two eyes were peeking out from the cloth. It was an archetypal assassin getup... but there was something about this guy that seemed different from your typical assassin.

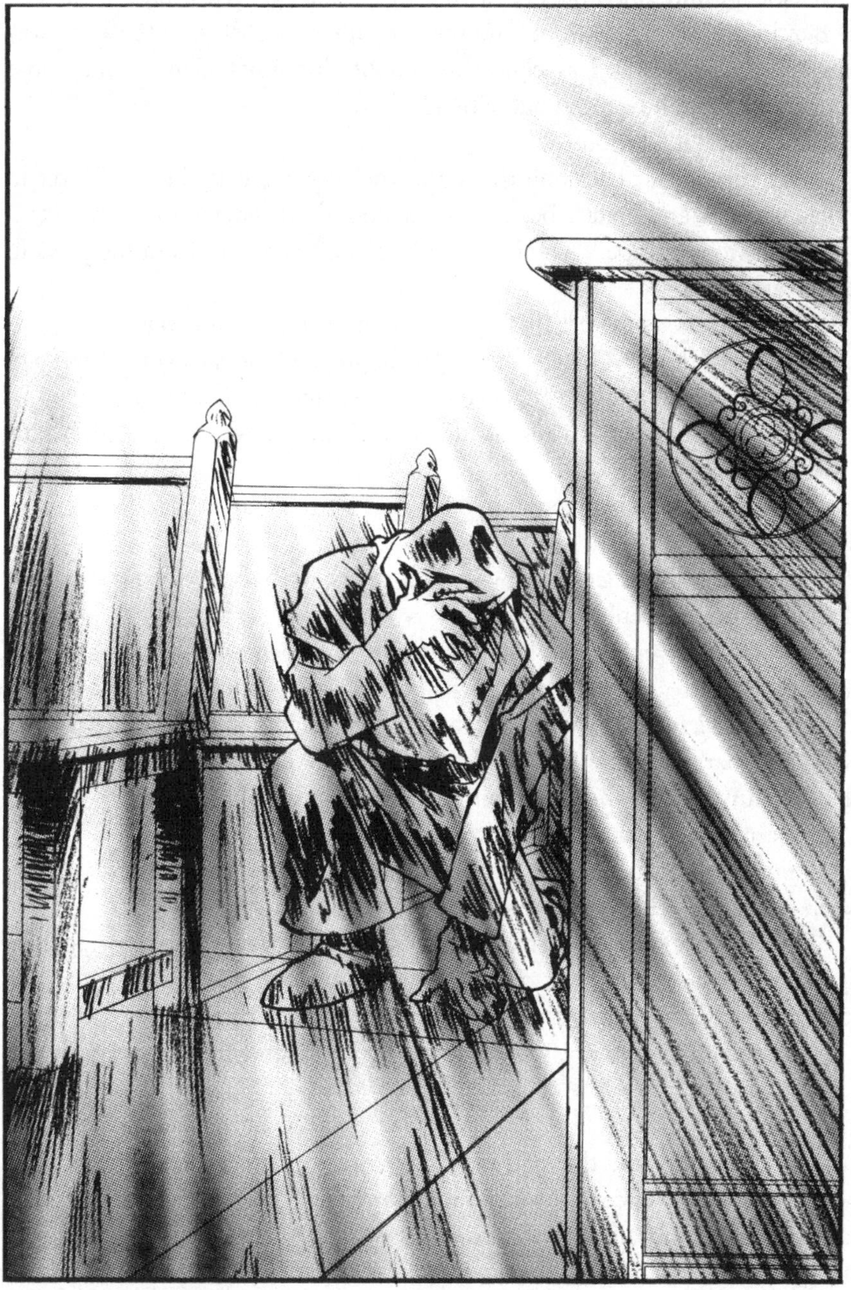

Gourry and I had tangled with a mysterious gang of thugs in the city of Bezeld over a magic sword, and their members had dressed the same way. But right now, I was less concerned about this guy's identity and more concerned about how to get out of here!

"Let's beat it!" I shouted.

We turned our backs on the man, who was currently hunched over to shield his eyes, and made a beeline for the door we'd come in through. But...

"You won't escape!" Another man in black leaped out from the pews to block our way!

There's more of them?! This new figure threw knives our way!

"That's nothing!" Gourry shouted as he stepped forward with a sweep of his sword. *Clink! Shing!* He knocked the knives right out of the air.

Perhaps realizing knives wouldn't work anymore, the man drew his sword instead.

Don't forget I'm here too, okay?! I waited for the man in black to get close, and then...

"Dam Blas!" I unleashed my spell at very close range. No way could he dodge this one! Except...

Crash! He swept his left hand at my sure-kill spell, effortlessly dispersing it!

Impossible! Dam Blas wasn't the kind of spell you could just bat away with your bare hands! The darn thing could smash through a wall! I hadn't detected any signs of the guy chanting a defensive spell either...

"Hah!" Gourry shouted, as if to rip me from my thoughts.

Shing! Sparks flew as his sword collided with the man in black's. At the same time, I felt a hostile presence rise up behind me.

I didn't even have to turn back. The man I'd distracted with my Lighting spell had recovered and was charging at me from the rear. But if he threw a knife at me and I dodged, it would hit Gourry! Which meant...

"Hwaaah!" With a cry, I took a flying leap and landed on Gourry's back!

"Bwuh?!"

"What?!"

Both Gourry and the man in black he was fighting let out startled cries. My sudden appearance in the fray had thrown them both off balance, sending all three of us tumbling to the floor. As we fell, I felt something rush over my head.

Hah! Dodged it!

"Hey, Lina, watch it!"

"Please save any and all complaints for later!"

Grabbing Gourry's hand as he stood up, I dashed through the door.

Wham! The dark of night greeted us outside, right along with the rallying guards. They'd be tough to break through—but the sky overhead was wide open!

"Lei Wing!" Holding on tight to Gourry's hand, I used an amplified high-speed flight spell to take off into the air. We sailed over the guards' heads, over the wall, and out into the city.

"Hey! Lina!"

I'd been flying for a while when Gourry called out to me. We were some ways away from the temple now.

"What?!" I called back.

"We're not going back to the inn, are we?"

"Where else are we supposed to go?!"

"Don't do it! They're following us!"

"What?!"

I quickly looked behind us. I couldn't see much between the distortion from my wind barrier and the darkness. Thinking about it, we were currently streaking over the city roofs with an enhanced Lei Wing. They shouldn't be able to follow us… Key word being *shouldn't.*

"Are you serious, Gourry?!"

"I'm sure of it! I can't see them, but I feel two presences following us!"

Gourry had the instincts of a wild animal, so if they were telling him someone was there, then I wasn't gonna doubt it. Two presences suggested it was probably the guys in black from before… meaning Gourry was right and it wouldn't be safe to head right back to our inn.

I changed course and took us down into a relatively dense cluster of buildings, dismissing the spell as we landed. All was silent. There was no sign of pursuit. But I could feel a tension in the ostensibly calm night air. Someone was there, concealing their presence, in the dark.

"Lina!"

Vm! I heard something tearing through the air behind us just as Gourry tried to warn me about it. *Fwsh!* I quickly moved to dodge, but the small flying object ripped my mask off! A throwing knife?!

"Guh!"

I turned to run, but a figure emerged from the black. As I thought… it was one of them! My torn mask fell to the ground, exposing my face to the moonlight.

"Oho…" he hummed as he caught sight of me.

"Guess there really is something in that building," I said, hoping to bait him.

"We just came by to finish off some illegal intruders," came another voice from behind me. I glanced over my shoulder and saw the second man in black come out from around a building.

I'm surrounded… "Gourry, cut us a way through. We're getting out of here," I whispered, standing back-to-back with him.

"We're not fighting?"

"I don't want to make trouble in the city. Not yet." I could easily bust out a big spell that would cause enough of a commotion to let us escape… But if I was too reckless in my escalation, any ensuing chaos would technically be on my head.

"I don't quite get it, but fine! Let's go!" Gourry agreed, charging at the man in front of him!

The man started in surprise, and I took the opportunity to follow after Gourry. He and the man in black drew their weapons at the same time! *Clash!* Sword met sword, and sparks scattered in the night.

Gourry slid his blade along his opponent's to throw it off course, then slipped past the man and dashed off. Our black-clad buddy briefly seemed uncertain about whether to pursue Gourry or meet my charge, though he ultimately turned his sword, glinting in the moonlight, on me. Too bad for him…

"Lei Wing!" The wind barrier created by my Lei Wing, activated at close range, blasted both the dude and his blade away! I then caught up with Gourry and dismissed the spell. We kept running together as I chanted my next one.

After fleeing down the main avenue and cutting onto a side street, we kept turning wherever we could. Keeping too straight would get us throwing knives in the back for our trouble. Continually snaking our course would help confuse our pursuers too. Of course, if they could keep up with my boosted Lei Wing, I kind of doubted that a few corners would be all it took to lose them…

As we ran, I spotted a narrow alleyway, gestured, and had Gourry enter ahead of me. Before long, the men in black appeared behind us! They were probably going to use more knives. It would be hard to dodge them like this, but I waited for the men to stop as they made to throw and…

"Diem Wind!" I took that brief opportunity to unleash the amplified wind spell I'd chanted!

Vroosh! The gust rushing down the alley roared into a full-on squall that blew back the men in black!

"Okay! Now book it!"

I sped up and encouraged Gourry to do the same. I'd sent our pursuers flying, but they'd be back on our tails again soon enough. We didn't have a moment to lose. Eventually, Gourry and I made it out of the alley and…

"Geh!" I let out a short groan as I came to a stop. There was a long wall stretching out in front of us.

Yup. It was one of the walls between city blocks. We couldn't turn back now, and if we ran along the wall, we wouldn't have any place to hide. That meant our only option was going up and over! I swiftly chanted my next spell, and…

"Lina!" Gourry shouted, pushing me before I could finish!

Bwoosh! After came a howl of wind. An unseen force shot out from the alley and crashed into the wall ahead of us—probably a pressure blast from some kind of spell. Shortly after, the two figures reappeared. I was shocked they'd caught up already.

Two of us and two men in black… The four of us squared off once more.

"You can't escape us," one of the men said lightly, without any sense of boasting.

I didn't doubt him. They clearly weren't going to let us go without a fight, and they knew the terrain much better than we did.

Guess we'll just have to throw down after all. But as that thought entered my mind…

"What's all this ruckus in the middle of the night?" came a new voice from atop the wall.

I looked up and saw a figure standing stoically against the backdrop of the night. It sounded like a man, but his face was hidden behind a cloth wrap. He didn't seem to be with the guys in black, but he was definitely a similar level of sketchy.

"Who are you?!" one of the men in black demanded.

"Don't make so much noise. You'll wake the neighbors… is all I'll say for now," the masked man atop the wall replied calmly.

"Are you with them?!" the man in black barked back.

"Certainly not, but—"

"Then keep your nose out of this! We're trying to arrest ruffians who infiltrated a local facility!" he now shouted shakily, perhaps a bit rattled by the interference of this unknown third party.

Meanwhile, the masked man just snorted in amusement. "Ruffians? You look far 'rougher' than they do, to my eyes. Not that I'm one to talk… But at the least, it's obvious from your dress that you're not agents of the law authorized to make arrests."

The guys in black fell silent for a moment, then… *Whoosh!* One of them threw something. The masked man on the wall made a motion with his hand, and the next instant, a small knife appeared in it.

"What?!" the man in black shouted in shock.

I was guessing he'd thrown the knife, which the masked man had then caught. Pulling that off in the dark took some pretty serious chops!

"I see. You've made things quite clear." The masked man tossed the knife aside. "You *are* the ruffians in this situation, which means I cannot let you go. I suppose a flashy battle here and now would cause a commotion… Rumors of it are sure to spread to other cities. Though that won't particularly bother *me*…"

"Ngh!"

I wasn't quite sure what the masked man was hinting at, but the men in black seemed distinctly shaken by the threat.

"Then… shall we?" the masked man proposed, beginning a chant.

"Let's get out of here," one of the men in black whispered forthwith. They then both leaped back and disappeared down the alley they'd emerged from.

"That… That seemed a little too easy," muttered Gourry.

"Y-Yeah. Speaking of…" After watching the men flee, I turned my eyes back to the top of the wall… only to find the masked man was already gone.

"Say… is it okay for us to just sit back like this?" Gourry asked quietly the next morning. Upon our table on the first floor of the tavern was a full spread of breakfast platters, which we were steadily making our way through. "Won't those guys be looking for us?"

"They might be, but to be honest… I'm not sure," I admitted, taking a bite of bacon and lettuce salad. "If the men in black are connected to the local lord, I figure they'll definitely show up again. They could make up any pretext they wanted to arrest us. But we now know that, for some reason, they don't want a big stink made out of this. And it's not like our break-in yielded anything incriminating. So rather than hunting us down and escalating things, they might have decided it's best to leave well enough alone."

I hadn't noticed any increased activity among the town guard since last night either, which implied someone was willing to let sleeping dogs lie. Nevertheless…

"I agree that the safest course would be to leave the city," I conceded. "But after all that, I'm all the more eager to find out what's going on. That masked man yesterday seemed to know something."

"Oh, him? He did seem pretty capable. And judging from his voice, he seemed on the older side…" Gourry said, taking a bite out of a croissant sandwiched around not-too-sweet whipped cream.

I paused my breakfasting, swaying my fork between my fingers. "So the real question is… are these the same black cloaks we fought before?"

"When?"

"You know, for the sword in Bezeld? When we teamed up with that weird couple, Luke and Mileena? And battled that big thing with the insta-regeneration?"

"Oh, right. I think I sorta remember that!"

"Remember the guys in black that kept hassling us? Let's just say they share a tailor with the guys we met in the temple."

"Which means…"

45

"Yup." I nodded firmly at Gourry. "The ruthless sword-hunters might be based outta here. Or maybe it's this Lord Langmeier guy himself who's behind the whole deal. Either way," I slammed my fork into a thick slice of ham and whispered, "this is gonna be trouble."

Hrk! Gourry's face froze over. "I think it might already be trouble," he said, pointing behind me... at the front entrance to the tavern.

"Hmm?" I turned around, brow furrowed, and...

Hrrrrrk! I immediately realized the cause of his expression. Standing at the entrance were two city guards. They glanced at the paper they were holding, then glanced back at me.

Hang on! So they did *decide to arrest us?!*

The two guards marched right up to our table. Gourry and I clamored to our feet, ready for action... but the two guards suddenly came to attention. "Pardon me. Would you be Mistress Lina Inverse, by chance?" one asked.

For a second, I considered telling him he had the wrong gal, but the paper he was carrying clearly either had my defining features listed or my likeness drawn on it. I wasn't going to be able to fib my way around that, and if they looked at the inn's logbook, the jig would be up anyway.

"I am," I answered warily.

The two guards quickly bowed. "We serve Langmeier, lord of this city!" one proclaimed with booming formality. "His regent has requested your esteemed company for dinner."

"Huh?" Gourry and I gawked in unison.

"Say... what exactly is going on here?" Gourry asked as we strode the sunset-soaked avenue toward the castle that evening.

"Dunno," I responded bluntly. Of all the things I'd been expecting, an invitation to dinner wasn't high on the list. "There're a lot of possibilities. First, it's total coincidence. Maybe the regent just happens to know who I am, just happened to hear I was in town, and just happened to be looking for me today..."

"Seems unlikely."

"Agreed. Another possibility is there are multiple factions at play here, and that the men in black and the regent are on opposite sides. Thus, the regent is reaching out to get our help putting down the men in black."

"Got it."

"And last but not least… there's a possibility that the regent is in cahoots with the men in black, and this invitation is a trap."

"That does seem to be the most likely suspect, yeah."

"Right? I agree."

"Um… Then why are we going?"

"Because!"

Wham! My flippant reply sent Gourry into a pratfall. "You took his invitation just 'because'?! You just said that it could be a trap!"

"Okay, well, let's say I turned the regent down. If he really is fighting the men in black, we'd be leaving him high and dry."

"Well… I guess."

"Conversely, if they're in cahoots and I turned him down, do you really think he'd just be like, 'Oh, okay, no problem,' and leave us alone forever?"

"Well… of course not, but…"

"Right? So either way, if we want to get the lay of the land, our best plan of attack is to accept the invitation. If it's a trap, then it's a trap, and we can bust through it when it springs!"

"That seems pretty reckless… though I guess that's nothing new."

"Live a little, man! And most importantly…"

"Most importantly?" Gourry asked.

I responded with a wink. "I just won't be satisfied until I've solved the mystery, y'know?"

"You're so weird…" My words brought a wince to Gourry's face, and he plopped a hand on my head. "But that's okay. I'll stick by you a while longer, at least."

"Thanks a bunch, self-proclaimed guardian man. Now…" I turned my eyes straight to the castle that was our destination. "Let's get in there, Gourry!"

"Pardon the delay," an elderly butler said with great formality as he arrived in the antechamber where we'd been waiting.

Following our earlier conversation, we'd marched boldly into the castle where we'd been received with a polite welcome. We were then shown to this small sitting room while dinner was prepared. No trouble thus far, at least, and no sign of hostility from the various servants who attended to us either.

The waiting accommodations were actually pretty cushy, so we'd just been killing time until the butler arrived.

"Dinner is served. The regent awaits," he announced.

Gourry and I shared a silent glance, then nodded. Shit was about to get real!

"Understood," I responded as we stood up.

The butler then showed us through the door and down a long hall to follow. "Right this way," he finally said, coming to a stop in front of a door.

Okay... time to find out what we're dealing with here.

"You may enter," he encouraged, opening the door to reveal...

"Huh?!" Gourry and I both halted in our tracks.

Inside the room was a long table covered in a white cloth and silver candlesticks. Magical lights blazed in sconces on the wall. And at the head of it all was a young man. He was probably a little over twenty, and was dressed in white in a fashion that could be called either "classy" or "pretentious" depending on your predilections. Either way, it made for a striking contrast to his fiery red hair. There was a beaming smile on his handsome face.

I presumed he was the lord's regent... But he wasn't the reason Gourry and I were so surprised. That honor belonged to the two bodyguards standing behind him—a raven-haired man and a silver-haired woman. There was no chance of mistaken identity. This was the odd couple we'd teamed up with to fight men in black before, Luke and Mileena!

Chapter 2: Not a fan of the Cloak-
and-Dagger Stuff, Y'know?

"Welcome, Lina Inverse. Do forgive the wait." The redhead's words snapped me and Gourry out of our shock. He stood up and beckoned for us to join him. "By all means, come sit. Make yourselves comfortable."

"Oh… sure. Th-Thank you for inviting us," I responded, still a little stiff as I stepped into the room.

"The pleasure is mine, truly. I'm delighted to finally meet the famous Lina Inverse."

"Famous, huh?" I whispered as we took our seats. I was hoping that whatever he'd heard about me hadn't come from the nasty rumor mill.

Once we sat down, the regent took his seat again. "Let us begin with introductions," he began. "I am Lavas Nexalia Langmeier, current regent of Welgis Castle. I've taken up the duties of my father, Lord Klein, who has been laid up ill for some time."

Gourry's attention remained on Mileena and Luke, who stood behind Lord Lavas. Luke, perhaps also curious, kept shooting looks our way, while Mileena was as expressionless as she'd been the first time we'd met her.

Lord Lavas, whether he noticed the exchanged glances or not, continued talking. "You might not think it to look at me, but I'm quite an aficionado of the magical arts… More specifically, of tales regarding them." A server came out of the door behind the regent, placed some potage in front of us, and left again. "There are many accounts out there, of course, but the ones I've found most intriguing of late are the stories of Lina Inverse."

"But aren't most of those stories really bad?" Gourry interrupted.

Hey! Why is that *the only thing you pay attention to?!* If we weren't in such a fancy-pants place, I would've smacked him one.

The regent winced at Gourry's words. "It's true that some of them are what I'd call… unsavory. But the more accomplished one becomes, the greater their renown—and the more gossipmongering arises to tarnish that renown. I personally believe that negative rumors are only ever half the story," he said.

He then looked at me and continued, "I hope you won't take offense when I say that I've collected quite the array of rumors about you. I've heard you were deeply involved with the power struggles of both the Atlas City sorcerers' council and the royal family of Saillune. There was also the elimination of an evil cult in Kalmaart, and the defeat of the mighty assassin Zuma. It's even said that you were party to the razing of the capital of Dils and Sairaag City. All events whose involvement would call for nothing less than a peerless sorcerer."

Oho… I let out an internal noise of appreciation. *Someone's done their research!*

"But hearsay is just that—hearsay. So while we eat, I was hoping that you might regale me with some of your accomplishments firsthand. But I suppose I have prattled on, haven't I? Do enjoy your soup before it gets cold," Lord Lavas said as he picked up his own spoon.

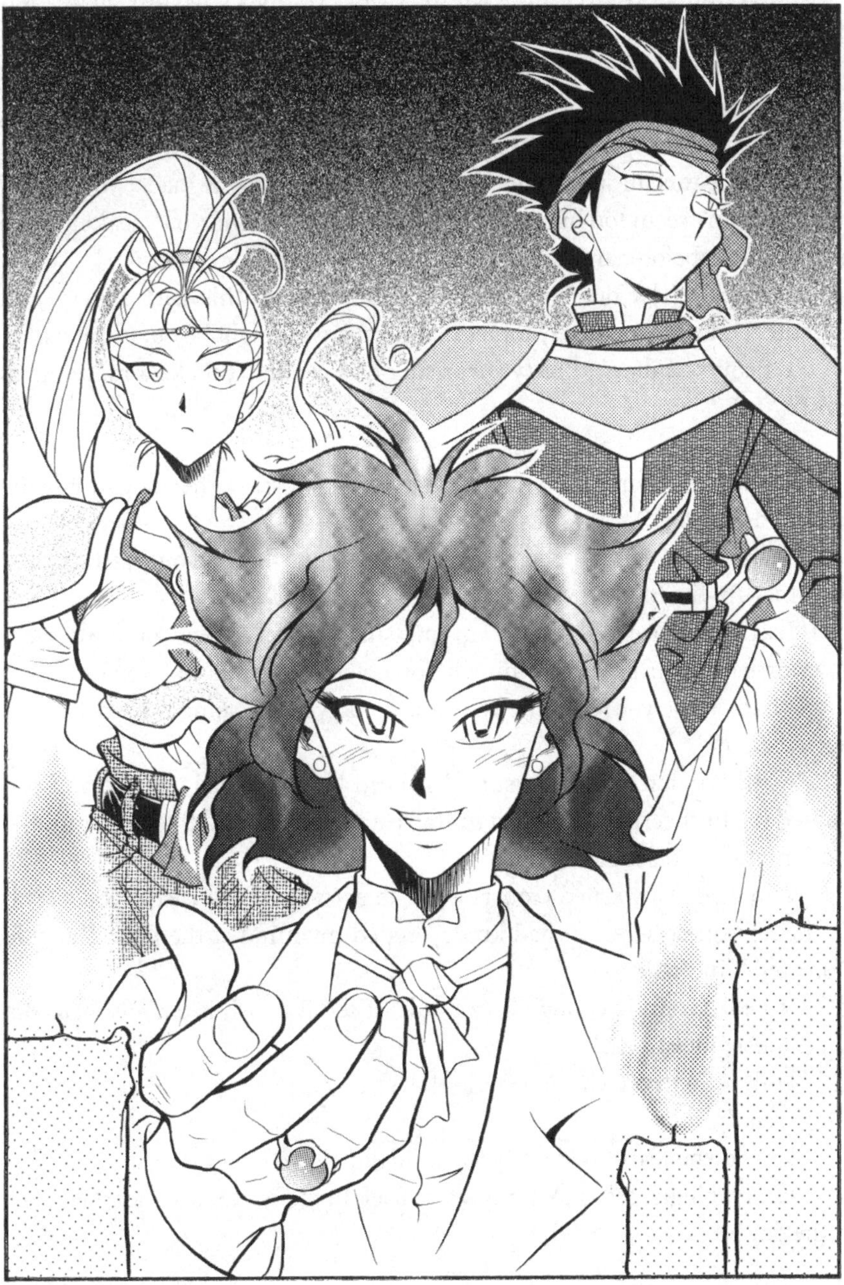

After dinner, Gourry and I left the castle. We were currently on our way back to the inn.

"Wow, what a meal," he remarked in satisfaction as we walked the night road together.

"I can't believe you stuffed your face like that."

"Well, it was all just so good... Nobles really have it made, you know? But you didn't seem too hungry yourself. What gives? Did you sneak in three or four meals beforehand 'cause you couldn't hold out for dinner?"

"Hahh..." I let out an exhausted sigh. "Listen, this isn't a matter of appetite. Did you completely forget that Lord Lavas might be out to get us?"

"Of course I didn't. Pretty surprising how he didn't make a move on us, huh?"

Ughhh...

"Well, what I mean to say is that I was worried the food might be poisoned."

"What?!" Gourry stopped cold in his tracks like that had only just dawned on him. "Th-The food... was poisoned?!"

"It could've been, although I'm guessing it wasn't since you don't seem any worse for wear after cramming it down your gullet the way you did."

"That's what you're going by?! You could've said something before we started eating!"

"As if! We don't know for sure that Lord Lavas is a bad guy yet, and you wanted me to cheerily sit down at his table and say, 'Careful there, big guy, the food might be poisoned'?!"

Why hadn't I warned Gourry *prior* to arriving at the castle, you ask? If I'm being honest here... it had kinda slipped my mind at the time. But shh! Don't tell him that!

"If I eat carefully enough, I can at least tell if a dish is empoisoned. But not if I just glut myself."

"Huh... So that's why you ate so slow?"

"Exactly."

"How'd you learn to identify the taste of poison?"

"Eh, no biggie. Just a skill my sister back home made sure I learned back in the day."

At this, Gourry fell silent for a moment. "I've been wondering this for a while," he finally said, "but what kind of person is your sister?"

"Don't ask. Please. Just let it be."

"O-Okay… I won't pry." Gourry must have noticed the terror deep in my eyes, because he fell silent again with a shiver.

"Anyhoo, I'm left wondering what that dinner invitation was really all about." I returned to the subject at hand, hoping to clear the air.

"I dunno. We did all that speculating about what he might be plotting on the way there, but all he wanted was to hear your war stories."

"Yup. Maybe hearing about me from his bodyguards, Luke and Mileena, piqued his curiosity… Although the timing seems a little too convenient for that, yeah?"

"Yeah. And speaking of, Lina, what're they doing there? The regent wouldn't hire those two if he was working with the men in black, would he?"

"Hmm…" I pensively furrowed my brow. Dude had a point. We'd teamed up with Luke and Mileena to fight the men in black over a sword back in Bezeld. Said sword was gone now, but even with the object at odds out of the picture, I was sincerely doubtful that the black cloaks would be so quick to hire former foes for protection. "Either way, our priority right now is dealing with you-know-who."

"Fair point."

Gourry and I exchanged a look as we continued to walk along. Ever since leaving the castle, we'd felt a presence tailing us. If it was a friend, they would have called out to us, so the fact that they hadn't suggested… trouble.

"Should we make the first move?" Gourry asked.

"Good question. All I know is we'd better not lead 'em back to where we're staying," I responded, coming to a stop.

There were no residences or bars nearby. It was only shortly after nightfall, but the streets were already empty of all but darkness and silence. Perhaps realizing we'd halted, the presence behind us seemed to hesitate momentarily before making its next move—coming straight for us!

Light burst forth from the black of night, riding a wave of hostile intent. The light took the form of a magical spear, but it was easily avoidable at this distance. Gourry and I leaped in opposite directions to evade it. But then—

"Huh?!"

Sensing a new wave of danger, I half-reflexively put a hand on my sword. A figure leaped out of the darkness right before my eyes! *Hey!*

Ching! I used the hilt of my half-drawn shortsword to block an incoming horizontal slash by a hair's breadth.

Wow, that was close! If I'd been a second slower, my opponent's blade would've buried itself in my side—or at least liberated me of a finger grasping my hilt. The attack had come way too fast for it to be the same guy who'd launched the spell, though. Were there two assailants?!

"Lina!" As I leaped back, Gourry interposed himself between me and my attacker, his sword drawn.

Clash! The man in black blocked a slash from Gourry with his own blade—one the color of darkness. From the same position, he then launched a spell at the big lug in retaliation! When had he chanted that?!

It should've been a surefire hit at close range, but Gourry managed to twist away and channel his momentum into a follow-up slash. This time, the man in black jumped back to dodge instead of parrying. He took some distance from Gourry, then suddenly turned and bolted.

"Is he running away?!" Gourry shouted.

"No!" I said, giving chase. "He wants us to follow him! He's luring us somewhere!"

"And we're just gonna play along?!" he whined as he ran to catch up.

"Of course! It's an obvious trap, so we're gonna spring it, bust through, and find our next step!"

"Gotcha!"

Gourry and I darted down the night-cloaked street in pursuit of the fleeing figure. I'd assumed there were two of them, but there was no sign now of a second. Maybe my mind was playing tricks on me... or maybe that was part of the trap. Whatever the case, chasing down this guy would get me my answer sooner or later.

We raced along, turning corner after corner. After a whole lot of running, the man in black finally passed through a certain gate.

"Hey, this is..."

Gourry and I briefly came to a halt, for we were right outside one of the mysterious off-limits facilities we'd scoped out before. It looked a little like a library or museum, but it was walled off and swarming with guards the last we saw... Yet there was no sign of guards near it now, and the gate stood wide open.

"Hey... Lina!" Gourry called.

There, I looked toward the building itself. The man in black we'd been chasing was standing at the front door, staring back at us.

"Got it. The old 'come and get me' routine..." I muttered.

"Are we... gonna go and get him?"

"You betcha!" I responded with a wink.

We then renewed the chase. Once the man in black was sure we were coming after him again, he disappeared through the door.

"This guy's really set on making sure we keep up!" Gourry remarked.

"A sign he's confident in his own abilities. Or in whatever trap he's set. Or... maybe both."

We were soon upon the entrance ourselves. A faint beam of light shone through the crack in the door, but there was no immediate sign of anyone inside. Of course, we knew someone *had* to be. They were probably just concealing their presence.

I recited a spell under my breath and signaled Gourry with my eyes. Then—*Bam!*—he kicked the door in, sword in hand! But...

"Nobody home," he whispered, looking around.

I took a moment and then peeked inside too. A large, circular entry hall opened up before us. At the end was a corridor, and on either side was a staircase leading up to the second floor. Candlesticks lining the walls cast the room in faint magical light. There genuinely didn't seem to be anyone around. Except...

The opening to the corridor in the back was flanked by two griffon statues, the rightmost of which was shifted slightly from its original position. Below it was a hole in the floor leading into the basement.

"Another obvious trap, I'd say," Gourry observed.

"Guess we better fall for it, huh?" I responded. "They've gone to this much trouble, after all."

We steeled ourselves as we strode across the room and sallied down the stairs to a hallway below. The ceiling itself seemed to have been enchanted with some kind of magical light, which cast a cold, inorganic glow over the austere, empty corridor.

After we walked a ways, the hallway culminated in a door that just screamed, "Hello there! I'm a trap!" Still, we couldn't exactly turn back now.

We made it to the door, reached for the knob, and... *Clack.* A chill air washed over us from the room beyond. On the other side of the door was... blackness. The light trailing in from the hall only revealed silhouettes lined along either wall.

"Lighting!" I incanted to brighten the place up. And then... "What is all this?" I found myself whispering.

The room was flanked with crystal tubes as high as the ceiling. Inside of them floated living things, seemingly asleep... Curious creatures that could be called neither human nor monster.

"Say, Lina, what is this place?"

"A chimera factory... and a big one, at that."

The rows of tubes extended beyond the light of my spell. There had to be a hundred or more.

"Chances the guy in black is farther in?" Gourry asked hesitantly.

"No contest, man."

The crystal tubes were set into the wall. It would be impossible for someone to hide behind them. Our guy probably intended to lead us deeper in, then release the chimeras from the tubes to surround us. But if that was the game, I had a little plan of my own.

I began to walk the narrow hall between the tubes, chanting under my breath. And before long...

"We meet again," came a voice as I felt a presence spring up behind us.

I quickly turned to see a figure standing at the door we'd come through, haloed by the light. No prizes for guessing it was a man in black. Of course, given the dress code, I technically had no way of knowing whether it was the *same* man in black...

"Do you remember my voice? It's me... Zain."

"Zain?!" I cried out, abandoning my chant.

"Who?" Gourry asked.

"From the whole Bezeld thing! You know, the black cloak who disappeared on us at the very end?!" I shouted. This guy wasn't a bad fighter, but we could beat him so long as we didn't let our guard down.

"I heard you infiltrated another of our facilities yesterday," he said. "I was rather surprised when my comrades mentioned your names."

"So this city is your home base after all, huh?"

"I can't tell you that."

"Aw, really? You always took the bait before. Kids grow up so fast!"

"Say what you like," Zain spat indifferently.

Huh, and he used to be so easy to manipulate too... There was definitely something different about him now.

"Either way, you need to die," he hissed, killing intent now flooding out of him.

I quickly chanted a spell, when just then...

Krrrik-ak-ak-ak! The crystal tubes that lined the hall between us and Zain audibly began to crack! *Crash!* So-called "water of life"—a culture fluid used for making chimeras—gushed forth, momentarily hiding Zain from sight.

The next instant... a hostile presence appeared behind us.

"What?!"

Gourry whipped around. Swords flashed. *Clang!* He skillfully managed to block the man in black's blade.

I knew it! There were *two guys!* That meant my job was to pin down Zain, who was still in front of us. But just as I settled on that strategy...

"As usual, not bad," whispered the man behind us—in Zain's voice!

What?! I looked back to the door ahead to see that the silhouetted figure was gone. *It can't be!* Even if he had a secret passageway or something, he shouldn't have been able to get behind us that quickly!

Nevertheless, we didn't have time to sort that out right now. The sealed chimeras were now starting to flood the hallway from their broken tubes.

I unleashed the spell I'd chanted on the nearest one: "Freeze Bullid!"

As its name suggested, Freeze Bullid fired a frigid projectile meant to quick-freeze an opponent. The corridor was pretty narrow, so if I iced the one in the lead, it should hold off the others behind it. Yet...

Crash! My spell hit the head chimera, but rather than freezing solid... the creature just shook it off.

It didn't work?! Did this particular chimera have a little demon in it?!

I didn't have time to cook up another spell with the monsters barreling toward me. Instead, I swiftly drew my shortsword and prepared to meet them. I'm not bad with a blade skill-wise, mind you, but I can't deny that I'm lacking in the brawn department. If Chimera No. 1 was a fusion of human and demon, I'd be hard pressed to fell it in one blow. That being the case...

The approaching chimera roared, raised its right hand high, and...

Whoosh! In that instant, I leaped close, keeping low in a crouch so that it might look to the chimera like I had disappeared. I then straightened up, thrusting my sword straight above me!

Krrkkh! The tip of my blade pierced the chimera's jaw from below! It let out a howl curdled by bloody foam, lashing out as it struggled in agony.

I quickly let go of my sword, drew back, and released the spell I'd been working on. "Blast Ash!"

Whoom! The flailing chimera and the one behind it took the spell head-on and turned to ash. See, this little black magic number would cremate anything with life or will—meaning it left my sword and the walls around us unscathed. I scooped up my weapon as it clattered to the floor and readied myself to face the next round of chimeras.

About a dozen were still crowding the hallway. I could beat a couple more the same way, but it would be slow and dangerous going. If only I had access to my good ol' Gaav Flare, which would both affect demons and penetrate multiple opponents... Too bad circumstances had conspired, let's say, to deny me that spell.

If Gourry got a free moment, I could order him to take point while I watched on from the sidelines. But, while I didn't have any time to spare him a glance, I could still hear the clashing of swords behind me. That meant the boys were still busy, so I was gonna have to do something about these chimeras myself! If I could just stymie the one at the head of the pack...

That's it! I quietly began chanting. I held the cautious chimeras at bay with my sword, and then...

Whoosh! The beast in the lead finally decided to charge.

But by then, I'd already finished my spell! "Dynast Breath!"

Shing! This time, the vanguard chimera froze entirely in place.

This spell summoned magical ice capable of freezing even demons, meaning it overpowered any magic resistance the chimeras might have.

It usually froze an opponent and then shattered them into little shards... But I'd adjusted the incantation slightly for all freeze, no break. If you truly understood a spell's chant, such modifications were pretty easy to make.

Okay! The other chimeras won't be able to get by the frozen one at the head of the parade, which means I can help Gourry out with Zain now!

I turned around, chanting a new spell.

Clink! Clank! Clang! Their battle was still going strong, as I'd expected. Gourry wasn't taking it easy on the guy either. Zain's slashes seemed to be coming harder and faster than they had the last time we'd tangled with him.

What the heck? How'd he get so much better so fast? Regardless, taking on me *and* Gourry at the same time would be his downfall!

I got around behind the big lug and unleashed my spell: "Flare Arrow!"

A dozen arrows of flame appeared in the air—right between Gourry and Zain!

"What?!" Zain shouted in surprise as the fiery bolts rained down on him.

Fa-fwoom, fwoom, fwoom!

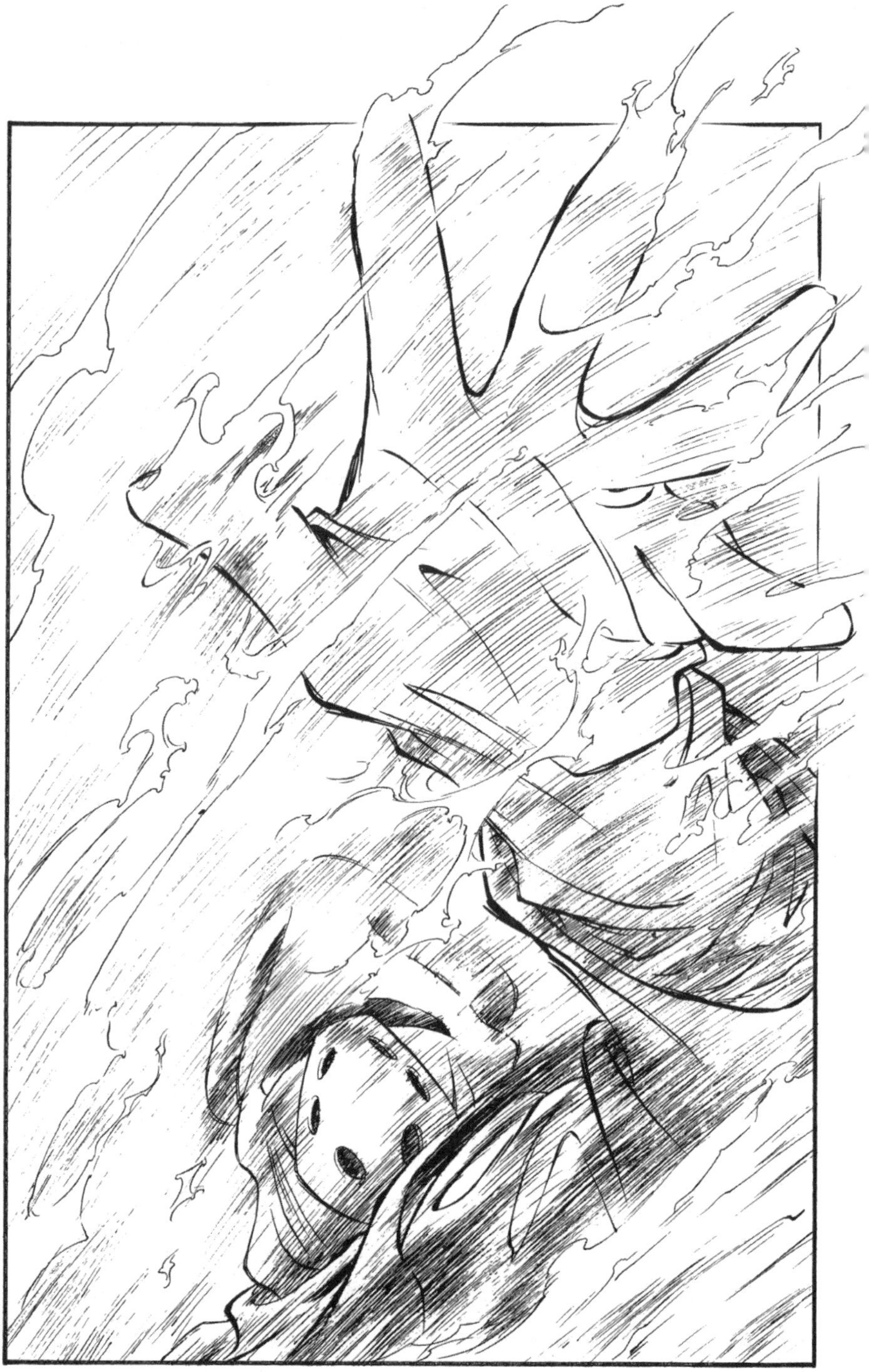

Conjured Flare Arrows ordinarily manifested in front of the caster, but I'd made a little modification to this spell too. *Okay! Now let's bust up those chimeras and...* I turned around, only to see...

"Bwuh?!" Gourry cried out in shock. The din of clashing swords followed. As for who'd attacked him, it was none other than...

"Sorry, little girl, but that won't work on me!"

"Zain?!"

For a moment, I couldn't believe my eyes and ears. His black clothing was clearly covered in scorch marks, but there was no sign of damage to the man therein. Had he anticipated my attack and cast a fire protection spell?! Or...

"Oh, damn!" Zain abruptly called out in fright before I could finish my thought.

Even as he continued to trade blows with Gourry, his eyes moved to me... No, behind me! I turned back, still wary of any sudden movement from Zain, and saw the vanguard chimera still frozen in place. I couldn't see anything amiss, but...

Oh, of course! The chimeras that had been crowding around behind the frozen one were nowhere to be seen, meaning... Wait, had they just up and left?! Was our buddy in black *not* in control of them?!

Realizing that the sound of swordplay had ceased, I looked back toward the boys in time to see Zain leap away. He put a wide berth between him and Gourry, then whipped around and dashed off into the darkness.

"Luring us again?" Gourry whispered.

"Doubtful!" I shouted back in response. "I think the chimeras got out, and all hell's about to break loose in the city!"

"Whaaat?!"

I quickly cast a spell. "Dynast Breath!"

Shing! This unaltered version pulverized the frozen baddie, and beyond it... just as I feared, there was nothing but an empty corridor. The chimeras that had been swarming behind it were long gone.

"What should we do, Lina?!"

"What else? If the monsters really have escaped topside, we can't just hang around here! We've gotta get back up there and see what's happening!"

I took off without waiting for a response from Gourry, who obediently followed behind. We ran back through the corridor, made a beeline for the top of the stairs, and found ourselves in the entrance hall once more.

"There!" I cried when I spotted a chimera standing up ahead. It noticed us and let out an intimidating roar, but before I could chant a spell...

Vwoosh! Gourry dashed out in front of me and slashed through the beast.

Gourry, you rock! If only you weren't as dumb as one!

"Was that the chimera you were talking about?"

"Yeah, but he's got buddies too."

"How many in all?"

"I can't say for sure... There should be about ten more, I think." I couldn't see any others nearby. There might have been some wandering around elsewhere in the building, but if any had gotten outside, they had to be our top priority. "So let's get out there!"

"Right!"

Gourry and I burst out the front door, and...

"Geh!" I stopped with a groan. The fight had already spilled beyond the compound walls, out into the city streets.

"I just don't get it," I commented to Gourry, who was waiting at our table, as I returned to the inn.

Last night, we'd managed to defeat all the chimeras running rampant in the city, make it back to the inn (acting as if nothing had happened), and get some shut-eye. But after breakfast this morning, I'd gotten curious about the status quo, so I'd headed out into town to run some recon.

"You don't get what? You mean nobody's talking about what happened last night?"

"Well, of course people are talking. There was an official statement and everything. Said it was the handiwork of a rogue sorcerer on the run, but that the culprit in question had already been apprehended."

"What's that mean?" Gourry asked, scowling.

"It means that the black cloak faction has suppressed the truth."

They probably wanted to keep things on the down-low here in their headquarters city. They even seemed to have lent a hand last night, as Gourry and I had stumbled across a few already-slain chimeras during our rounds.

I mean, no surprise the black cloaks didn't wanna publicly admit the real cause of the chaos, but...

"But still, they easily could've blamed all the trouble on you and me. They control the authorities and the flow of information, after all. But they didn't—that's what I don't get."

"Hmm..." Gourry scratched his head, puzzled.

"Want me to explain it to ya?" came a new voice.

"Huh?" I looked over to see a familiar face. "Luke?!"

Indeed, it was Luke, the black-haired warrior with the sour face. He'd appeared at our table at some point, sans Mileena for once.

"Hey," he said bluntly, taking an empty seat. He was scratching his head awkwardly. "I ain't a fan of this messenger boy crap, but ya can't say no to a client... This is why I hate hired gigs."

"That's a lot of griping from a guy who approached us. And what kind of mercenary hates hired gigs?"

"Who're you callin' a mercenary?! Me an' Mileena are treasure hunters!"

"Really?"

"Yeah!"

As the title suggested, treasure hunters sought out ruins and the like for loot to sell at a profit. Most folks would say that's not much different from what Gourry and I did, mind you... But whatever floats your boat as far as labels are concerned, I guess.

"Come to think of it," I said, "you guys got involved in the whole Bezeld drama because you were after a sword, right?"

"That's right! We hunt down storied treasures, surmount trials to find 'em, and then seize 'em for ourselves! A real life of adventure! I ain't no mercenary waggin' my tail for some bored rich jerk."

"But you're wagging your tail for Lord Lavas right now."

"Waaaaah," Luke suddenly bawled, sobbing in response to my comment. "L-Look... I ain't workin' for that guy 'cause I wanna be! I just..."

"You just... ran out of money?"

"No way! I just... Mileena took the job without even askin' me!"

"You could have turned *her* down, y'know."

"You stupid or somethin'? I could never turn my sweet Mileena down!"

"For all your big talk about adventure, you're pretty gutless when it comes to her..."

"Hmph. I'm a slave to my love!"

Or you're a slave, period...

"A slave to love? Come on, man..." Gourry said with a wince. "I think she's just got you whipped, is all. It's sad to see a man fall so low."

"As if you got a leg to stand on," Luke said, glaring at me and then at Gourry.

"Hang on, it's not like that. Lina doesn't have me whipped at all. It just looks that way because I don't like thinking for myself."

Sheesh... How you live your life is up to you, granted, but this is... It's just pathetic, both of you...

"So, anyway..." Realizing this train of thought was only going to get *more* depressing, I cast a glance at Luke. "Back to the subject at hand, what are you doing here? You made it sound like you've got some insider knowledge."

"Oh, right, yeah." He snapped back to himself at last, glanced around cautiously, then whispered, "You know the chimeras that were all over town last night?"

"We've heard rumors."

"Don't play dumb. The regent thinks you were involved. He's the one who covered it up."

"Oh?" I asked, keeping my own voice hushed.

"Yeah. He wants your help."

"Hmm." I thought for a minute. "This wouldn't happen to be... some kind of familial power struggle, would it?"

"Heh. Good call," Luke responded with a grin.

Not that it was especially hard to figure out. If there were two parties in conflict and one was a regent, it was reasonable to assume that the other was of comparable standing. A blood relative was the most likely candidate.

"So get this," Luke began. "Lord Lavas's got an older brother named Veisam. He's pretty ambitious, and he ain't satisfied with bein' in charge of one measly territory. So he starts plottin' all kinds of rotten stuff. An' now that their old man's fallen ill, he's left runnin' things to his little brother while he takes advantage of the money and power."

"Brothers, huh?"

"Yeah. But if what the older one is doin' gets out and the king hears about it, he'll strip 'em both of their rank an' titles. They could even end up with their heads on pikes. So Lavas's doin' what he can to stop his brother as quietly as possible. That's why he needs strong people on his side. One of the spies he sent to keep tabs on his brother reported that you guys were in town, so he wants to hire you."

"I see…" I remarked. It certainly added up.

"But that'd all be down the drain if you got arrested over the chimera business, so Lavas cooked up a story to feed the public and sent me to fill you in. Now, here's where I ask: You wanna help the regent out?"

"Hmm…" I scratched at the back of my head thoughtfully. "If you don't mind my asking, Luke, have you ever met this Veisam guy yourself?"

"Nah, no way. They say he ain't in the castle no more."

"I see. I'll pass, then."

"Got it. I'll let 'em know." Luke nodded easily and stood up.

"H-Hang on! You don't want to know why I turned you down?" I demanded. It was apparently my turn to lose my cool.

"I told you that I hate this messenger boy crap," he said in annoyance. "What you do ain't no business of mine, so it don't much matter to me *why* you do it."

"Mileena's going to be mad that you didn't ask."

That sent a full-body twitch through the self-proclaimed treasure hunter. He then sat back down. "W-Well… maybe I oughta hear you out after all."

"Man, how whipped does she have you?"

"C-C'mon, out with it already."

"Nah."

" … "

" … "

"Hey now…" Luke said, rubbing at his head hard. "Are you messin' with me or somethin'?"

"Kinda!"

Luke was at a loss for a response.

"But there *is* a good reason I'm not telling you," I offered. "And now that you've inquired, you can tell the regent and Mileena, 'I kept asking and she just wouldn't say.'"

"Got it." There, Luke stood up with a scowl and made his exit.

"Hey, Lina, why'd you refuse?" Gourry asked once he was out of the building. "It seems like the regent's in real trouble."

"That's assuming Luke... rather, that the *regent* is telling the truth," I explained. "I mean, the setup all sounds legit, but that doesn't mean it actually is. For example, what if their positions are reversed?"

"Reversed?"

"Maybe the regent's the one plotting the nastybads while the older brother Veisam is trying to stop 'im. Maybe Veisam fled the castle because his brother tried to kill him, and the regent wants to hire us as a distraction—or even to finish the job. Either way, we need to figure out what's what before we take sides. Moreover..."

"Moreover?"

"You remember the masked man who jumped in when the black cloaks were after us two nights ago? Who the heck was he?"

"Don't tell me... it was Veisam!"

"Doubtful, but..."

"We've seen royals acting as crusaders of justice before. Nothing weird about a noble lord putting on a mask and jumping up on walls, is there?"

"Huh... You got me there."

"Right?"

"Anyway, our top priority is still getting to the bottom of all this. In other words, it's time to ask around!"

"Say, Lina," Gourry called out.

"What?"

"I'm starting to think that sneaking into the castle, even if it is to get to the bottom of things, might be a tiny bit reckless," he continued in a whisper.

For, you see, we were currently both hiding in the shadows dressed in black clothes and black masks. Indeed, after an eventful day, we'd decided to infiltrate the castle in the dead of night. I cast a glance down the dark road to see its spires silhouetted against the moon and stars.

"C'mon, don't wimp out on me!" I hissed. "When I suggested sneaking in, you were all for it!"

"I don't remember you saying we were sneaking into the *castle*!"

"Of course not! I didn't tell you that part!"

"Okay, right…" Gourry whispered in exhausted response.

Earlier in the day, after Luke had slunk off, I'd gone around questioning the locals and learned a couple of things. First, there was indeed a man named Veisam in the lord's family. Second, Lord Lavas was new in town. The citizens had never heard of him until recently. Could it be a bastard son situation? Word on the street suggested as much.

But more importantly, people were saying that Veisam's disappearance, the lord's illness, and the sudden mysterious facility boom in the city center all coincided with Lavas's arrival. That seemed like a pretty big red flag. Of course, the idea that the appearance of a bastard brother had spurred Veisam to begin pursuing his own foolish ambitions wasn't one I could rule out…

I guess, in a way, we hadn't actually learned much relative to the amount of walking around we'd done. Our goal was to figure out which brother was the bad egg, help the other one come out on top, then take a couple magic swords and a couple hundred gold pieces as a reward. That meant we needed to sort out the intrigue ASAP.

"But Lina, will sneaking into the castle really tell us what we need to know?"

"Dunno."

"Come on…"

"Well, it's a lot more likely to yield useful information than sneaking into those other facilities at random. Take the one from yesterday. It had a hidden staircase and a bunch of chimeras in the basement, but that's not proof of a rebellion—and it certainly doesn't tell us which of the two brothers was behind it. But if Lord Lavas is the one plotting an insurrection, the castle's the best place to find evidence. For instance… if we're found sneaking around in the castle and the men in black attack us."

"That's even more reckless!"

"It's just one example. It's not like I'm gonna get us caught on purpose," I protested.

"I sure hope not. But if we search the place and find nothing, does that mean the missing brother is masterminding the rebellion and not the regent?"

"It could just mean that Lavas is cautious as hell. Either way, let's get going already."

I took Gourry's hand and began chanting a Levitation spell.

Infiltrating the castle itself wasn't hard. I did my usual—levitate us over the outer wall and land on the roof of the main building. I then cast an Unlock spell on the skylight of an empty room and slipped inside. The real work was yet to come.

If the regent *was* the mastermind and there *was* proof, where would it be hidden? Security outside wasn't too heavy, but there would probably be patrols in the castle itself and watchmen at key locations. It wouldn't be easy to slip through all of them and uncover the truth.

I mean, ideally we'd stumble upon a bad guy monologuing about his evil plan to his flunkies like in the old heroic sagas, but… you know.

Hmm… Where would I hide my incriminating evidence? I stood in the moonbeams streaming through the skylight for a while, my head pensively cocked to the side. "Okay," I whispered softly. "I know what we're after."

"What?" asked Gourry.

"We're gonna pay the bedridden lord a visit."

"Hey now…"

"Security will probably be tight, but we can learn the whole story if we find him."

"You really think he's gonna tell us?!"

"Depends on how we broach the subject. I have an idea, though. Leave it to me."

"Well… if you insist." Gourry sounded hesitant but seemed to accept my assurances.

While carefully scanning for nearby sounds and presences, Gourry and I opened the door and set out.

"Hey… do you think we're maybe going in the wrong direction?" Gourry whispered after we'd stealthily scuttled a ways down a dim, empty hall.

Upon leaving the room we'd come in through… Well, we'd started our search, but the place was just crawling with patrolmen. We'd gone from lighter security area to lighter security area, but all we'd found so far were boring places that probably didn't see much use. The corridors here were almost pitch black, with only the occasional sconce on the wall and absolutely zero guards.

"Maybe, sure… But what recourse do we have?" I whispered back.

"Why don't you put the guards to sleep with your magic?"

"Y'know, Gourry, for how much you call me reckless, that's a pretty reckless suggestion. Even if I did put a soldier to sleep for us to sneak by, another soldier would come along soon enough, find his passed-out buddy, and sound the alarm. We'd have to tuck tail and run with nothing to show for it."

"Yeah, but still… wandering from empty room to empty room isn't getting us much either."

Ack! Surprisingly keen insight from the big lug!

"F-Fair… So, okay, let's go somewhere else!" I said, setting off once more.

If we retraced our steps, we'd be backtracking into a patrol unit. The route ahead seemed safe enough, so I figured we'd continue on while looking for alternative paths. We thus darted around in the dark at random for a bit, and then…

Gourry and I stopped in our tracks at the same time. The hall we'd been following for a while suddenly split in two. Off to our right, I could feel human presences.

If people were around, you'd think they'd have lights with them… yet the corridor in question was just as dark as the others. The word "ambush" popped into my head, but I didn't get any sense that these folks were trying to cloak themselves.

Hmm… I stood there in the darkness pondering the situation. If someone was here, surely it was for a reason. It was unlikely that another party of intruders just happened to be invading at the same time we were, and even if that was the case, they wouldn't just be standing around like this. The lack of hushed voices probably ruled out a clandestine meeting too.

What could it be, then? Curiosity began to gnaw at me.

Welp, time to find out! If we just strode over there, then the persons in question were bound to notice us. But fortunately, there were no patrols around, which opened up my options somewhat.

I recited a spell under my breath. "Sleeping!" Within moments…

"Ugh... Mm..."

"Mrrgh..."

I heard a set of soft groans from down the corridor, in the direction of the presences, followed by the sound of people hitting the floor.

Okay! I signaled to Gourry and we advanced together. We turned the corner to find two guards, collapsed under my spell, in front of an unassuming door. Given its location and rickety appearance, I would've guessed it was a broom closet. But who in the world would put guards on a broom closet?

"What's in here?" Gourry asked quietly.

"Dunno. No idea what they're protecting all in secret like this... but the best way to find out is to see for ourselves," I said, reaching for the knob. It wasn't locked.

Wreeeeek... The door opened with a slight squeak. The air inside was stagnant. At the center of the room was a single lamp casting a dim light over the walls and an old canopy bed. On it lay a frail old man. He showed no sign of stirring upon our entry, just let out the unsteady sounds of sleep unique to the bedridden.

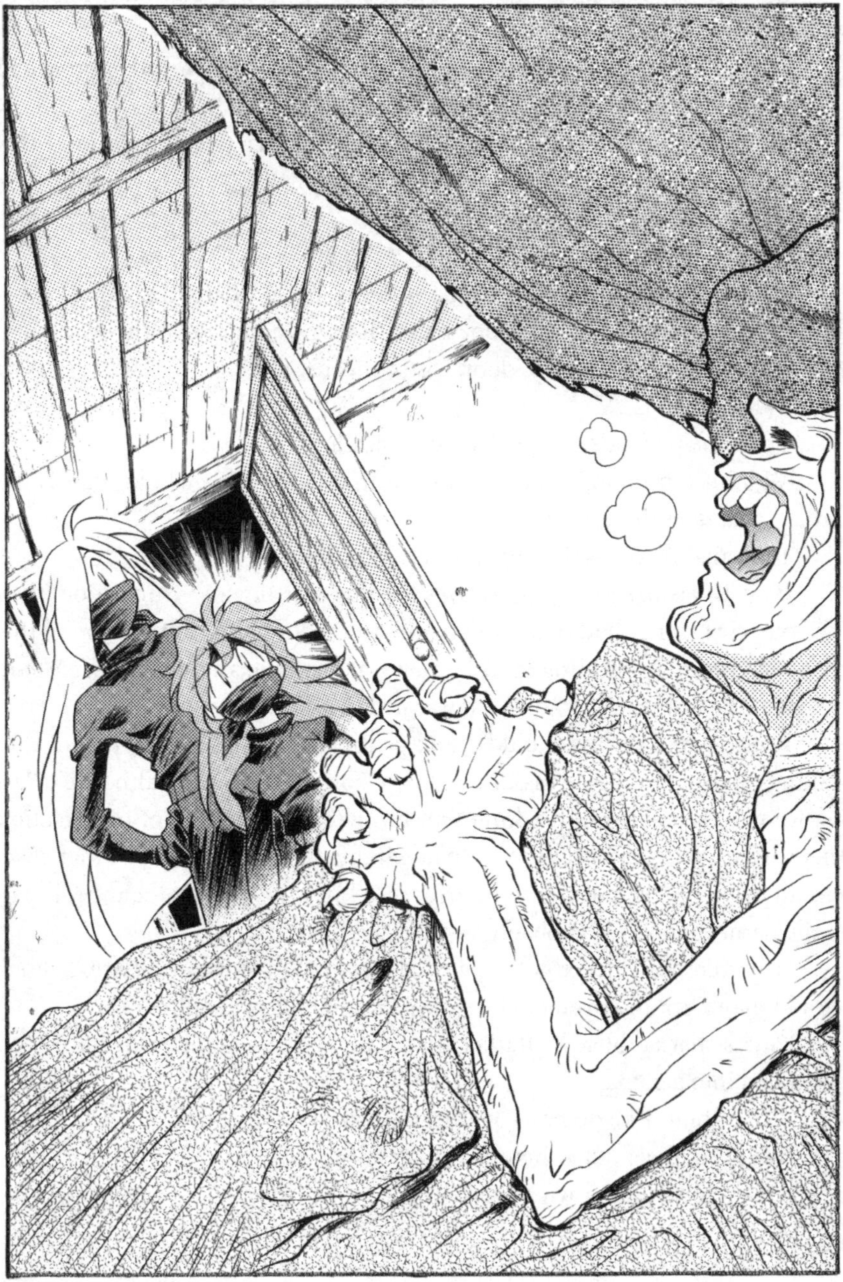

But… what was a sick man doing here? If he was quarantined, there wouldn't be any guards on the room…

"Hmm?" I sensed something in the man's countenance and approached. I took his pulse, inspected his skin, and smelled his breath.

"Hey, what're you doing, Lina? What can you learn from prodding at that old guy?"

"That he's been poisoned, for one thing."

"What?!" Gourry breathed.

"By the kind you feed someone little by little. That's the cause of his current condition. He was poisoned and thrown in an out-of-the-way room with two guards posted at the door, which means…"

"Which means…?"

"I can't help wondering if this is our 'sick lord.'"

"W-Wait a minute!" Gourry shouted in a panic. "If this old man is the lord… what *does* that mean?"

"It means Lavas is spinning lies," I said softly.

If, as Lavas has said, Veisam was the one plotting an insurrection, then the younger brother had no reason to poison the lord and shut him up in this cheap old room. Presuming this old man was the lord, anyway. To make sure of that… the fastest way to find out was just to ask him.

I put a hand on his shoulder and gently shook him. I didn't want him waking up and making a fuss, but I knew how to keep him calm. We'd just say we were scouts from the king sent to investigate rumors of insurrection. That way, drawing attention wouldn't be in his interest. Of course, that cover was all just a big lie, but a certain princess I knew would have said, "All's fair in the name of justice!" Probably, anyway.

Regardless… I never got a chance to put my plan into practice. I shook the old man over and over, but he showed no sign of awakening.

"Guess that's a bust…" Rather than simply sleeping, he must have been enervated into a coma.

"What should we do now?" Gourry asked.

"We need to get out of here."

"I'm all for that, but what then?"

"Good question. Why don't we wake up one of the guards and ask them? If this old man is the real lord, that means Lavas is the one usurping his position to raise a military force."

"I see. Let's get to it, then."

Gourry and I exited through the door, back into the hallway. There...

"Hey, you two!" cried a familiar voice.

Geh! I didn't know what the hell they were doing here, but I looked up to see... Luke and Mileena.

Chapter 3:   Battle Breaks over Solaria at Night

"Who's there? Don't move!" Luke drew his sword and dashed straight at us.

Whaaa?! Gourry and I reflexively ran in the opposite direction!

"Don't try to get away, you bastards!" he shouted as he gave chase.

A pretty absurd request, if you ask me. When a guy charges you with a sword, you get the hell outta there! Granted, I'll admit that we looked pretty darn suspicious under the circumstances. Faces covered, dressed all in black... and while we weren't armored, we *were* armed. All that, plus two guards collapsed by the door? It was no wonder Luke was after us.

The question now was how to handle the situation. Should Gourry and I peace out, or reveal our identities and explain ourselves? The answer came to me easily enough—*Let's book it!*

With Luke's shouting and carrying on, there were bound to be other guards on the way. And amidst all the coming kerfuffle, we'd never get a chance to tell our side of the story. We were just gonna have to make tracks for now and get back in touch tomorrow to lay out the sitch. Now, as for how best to make our getaway...

I chanted a spell under my breath. "Dam Blas!" Then I whipped around and unleashed it!

Crash! Just as I'd planned, the blast broke through the ceiling between us and Luke, raining debris down to block their way.

"What?!" Luke backed off to avoid the shower.

Meanwhile, I chanted another spell, took Gourry's hand, and... "Lei Wing!"

I used that to take us out the hole in the ceiling and land up on the roof. I theoretically could have just kept going, but Lei Wing's speed, altitude, and carrying capacity all varied greatly based on the magical power at the caster's disposal. With Gourry in tow, it took all my concentration just to get us this far. My Demon Blood talismans would let me tote him with ease, but I hadn't had time to cast the amplification chant with Luke on our heels.

So I waited to cast it until now, as we reached the edge of the roof.

Hail, Lords of the four worlds' darkness
I beseech your bond and beg you this boon
By your powers combined, entwined,
Bless me with magic mightier than mine

And with that one little recitation, the Demon Blood talismans on my neck, both wrists, and belt buckle began to shine. I could feel their power filling my body. I then started chanting a new Lei Wing. When I did...

"Get back here!"

Luke and Mileena appeared on the roof too, probably courtesy of a Levitation spell.

Man, talk about persistent!

Luke darted toward us, but just before he could close the distance, I finished my chant!

"Lei Wing!" With far greater speed than the last time, Gourry and I took flight and fled into the night sky. Now, once we shook these guys off—

"Lina! They're after us!" Gourry shouted.

"Whaaaaaaaat?!" I couldn't help screaming. "You gotta be kiddin' me! First those men in black, now Luke and Mileena?!"

"Guess your spell isn't all that fast..."

"Yeah, right! There ain't a sorcerer around with a spell that can keep up with this baby!"

"Except them, I guess. Oh, I know!"

"You know what?!"

"Last night, your spell didn't work on the man in black either. Must be that time of the month!"

"It is not!" I barked.

Gourry was right that I'd failed to defeat opponents I should've trounced and outrun opponents I should've left in the dust... But my magic wasn't compromised in any way. The speed of my Lei Wing just now and the force of the Dam Blas I'd used on the ceiling earlier were up to snuff. That meant we had a different problem on our hands—our opponents were more powerful than usual.

A normal Lei Wing could never keep up with my amplified one. But one with an artfully altered chant? An enhancement like that might get the job done. It seemed Luke and Mileena had quite a few tricks up their sleeves... I'd have to ask 'em about it later. For now, however, our top priority was filling them in.

I flew out to one of the city's meandering walls some distance from the castle, touched down in an unpopulated area, and dismissed my flight spell. Not long after, Luke and Mileena followed suit. It looked like Luke had been pulling Mileena by the hand through the air, but I suspected both could use Lei Wing. If you combined two spells just right, maybe you could boost their effectiveness. But all that aside...

Hang on, you two! I wanted to cry, but before I could... a ball of magic appeared in Luke's outstretched hand! *Oh, for the love of...!*

"Prepare for pain, assholes!" Luke shouted and released the orb. It broke up in midair, sending countless small glowing bullets showering down on me and Gourry.

"Gwaaaah!"

Pow! Powpapow! Gourry and I split as they rained down around our feet. They didn't seem particularly powerful on their own, but I wasn't anxious to taste one.

"You ain't gettin' away from us!"

"Hold your freakin' horses, darn it!" I shouted, turning back toward Luke as I pulled the cloth off of my face. "It's me! It's us!"

"What the...?!" Luke stopped, understandably surprised, while Mileena observed us as stoically as ever. Had she already figured us out, perhaps?

"It was you guys?!" Meanwhile, Luke seemed absolutely flabbergasted, suggesting he definitely hadn't. "Finally turned to dirty dealings, did ya?!"

"Why would you assume that?!"

"Shut up and eat this!" Luke extended his hand, another ball of light forming in it...

"I'd advise you to hear them out!" a familiar voice boomed out, interrupting him.

"What?!" Luke called off his attack, looked around, and froze when he saw something.

I followed his gaze and spotted a silhouette standing on a roof near the wall. It was the masked man again!

"You there, raven-hair. Are you doing this with full knowledge of Lavas's plot?" the masked man boomed again.

"What?!" Luke stammered, looking shaken by the accusation. "Lavas's plot? What're you talkin' about?!"

"Lavas is leading the men in black we fought in Bezeld!" I threw in this time.

"For real?!"

"We're not sure yet! That's why we snuck into the castle!"

"For your information, Lavas's plot does not stop with merely amassing forces…" The masked man glanced around him. "But it seems I've no time to explain."

I heard a rustling on the wind and suddenly felt presences appear all around us.

Of course… Luke and Mileena weren't the only ones who'd followed us. The figures that came into view, rising up out of nowhere like moonlight taken form, were the all-too-familiar men in black. More than ten of them, at that.

"Beware," said the masked man, his eyes cautiously scanning their ranks. "Several of these men are fused with demons."

What?! I looked back at Mr. Mask in shock. And I wasn't the only one taken aback.

"You… Who are you?! How much do you know?" one of the men in black demanded anxiously, lending credence to the man's declaration.

But it made perfect sense! That explained how Zain had gotten so much stronger than before, and how his buddies had kept up with my amplified Lei Wing. They had demonic power now!

Still, if that was the case, it was hardly good news. What I'd witnessed so far (these guys quick-casting spells and blocking them barehanded) didn't mean they'd been sneaking chants past me somehow; it meant most magic didn't work on them at all.

"Take the masked man alive. Kill the others."

On the lead man's order, the other black cloaks sprang into action. One of them jumped up on top of the wall, produced a spear of light in his hand, and let it fly. His target? The masked man on the roof!

But the masked man just calmly and quietly brought his right hand forward. "Vas Gluud." As if he'd expected the black cloak's play, he created a magic barrier the size of a small shield. *Plink!* It dispersed the spear of light effortlessly.

"What?!" The man in black froze for a second, shaken.

Ah, never let your guard down, as they say! I'd already finished chanting my spell. "Blast Ash!"

Vwsh! Before he could even scream, the man in black on the wall turned to dust.

"Don't underestimate them!" spat one of the men in black. It sounded like Zain! "I'll start with you, Lina Inverse!"

With that, Mr. Probably Zain came straight for me! Still, he had a lot of ground to cover, and I could chant pretty darn fast! I completed my next spell before I was even in his sword range.

"Blast Ash!" I aimed it right where I expected him to run. About the only spells in my repertoire with a fairly wide area of effect that would *also* work against targets with beefy magic resistance were this and Dragon Slave—and I couldn't go chucking Dragon Slaves in the middle of a city.

My Blast Ash caused a black something-or-other to wreath any swath of air I targeted. The dark field would expand and then disappear, reducing any opponent caught within it to ash. I watched as it encircled Zain, and when it disappeared, I saw... nothing.

"Lina!"

The second Gourry cried out, I felt a chill run up my spine and immediately leaped forward.

Whoosh! Something brushed by my back. I quickly took my distance, turned around, and saw a man in black standing there, sword in hand. There was no way it was reinforcements. The men in black already had us surrounded. Which meant... this could only be...

"He... He just came out of nowhere!" Luke shouted, confirming my theory.

"Is that your power, Zain?!" I demanded.

"It is," he responded quietly.

Just as I thought. In the moment I'd cast my spell, Zain had warped behind me in an attempt to sneak in a backstab. The ability to blink through space... That explained his impossible moves in our battle last night as well. It was something I'd seen powerful pure demons do from time to time. But to see a human do it, even if he was fused with a demon... That'd only be possible by combining the magic power he'd acquired through the fusion with a certain degree of innate magic skill as a human. That added up to a tricky opponent.

I'd so narrowly dodged his blow that it had caught the edge of my clothing, but I might not be so lucky the next time. If the masked man was to be believed, Zain wasn't the only one with a deadly trick up his sleeve either. And that was all without acknowledging that these guys had us outnumbered two to one, which wasn't the best of odds even if they'd been normal humans. Yeah, this was gonna be a tough fight.

While we were panicking over the reveal of what Zain could do, the other men in black began to close in. *If the five of us could work together, then maybe...*

But just as I was thinking that—*Tnk!*—the masked man suddenly leaped from his roof to the top of the wall. With another jump, he then vanished into the adjacent block.

That little sucker ran off on us! I wasn't the only one distraught over his actions. Zain also let out a cry of surprise, briefly stopping in place.

"Raza Clover!" In that instant, Mileena unleashed a spell.

Zain leaped up and dodged it with ease. "You four, after him! The rest of you, finish them off here!" At his behest, several of the men in black disappeared over the wall in pursuit of the masked man.

Aha... The black cloaks' priority was pinning down the masked man and what he knew. Him fleeing the scene had taken some of the heat off of us. But even so, we were still outnumbered. We'd have to approach this carefully.

Zain, who'd remained on our side of the wall, dashed straight at me again!

Clink! Two flashes of silver clashed, a metallic ring resounding through the air. Gourry had dived in to parry Zain's blow before it could reach me.

Then, as if intent to finish their business from the night before, they launched into a fierce back-and-forth.

Too bad I didn't have time to stand around and watch it. The remaining men in black set upon us immediately. I drew my sword, on my guard for the first one charging at me. Needless to say, I was also chanting a spell!

Shing! I blocked the incoming strike just as I finished my spell. "Freeze Arrow!"

Fwsh! Responding to my words of power, a few dozen bolts of ice manifested in front of me. A normal casting of this spell would only summon a fraction of that, but this puppy was amplified!

"Wha?!" Clearly terrified by this, the man in black leaped back.

"Go!" I fired my spell into the densest part of the black cloaks' ranks.

Fshhfshhfshh! Countless streaks of light audibly tore through the air. It was such an overwhelming ice storm that there was no way to dodge it all, even if you were fast.

"What?!"

"Gwah!"

Were those screams of shock, or pain? Either way, I heard quite a few and saw two men collapse. Ice magic probably wouldn't work on the demon-fused guys, but quite a few of the black cloaks seemed to be plain ol' humans, and my goal was to sift out a few of their number. Fortunately, my plan had worked perfectly. I started my next spell…

Clank! Clang! I could hear the ringing of metal on metal directly behind me. At some point, Mileena had moved to stand back-to-back with me, her sword drawn. Beyond her, some distance away, two men in black had thrown something at me—maybe knives—which she'd knocked out of the air. The men's hands were raised like they were about to throw something again…

"Fight like men already!" Luke shouted as he swung his sword. *Whoosh!* A burst of wind from his magical blade sent the men in black flying.

And as if she'd been waiting for just that… "Fell Zaleyd!" Mileena incanted, unleashing a swirling bolt of white light that mowed one of them down!

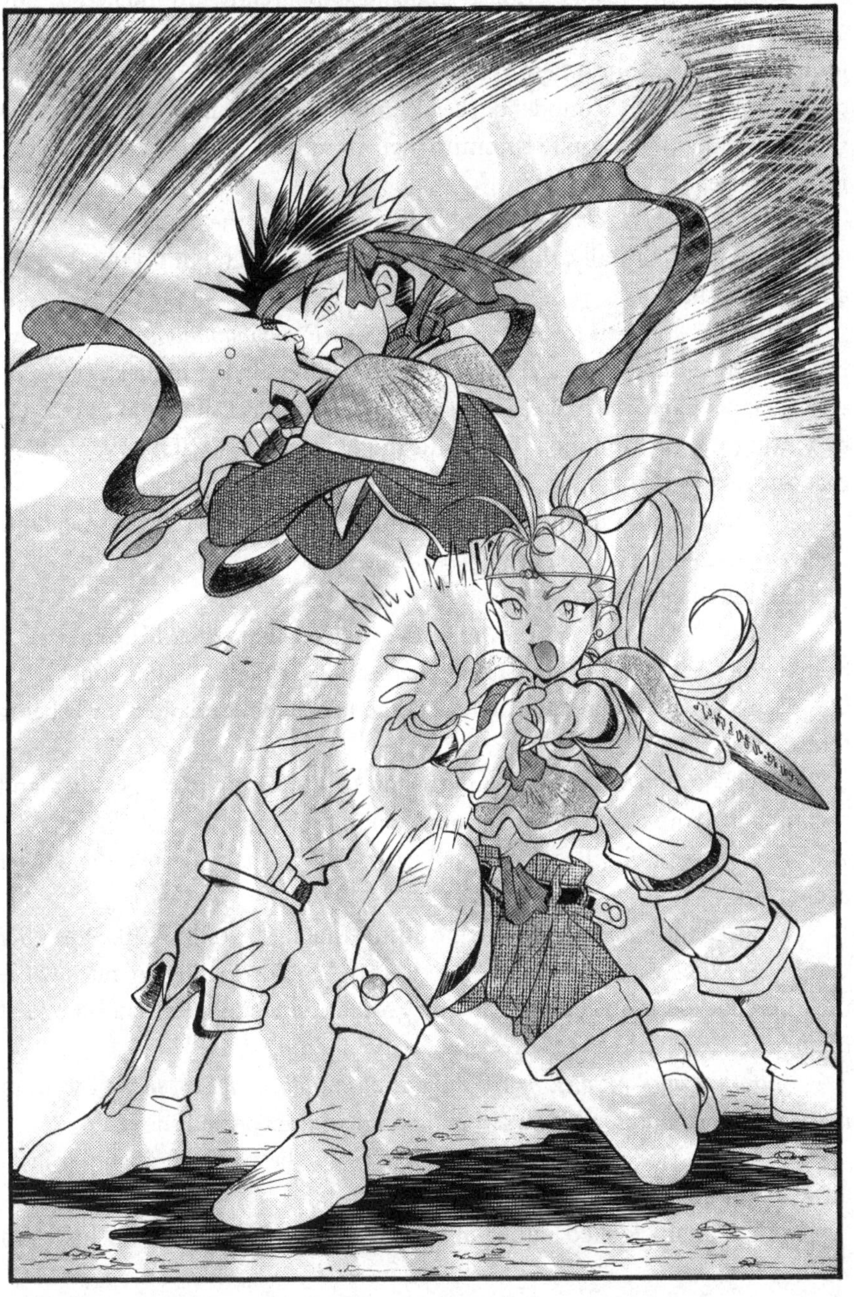

Their teamwork was seriously amazing. Apparently intimidated by how quickly we'd dispatched so many of their buddies, some of the men in black looked hesitant... but others yet were still raring to go. Were they just that cocky, or was this the confidence their demonic powers afforded them? It was safe to assume that, despite thinning their numbers, we still had quite a few formidable enemies left to face.

So... what if I do this?! I released the spell I had at the ready.

"Fireball!" Normally, this baby exploded on contact, but I'd tweaked the chant a little bit.

"Break!" I snapped my fingers, and then... *Fwooobababoom!* High above my head, the Fireball burst, creating crimson flowers in the night sky.

Two days ago, the masked man had forced the black cloaks to retreat just by hinting at the commotion their battle might cause. So what if I *intentionally* made a scene here and now? I was betting it'd chase them off again.

"Damn it! This ain't no time for playin' around!" Luke yelled at me, none the wiser to my plan. It certainly gave the black cloaks pause, however...

All but one of them.

"Graaah!" The man who refused to be cowed charged at Mileena with a bestial howl. With the force of a berserker, he piled on attack after attack.

"Tch...!" Barely managing to deflect the strikes, Mileena was slowly being forced back.

"Hey! Lay off my Mileena!" Luke bellowed, moving in to support her (and sneaking in some shameless self-promotion in the process).

"I'm not yours," Mileena objected, as cool as could be despite the danger she was in.

I was chanting a spell in the meantime, natch. I would've liked to offer Gourry or Mileena a little magical backup, but I couldn't really do much while they were locked in melee combat. Too great a chance that I might hit one of them.

Should I work on picking off the rest of the black cloaks, then? I went to release my spell and... that was when I heard an unexpected shout.

"What?!" cried an old man on the side of the road—probably a local attracted by all the ruckus.

"Tch..." Zain looked rather disturbed and leaped back from his clash with Gourry.

Yes! Success! If we could draw a big crowd, the men in black would be forced to retreat!

Or so I thought, except the man in black attacking Mileena didn't react the same way. He did break away from their skirmish, but...

"You're in my way," he said casually. His left hand flashed.

"Geh!" The onlooker let out one final shout as he hit the ground with a thud.

What the...?!

"What are you doing, Zord?!" Zain reproached him.

"Getting rid of a witness!" the man called Zord responded with unsettling glee. "Anyone who interrupts our battle must die!"

"Are you insane?! You just made things worse! He won't be the only one who comes!"

"Then I'll kill all of them!" Zord said, his left hand now flashing... in my direction!

Sensing a danger that I couldn't put into words, I jumped to the side. An unseen blade severed a lock of my hair.

My beautiful tresses! How dare you?!

But this was no time to be petty. This was probably the same move he used to kill that innocent old man. I'd thought it was a throwing knife at first, but I hadn't seen anything moving through the air. My hair was there one minute and simply gone the next.

An invisible shockwave, then... Zord must have produced one the size of a knife when he flicked his hand.

This is so not cool! I decided. Watching Zord's movements and dodging when he seemed about to attack was going to be the only way to deal with it. But with other enemies around, I couldn't afford to focus solely on him. In other words, we were gonna have to finish him off first!

I released my next spell, another Blast Ash, even knowing how easily these guys could dodge it! *Don't get caught up in this, Mileena!*

"Blast Ash!" I aimed straight at Zord's back.

He must have realized it was coming—either that or he had good instincts—because he ran forward to avoid it. When he did, though, Luke leaped in! *Vwoosh!* With a magnificently timed sweep, he cut deep into Zord's side.

Yes! Now we just— But my celebration was premature. Zord immediately swung his own sword right back at Luke, with a speed that suggested he was totally unfazed by his gaping wound.

"Huh?!" Luke managed to block the strike despite his surprise. "How in the hell…?!"

"Wahaha! You'll need more than that to kill me!"

H-Hang on a minute now! This guy's tough as freakin' nails! If we don't beat him fast, we're in trouble! Yet before I could make my next move…

"Withdraw!" thundered Zain.

The other men in black immediately pulled back. Everyone except for Zord.

"Zord!" Zain scolded.

"Go on if you want to! I'm not done here!" he replied in a crazed tone.

Word to the wise: don't give crazy dudes superpowers. Or… was his madness a byproduct of the demon fusion?!

"What will *he* think of your insubordination?!" Zain shouted.

Twitch! That threat seemed to register with Zord. He quickly jumped back, got some distance from the group, and hurriedly said, "F-Fine! I'm sorry!"

Huh? He seemed completely docile now.

"Let's go."

With Zain's second order, the men in black at last all disappeared into the darkness. Zain withdrew with them, leaving the four of us to a growing crowd of rubberneckers.

"Anyway… we'd better get going too," I said.

"Indeed." Mileena nodded in response. "We should head somewhere we can have a quiet talk."

"Aha… so that's the deal," Luke whispered grumpily, sipping his cup of wine as I finished my story.

After the men in black had retreated, Gourry and I slipped back to our lodgings, picked up our luggage, and got some distance from the walled-off central block of the city. We'd then made our way to this inn-slash-tavern (which seemed weirdly run-down despite not actually being that old) in a burgeoning outer district. The houses here looked like they'd been built willy-nilly with no actual attempt at city planning, giving the place a real "wrong side of the tracks" vibe. The joint was packed with seedy and suspicious characters too—the perfect hiding spot, if you ask me.

"So can we say for sure that the regent's in league with the guys in black?" Luke now asked.

"Seems like it to me, yeah," I replied as I took a bite out of the salmon sandwich I'd ordered off the late-night menu.

"Tch. He really pulled the wool over our eyes, huh?" he said in frustration.

Mileena interjected calmly, "Not *ours*. Just yours."

"Huh?" Luke looked stunned at this. "W-Wait a minute... I thought you trusted the regent, Mileena."

"Why would I? I've never liked redheads."

"W-Well... that's kinda prejudiced, if you ask me..."

"Weren't you the one who took the bodyguard job?" I had to ask. I was pretty sure that's what Luke had told me.

"I was. But I had my reasons." The silver-haired sorceress then began to explain in her ever-calm voice...

Many nights ago in a city not too far from here, Mileena—fed up with Luke's incorrigible lovey-dovey overtures (her words)—decided to leave their inn and take a stroll. While she was out, she encountered a man who claimed to be a servant to Lord Langmeier of Solaria. He said the lord had been usurped, and that his entire family might be killed if nothing was done. He was allegedly on the way to report the situation to the king himself, and he was looking for protection for the journey.

Mileena had turned him down. Not because she hated mundane errands (unlike our whiny buddy Luke), but because she doubted the man's story. This was entirely understandable, of course. Who comes crying to a random merc on the side of the road—that they haven't even hired yet, no less—about how their lord has been usurped? Mileena figured it must have been some kind of scam.

But the next day, when she found that same man dead on the street, she had to wonder... *Could* he have been telling the truth? Had he unloaded on her out of desperation, knowing his pursuers would catch up to him soon? Was it a last-ditch effort to ensure that the knowledge didn't die with him? Mileena had come to Solaria to find out for herself.

"But if the regent's got the men in black, why hire you guys?" Gourry asked skeptically as Mileena wrapped up her tale.

"He's probably the opportunistic type," she replied, taking a sip of brandy-infused tea. "I wanted to stay at the castle a bit longer to investigate, but of course, things have since changed."

"Ah, so you were investigating too when you stumbled across us, huh?" I mused when it dawned on me.

Mileena nodded silently.

"There was a man laid up in that room we broke into," I shared. "He'd been drugged."

Twitch. Mileena's eyebrow arched slightly.

"I'm assuming... that he was Lord Langmeier."

"So he really did get usurped," Gourry remarked with a frown. "Wait, then who's this Lavas guy really?"

"Our enemy—I can tell ya that much," Luke said as simply as ever. "But the one I'm wonderin' about now is that masked guy. Just who is *he*?"

"Well... probably not our enemy, at least," I offered.

"You sure about that? What if he's an agent of the king, who's just usin' us to keep Lavas busy? Or what if the lord's other son, Veisam, got out alive and this dude's workin' for him, huh? That'd explain how he knows so much. If that's his angle, he might play nice as long as we're handy... and then throw us to the wolves once Lavas is gone."

"Fair enough. We won't slot him in the ally column just yet, then."

"The smartest thing to do, if you ask me," Luke said, with a glance at Mileena, as he scratched his head, "is to say bye-bye to Solaria, give the king a heads-up about what's goin' on here, and leave the rest to him."

"You can do that if you like. But I won't be going with you," Mileena said harshly.

"Mileenaaa..." Luke whined, turning teary-eyed.

"Can I ask a question? What should *we* do next?" Gourry asked, wincing in anticipation of my expected reply.

Far be it for me to disappoint him, I delivered with a bright smile. "The same thing we do to anyone who picks a fight with us, be it cat or bird or regent lord!"

"Then it's decided," Mileena said, expression unchanged.

Luke smiled through a grimace. "So we wait for things to quiet down and strike back?"

"Oh, don't be such a wimp," I said, rising to my feet after polishing off the last of my sandwich. "We strike right now—while the iron is hot!"

Solaria that night was as busy as I'd ever seen a city. That was to be expected, given that there'd been trouble two evenings running. The site of our last battle was packed with onlookers, as well as guards marching this way and that to investigate the scene and keep traffic moving.

We gazed down at it all as we flew overhead through the darkened sky. We were backtracking to the temple-like building that Gourry and I had infiltrated on our first little mission, but there were a few key differences now. For starters, we had a bigger party... And more importantly, this was no stealth operation. We were going to pick a fight this time.

I figured there had to be a pretty important facility under there, see... Possibly a facility creating demonoid humans like Zain and Zord. We needed to find it and crush it.

Of course, the quickest way to wrap this whole business up would actually be to head to the castle, tie Lavas up, and beat a confession out of him. In fact, that *was* my original plan, but Mileena had poo-pooed it. It was clear that Lavas was our prime suspect, but we still didn't have solid proof against him yet. She was concerned that if we came for Lavas and it turned out he wasn't the mastermind after all, we'd be up a certain creek without a paddle.

(My thinking was that a little "Teehee, whoopsies! Wrong guy!" would be enough to cover our asses in just such a situation, but Mileena had poo-pooed that too.)

Hence we'd shifted our sights to the facilities in the heart of the city. Whether or not Lavas was behind them personally, it was clear that they were important to the men in black. Striking one might enable us to put a dent in their forces, and if things went *really* well, we might even be able to identify their ringleader and bag some evidence of the rising insurrection.

It was also possible that Zain and his goons were busy reporting to their boss right now, so they might not even be around. It was highly unlikely that they were expecting a reprisal from us so soon, which meant security on the facility should be fairly light. Talk about a golden opportunity!

"There it is!" I whispered quietly—"it" being the temple-esque building with the domed roof.

I shepherded our group closer. Because of the darkness of night and the distortion of our wind barrier, it was hard to be certain, but it sure seemed like there were fewer guards than last time. The four of us touched down on the roof.

"Mileena, put up a wind barrier," I said.

"Why?"

"Sound dampening." She caught on quickly, chanted the spell, and conjured a wind barrier surrounding us. As for me... "Dam Blas!"

Crash!

The attack I unleashed broke through the floor at our feet with a big boom, but Mileena's wind barrier muted most of it. We then levitated down into the building through the hole I'd made. It was as dark inside as it had been on our last visit, but this time, we didn't have to keep quiet. Just as I was about to chant a light spell...

Wham!

"What is it?!"

"Who are you people?! Hold it right there!"

The outside door flew open and security forces poured in, rabbling at us.

"No fair!" I cried. "We muffled the sound!"

"They could still hear the rubble falling, dumbass," Luke whispered in response.

Ah... fair point. Our wind barrier prevented sound from leaking out roofside, but it didn't do much about the debris hitting the ground below. That had, um... probably made quite a lot of noise, in fact...

Welp, whatever! No use crying over spilled milk, right?

I quickly chanted a spell, got around behind the pews, and turned toward the approaching soldiers. "Sleeping!"

The crowd collapsed with a frankly comical *thumpa-thumpa-thud*. The fact that they'd all gone off to dreamland so easily suggested that there weren't any demonoids like Zain and Zord among them.

More soldiers kept coming, but Mileena and I put most of 'em to sleep with more magic. Any that managed to get through were quickly knocked unconscious by Gourry and Luke. Soon enough, we had a cathedral packed with snoozing soldiers, and no more reinforcements to go.

There had been two men in black present here last time, but maybe they'd been sent out to find us and weren't back yet. Maybe they were lying low for some other reason. Or maybe they were hiding in the main facility underground, just waiting for us...

At any rate, I cast another spell. "Lighting!"

Pop! The light I threw up toward the ceiling hung in the air overhead and illuminated the room around us. Lines of pews, a central walkway... and at the head of everything, a rather grand altar with a divine statue behind it. The building could certainly be used as a real place of worship. If not for all the security, I would never have pegged it for a front.

There was probably a hidden door somewhere around, but we didn't have time to search it out the old-fashioned way. I began chanting under my breath... "Dam Blas!"

Crash! My amplified blast tore through the floor below! And beneath it was... dirt.

"Tch. Not here, huh?" I was hoping to hit the jackpot on the first blast. I began chanting again.

"Hey... you're not gonna keep blasting the floor until you find a way down, are you?" Gourry asked in disbelief.

But of course I wasn't. I placed a hand on the exposed earth... "Bepheth Bring!"

This was a burrowing spell I used to create a long, narrow tunnel through the ground. My thought was that if I cast enough of these in various directions, we'd eventually connect to the underground facility. But I didn't even have to run a second chant. There was already light at the end of my tunnel.

"Found it." The facility seemed to be hidden pretty far below. I cast another spell to widen the hole, and then... "Actually, scratch that." I'd been thinking about using Levitation to take us down, but I changed my mind and switched to a different incantation. Right down the tunnel, I sent a... "Fireball!"

Fwoosh! Once the flames in the depths died back, Luke and Mileena levitated down through the tunnel. Gourry and I followed suit a second later.

We found ourselves in a straight, empty corridor with white walls, partly charred black by my Fireball. I'd shot the blast in the event that there was an ambush waiting for us inside, but there were no enemies in sight. The sound would probably bring them running soon, though, and knife-throwing enemies in a narrow place like this would probably make short work of us. In other words, we needed to get a move on!

I chanted another spell, and... "Dam Blas!" I fired at one of the walls based on nothing but a gut feeling.

Crash! And... pay dirt! I'd opened a huge hole that revealed a vast room on the other side. I darted in without looking and...

"Wh-What?!" There were a total of five sorcerers inside. They cast flustered, fearful gazes my way.

Now, I pegged them for sorcerers, but based on their appearance and bearing, these guys looked the research kind rather than the casting kind. And they weren't the only people around.

Well... "people" might be putting it loosely. There were several dozen chimera-growing crystal tubes in the room. And suspended in the so-called water of life within... were probably the fruits of their human-demon fusion experiments. Men who seemed half human, half lesser demon. Women with twisted bodies below the neck. And... children, equally deformed.

It was clear that none of these once-human creatures had volunteered to be part of this.

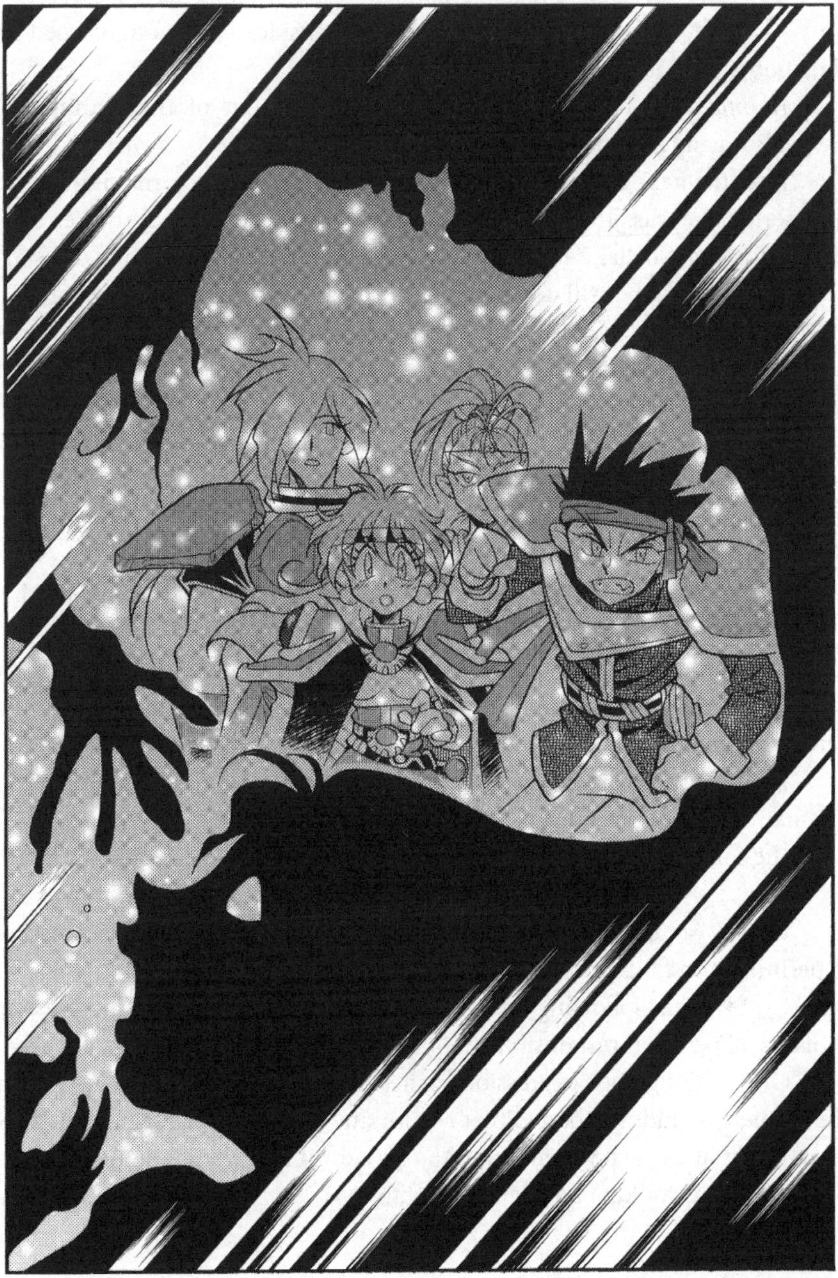

"You sons of…!" Luke raged, grabbing the collar of the nearest sorcerer.

"Ah! Ahh!" One of the sorcerers on the other side of the room reached for the knob of a door when…

Thump! Luke's sword was suddenly sticking out of the man's back. He fell limp and slumped to the floor.

"I kill the next guy who moves," Luke said in a low voice, making it clear how serious he was. The sorcerers all froze in place. He turned his eyes back to the guy whose collar he was holding and said, "Tell me everything or I start breaking fingers. You still don't talk, I kill you and move on to the next guy."

His eyes were dead serious. He seemed like he'd really do it if we let him… And after seeing what was inside those tubes, none of us were inclined to stop him.

"F-Fine! I'll talk!" Realizing that silence wouldn't save him (or perhaps just because he was a coward), the sorcerer readily capitulated. "They're… They're making us run experiments here! Experiments forcing humans into becoming hosts for demons summoned from the astral plane!"

Hmm? The sorcerer's words tickled something in the back of my mind.

"We study what happens if you use humans who haven't yet developed a strong sense of self—children—as hosts, their differences in stamina, compatibility… external appearance when using men versus women, adults versus children…"

"I don't give one damn what you're studyin'," Luke hissed, interrupting the man's terrified ramblings. "Who put you up to all this?"

The sorcerer hesitated for a moment, then said, "L-Lord Lavas."

Aha!

"Got it. So it's the regent who's orderin' you to do these disgusting experiments on folks."

"I… I was just following orders! I-It wasn't my fault!" shouted the sorcerer, refusing all personal responsibility.

"Oh?" A dangerous expression flashed across Luke's features. "I'm bettin' the women an' kids in there didn't ask for any of this. You're sayin' you bear no part of that 'cause it was an order? So it's okay if I kill you on someone else's orders, huh? It wouldn't be my fault, right?"

"Wha—"

A shudder ran through the sorcerer's body. Gourry and I gasped. I didn't know where he'd been hiding it, but Luke had produced a dagger in his free hand and plunged it into the man's chest.

Whud... His neck released from Luke's hold, the sorcerer collapsed to the floor.

"That's too far, Luke," Mileena said calmly.

"Don't you see what they're doin' here, Mileena?!" he responded angrily, uncowed for once. "He said he was 'just following orders'! These assholes don't even think what they're doin' is wrong!"

"We have more pressing concerns at this particular moment."

Luke gritted his teeth at Mileena's words. "Seeing this crap... It's enough to make a guy hate the whole of humanity..."

"I'm human. As are you."

Her words seemed to release some of the tension in Luke's shoulders. "Yeah... I guess. So what do we do with the rest of 'em?" He glanced at the remaining sorcerers, who suddenly huddled together in fear. And then...

"Sleeping!" The spell I incanted sent them all into slumber. "Why don't we just leave them here for now?"

"Fine," Luke said bitterly. He still seemed infuriated, but he was above killing men in their sleep.

"Quit worrying about these maggots. Now that we know Lavas is calling the shots here, it's time to go beat his ass! We can see that these guys get their just deserts later."

"But... I don't think we'll be able to leave just yet," Gourry said, peering through the hole in the wall that led back out into the corridor.

"Enemies?!"

"Yeah. Incoming." He drew his sword while keeping his eyes on the corridor. "I can't see them yet and they're masking their presences, but... I think they're surrounding us."

"You can tell all that?" Luke looked at Gourry skeptically.

The rest of us couldn't sense squat, but Gourry had a kind of bestial instinct that, as far as I knew, had never been wrong. Now, if the enemy had us encircled, what was the best way to respond?

I know! I quickly began chanting a spell under my breath.

"Okay, let's do this! I was lookin' for someone to vent on!" Luke, taking the news of an ambush *extremely* well, marched toward the door and yanked his sword out of the dead sorcerer. Just then…

Crash! The door came flying off its hinges—probably the work of a Dam Blas from the outside. Gourry had been right!

In that same instant, I erected a wind barrier on the knocked-in door with the spell I'd been chanting. *Whoosh!* It wavered and swelled, streaked with the colors of fire. Someone outside had chucked a Fireball at us!

In other words, the enemy's plan had been to blow in the door and follow up with a Fireball to finish us all off—including their own sorcerers who were trapped in the room with us. They'd probably also set this up so that if we'd jumped through the hole in the wall opposite to escape fiery death, we'd get pincushioned by throwing knives from men lining both sides of the hallway. The reason for their delayed attack was to give them time to close the snare. Too bad for them that Gourry's instincts were so sharp!

The second the fire died down and I released my wind barrier, I turned and saw Gourry leaping out the door. Luke and Mileena looked at each other, nodded, and followed after him. I was about to do the same… but a flash of inspiration hit me. I chanted a spell to set up a little trap before leaving.

When I caught up with the others, I found them in an even larger room than the one we'd come out of. It had to be a laboratory, lined as it was with strange devices I didn't recognize and more crystal tubes. And as expected, there were about ten men in black inside. Maybe they'd let their guard down, assuming they'd finished us, or maybe they were just kinda crummy in a fight, because by the time I made it through the door, two of them were already on the ground.

Intimidated by Gourry's skillful swordplay, one of the men in black drew back, and…

Swish! Suddenly, another man—leaping out from behind an empty crystal tube—flew at Gourry from the side, his sword swinging! He'd have to do better than that, though!

Gourry took a half step back, putting a small bit of space between him and the closer man, then pivoted on his left foot. He channeled his momentum into a slash at the man's stomach, and when he slumped forward, Gourry kicked him into the incoming ambusher!

The ambusher reflexively caught his comrade's body, and when he did... Gourry took the opportunity to cut them both down together.

While all that was unfolding, Luke and Mileena worked together to take down another black cloak, and I finished my spell... *Kra-kash!*

"Wah?!" came a cry of distress behind us with a crash.

Ha! Got 'em!

"Fireball!" Whipping around, I fired the spell I'd chanted at the men caught in my pit trap!

Fwoosh! Needless to say, they had no way to dodge it. They took the explosion head-on and were fried head to toe.

This had all worked out thanks to the little trick I'd taken the time to set up earlier. Assuming that the guys in the corridor would come swarming in, I'd used a Bepheth Bring on the ground in front of the hole in the wall in the previous room to dig myself a pit. I'd then left some flooring on top of it—just enough to crumple immediately if someone stepped on it. The men in black in the hallway, realizing that the earlier Fireball hadn't done the trick and sensing fighting deeper within, must have charged in in a panic.

Unfortunately, I'd probably only taken out a fraction of their number this way. More would likely be coming from that same direction soon. That meant I should leave the lab fight to my friends while I picked off the enemies pouring in from the rear! Fortunately, there didn't seem to be any of the fused demons in the group so far, but they could still show up at any time. I had to thin the crowd while I had the chance!

"Blast Ash!"

Vwmm! The spell I unleashed cleared out the next couple of black cloaks appearing from the hallway. Of course, if I limited myself to this pattern, the next one would probably just toss a Fireball or some other projectile into the room. Which meant...

I chanted another spell. Then, almost as if he'd waited for me to finish, another man in black appeared beyond the broken wall. An orange ball of light was already in his hand.

I knew it! Since I'd seen this coming...

"Fireball!" he shouted.

"Diem Wind!" I incanted in the same breath.

Our spells activated simultaneously. A normal Fireball, with no extra bells and whistles, was an orb of light that exploded on contact with a blast of flame. The orb in flight, however, wasn't powerful enough to push through my Diem Wind.

The man in black flinched. He probably hadn't been expecting his Fireball to come sailing back at him. Even if he processed what was happening and tried to flee, he wouldn't get far amidst the gust my spell produced. As a result...

Ba-bwoom! The Fireball fried its own caster.

Okay! That should keep the guys in the hallway at bay!

But as I was chanting my next spell, I felt a wave of hostility rising up nearby. And then, suddenly... a dark figure appeared in the corner of the room.

The ability to blink through space...

"Zain?!"

"Sorry I'm late."

The figure in question, possessing the power of both human and demon, zeroed his attention on me.

Chapter 4: The End of a Lost Kingdom's Dream

Brr! I felt a chill run up my spine. I was in real trouble here.

Zain was close. I wouldn't have time to chant a spell. No sooner than I opened my mouth to chant, he'd leap into sword range and slice right through me. I probably couldn't out-fence him, and escape was out of the question. The second I turned to run, I'd get a blade in the back for my trouble.

My best hope was Gourry and the others picking up on my predicament and coming to my aid, which left me with only one recourse in the moment—buying time!

"I see… You're the only one with the ability to blink through space, then?" I asked.

"You're free to think that, if you wish," Zain responded coldly. (Which was fair. It would've been weirder if he'd responded cordially.)

"If there were others with the same ability, they'd have shown up with you. Strength in numbers, right? But the fact that they *didn't* means that they *can't*. I'm gonna go out on a limb and assume you've all got shared basic properties like magical resistance and simple no-chant spells, and then each one of you has a little something special on top, right? You can teleport, that Zord guy can create shockwave blades without incantation… et cetera."

Zain remained silent, refusing to take the bait.

"Boy, you really have changed. Is that the demon fusion at work?"

"No," he whispered quietly, his voice filled with rage and hate. "It's because I learned the name of the person who destroyed our kingdom."

The person who destroyed his kingdom? I was about to scowl in confusion, but I held my face steady. The way he was going on made this sound like a buildup to a classic "It was you, Lina Inverse!" reveal. But not even *my* magic could wipe out a whole kingdom. Still, if I hinted that I was about to respond with a classic of my own—"Dunno what you're talkin' about!"—in a sweet li'l thing voice, he'd probably rush me on the spot.

"It was after the Bezeld incident that I learned of it… and it was then that I decided to forsake my humanity." Zain's aura of malice swelled.

Would you guys freakin' catch on already? Gourry, Luke, Mileena! Someone!

"Now…" Zain whispered, almost as if to steel himself, then made a slight movement.

He's coming! I thought. But just as I braced for it…

"Lina!" Gourry burst through the door and flew to my side. But it didn't seem like he was rushing in to save me. "You've got your hands full too?!"

"*Too?*" I asked.

Before Gourry could even respond, Luke and Mileena entered the room, backing toward us as if cornered. Luke cast a glance our way.

"More on this side, huh?" he spat out. Which meant…

"It seems our reinforcements have arrived," Zain said.

As if on cue, more men in black appeared behind him, beyond the broken wall. There were five or six of them in total.

Zain turned his cold eyes on me. "You thought you were delaying me long enough for your comrades to arrive… but I was buying time for reinforcements as well."

Geh! We were totally surrounded now.

"Galzard," Zain called.

"Sir," one of the men in black standing just outside the broken wall responded.

"Throw a Fireball into the room. Don't be afraid to hit me too."

"Sir."

"What?!" the four of us called out at once.

"Carmine, a barrage of Freeze Arrows. Jake, a Dug Haute. Release them all on my signal," Zain continued to order.

I heard someone start to chant from beyond the wall, and someone else behind the door. *Not good!* I didn't have a defensive spell strong enough to protect us from all of those puppies at once, and Zain's presence would keep us from finding cover without posing any risk to himself. He was taking pretty clever advantage of his demonic magic resistance.

"Not so fast!" Gourry charged the men at the door. But...

"Diem Wind!"

"Grh!"

A spell from one of the black cloaks kept him at bay. And just as the others finished their chants...

"Blast Ash!"

Fwom! The men past the hole in the wall were all annihilated in one hit.

"What?!" Zain turned back, aghast.

"Pardon the intrusion. I thought it might be time for a showdown, is all." Walking slowly to where the men in black had just been standing... came the masked man.

"You!" Zain hissed.

"Oh, calm down. What kind of self-respecting royal guard has such a short temper?"

Oho? "Royal guard"? The mention of those words sent a note of panic running through the black cloaks. And just then...

"Arc Blas!"

Crackle, crackle, crack! The spell Mileena shot over her shoulder zapped the guys clustered around the door. It was an area-of-effect lightning number that wouldn't kill in one hit, but rather would paralyze its targets and render them briefly immobile.

Next up... *Whoosh!* Luke ran at the men in black and felled them one after another.

"Most would call this 'the tables turning,' wouldn't you say?" the masked man said airily.

At the very least, we only had Zain left to contend with now. He was no slouch, mind you, but there were five of us and only one of him. Pretty good odds for our side!

"Who *are* you?" Zain whispered, his eyes locked on the masked man. He seemed to be shaken more by the callout than by the loss of his comrades.

"If I said I was your fellow countryman... would you understand then?"

Zain chuckled. "Aha. Of course..."

"Someone wanna fill me in?" I asked.

The masked man replied flippantly, "Do you perhaps recall a country named Ruvinagald?"

Ah! Ruvinagald... That name snapped everything together in my mind. The Ruvinagald Republic was a country on the edge of the Alliance of Coastal Nations. Most people knew that it had been a monarchy until a few years ago, but very few knew the reason for the royal family's dissolution.

You see, the kingdom had embarked on some secret research. That is, using humans as hosts for demons. Their objective was to strengthen their army through the mass production of demidemons that could be controlled by people other than just their summoning sorcerers. To serve as guinea pigs, they kidnapped people with an underdeveloped sense of self—in other words, children—and summoned demons from the astral side to possess them. This horrific plot was easily crushed by me (in pre-Gourry times) and a few others. This, in turn, led to the royal family's evil deeds coming to light.

I hadn't kept abreast of what went down afterward, but I'd heard rumors that when other countries caught wind of the incident, the Ruvinagald monarchy was dissolved and the country was reestablished as a republic. But what if the royal family behind the plot hadn't learned their lesson? What if they'd just gone underground? The Solarians said that Lavas had appeared out of nowhere... What if he was reviving his old ambitions here, even bigger than before? That would also explain Zain's comment about how I'd destroyed their kingdom.

In other words, Lavas hated me. It was misplaced resentment since, if you ask me, he was just reaping what he'd sown... but I wouldn't expect a guy trying to fuse humans and demons to be the self-reflective type. The fact remained that he hadn't resorted to the easiest method of getting rid of me and Gourry (putting a bounty on our heads to drive us out of town), however. He'd even gone so far as to try to hire us. Why? Probably to keep us close at hand for our inevitable slaughter. As for why he'd hired Luke and Mileena... it could have been mere caprice. Or a similar desire for revenge over the whole Bezeld debacle. I couldn't be sure either way.

"I see you've finally caught on," the masked man said, a smile in his voice as he noticed my expression.

"I'd say so, yeah. The only thing I can't figure is how he got in the lord's good graces."

"The man calling himself Lavas is a distant relative of Lord Langmeier. I suspect he offered him asylum."

"Impressive intelligence," Zain whispered, confirming the masked man's words.

"Despite appearances, I'm known to the local ladies as the sharpest inspector in the land."

"I see... That explains why you were hiding your face like a freak, even after coming so far to pursue us," Zain continued.

"There are many of our brethren here. Some will likely recognize me. And if you'd known who I really was, you likely would have focused your efforts on me rather than them," the masked informant said with a glance toward us. "To be honest, I was struggling to find hard proof, so I'm grateful that their meddling brought out your true colors."

What am I, your stalking horse?!

"Heh." Zain chuckled at his words. "Then I suppose it's time for a showdown indeed." With that, he immediately began chanting a spell.

Not that I was gonna let him get away with it! I unleashed my own spell, which I'd been chanting while they were talking. "Blast Ash!"

"Void!" But a split second before it hit, Zain vanished. My spell struck empty air where he'd just been standing.

More blinking?!

"Where'd he go?" I asked, scanning all around me.

"To the castle, most likely," the informant responded. "To report to Lavas about us." There, he reached for his mask. "Sorry for the delayed introduction."

Behind the mask was the face of a man in his early forties, with short, brown hair and a stern but distinguished countenance. One that I recognized, natch.

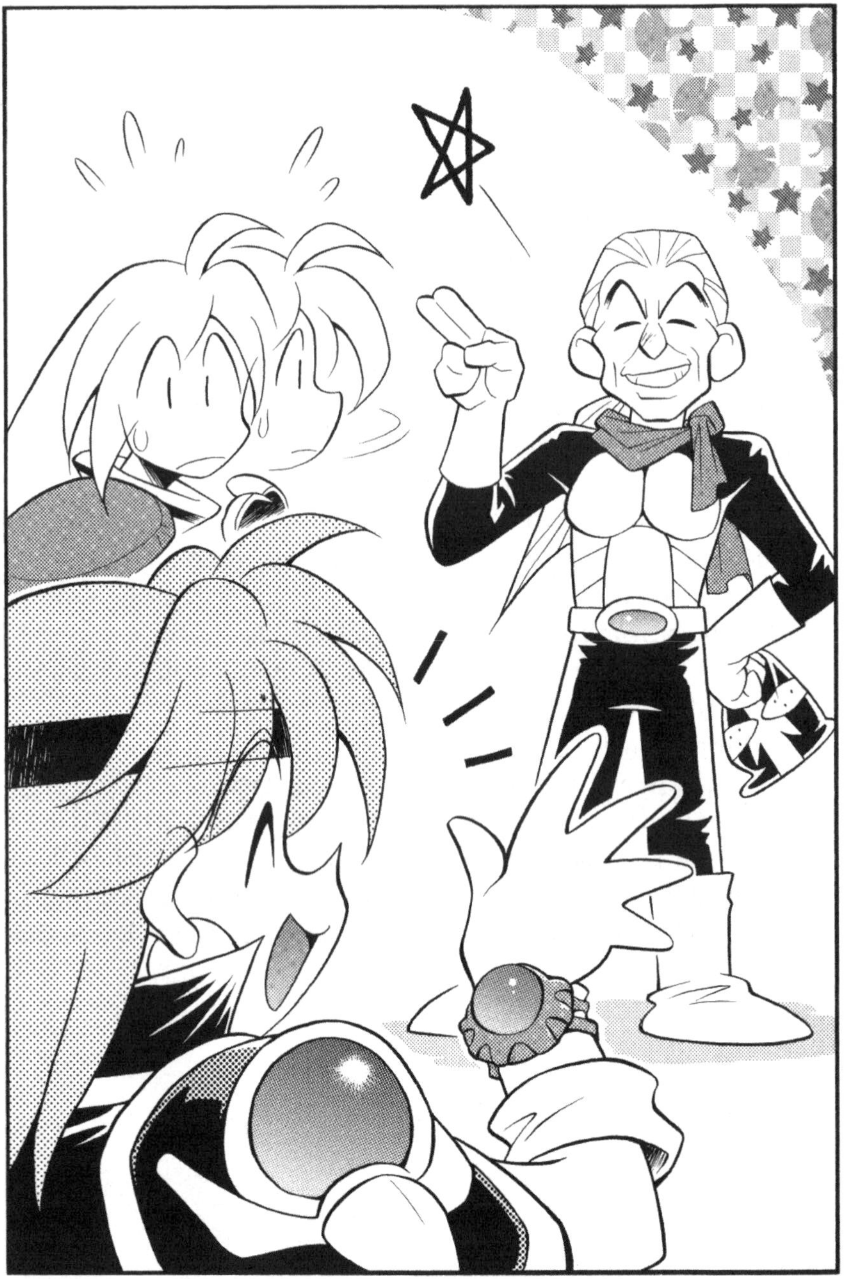

He rummaged around in his pocket and eventually produced a pendant with a crest on it. "I am Wizer Freion, inspector for the Ruvinagald Republic. I'm pursuing its former king, Belgis, and his royal guard for illegal magical experiments… Just as you surmised, Lina Inverse."

"I see. So that's Lavas's real name. It's been a while, old man. You really are pretty strong, huh?"

"You know this guy, Lina?" Gourry asked.

"A little, yeah," I answered with a wink. He was one of the people I'd worked with to bust the operation in Ruvinagald. "I'll tell you the whole story some other time. For now, let's get our butts to the castle!"

The city that night was totally silent as the five of us quietly walked the empty streets toward the towering castle. After the immediate commotion died down earlier, we'd tied up the (living) sorcerers still snoozing in a corner of the room despite all the ruckus. We'd then set out for the city center. I was expecting some resistance along the way from the men in black, but we had yet to detect any.

This was all feeling… not super great, honestly. Zain had probably reported the evening's events to Lavas, which meant the lack of attacks thus far indicated he was concentrating his forces in the castle. Forces which included demonoid fusions.

"Hmm…" I hummed, still walking. "Seems to me it'd be pretty easy to just blow away the whole castle with a Dragon Slave from here. Whaddya think?"

"No way!" Gourry shouted, apparently thinking I might be serious. "The real lord is in there, remember? And probably a lot of soldiers who are just following orders without knowing any better!"

"Yeesh, chill out, man. I was just joking, okay? Though I wouldn't have minded if someone gave me the go-ahead…"

"You mean you'd do it if they did?!"

"Well… uh… Anyhoo, the big question on my mind is what happened to the lord's real son, Veisam."

"It stands to reason that he's dead," Mileena replied, as monotone as ever. "The lord himself is still useful to Lavas. He could shift responsibility to the old man if things get hot, for instance. But Lavas would have had no such reason to keep Veisam alive. In fact, he was probably the first to be killed."

"What difference does it make?" Luke said, coming to a stop. We all did the same, for we'd arrived at the castle gate. "It don't change what we're here to do—beat the crap outta that Lavas asshole."

Fwooom! An indiscriminate boom disrupted the dead quiet of the night. The oak planks of the wooden gate scattered like scrap paper in the face of my amplified Dam Blas. We then floated over the not-so-wide moat with Levitation and descended into the castle grounds.

I know what you're thinking. "If you could levitate, why smash the gate?" Silly reader! Did you forget that we'd come to pick a fight? It's best to open with a bang! Unless your opponents are especially clearheaded or just way out of your league, scaring the pants off of 'em is a sure path to victory!

"Wh-Who are you people?!"

"Where'd you come from?!"

Guards began to gather in a panic, apparently none the wiser to what was afoot. There were about ten of them in all—none of which were our old pals, the guys in black. These dudes were just an appetizer before the main course.

Okay! Time for a little warm-up rampa—

Before I could get off my spell, Luke and Mileena dashed in and... "Sleeping!" All the soldiers were out like lights.

Seriously, guys, that was... anticlimactic. What was I supposed to do with my chant now?

"Look! Above us!" Gourry's voice rang out.

Above us? I looked up like I was told, and... just managed to keep from shouting. Standing atop the outer walls and castle roof were dozens of men in black. Their hands were outstretched, crimson orbs of light forming in them— Fireballs!

Of course! Their plan had been to fill the courtyard with ordinary soldiers to mask their own presences. Then after waiting for us to reach the center of the courtyard, they were all going to fire at once... even if it meant killing the collapsed soldiers in the process.

"Fireball!" came a chorus of incantations. Burning balls of light rained down on us en masse.

They were going to firebomb the entire area! There was no way to escape it. At least, there shouldn't have been. But luck was on our side! The spell I'd been casting happened to be...

"Bom di Wind!"

Whooooosh! My words of power conjured a massive gale. I had originally meant to blow the soldiers away with the explosive blast of wind this spell conjured, but I'd now released it overhead instead.

Krakakrakroosh! The fiery orbs scattered, buffeted by the wind. My spell had knocked them all off course, sending them in various directions... and exploding on impact. Several of the men in black were blown away in the ensuing firestorm, while all we felt was a slight prickle of heat against our skin.

Before the flaming winds could fully die down, the five of us made a dash for the main castle's front door.

"Hah!" With a cry of exertion but little actual effort, Gourry tore through the oak planks with his sword.

"Don't let them escape!"

"After them!"

The men in black on the castle wall jumped down into the courtyard and poured toward the entrance after us. I know they were panicking over the fact that we trashed their super cool trap and all, but seriously, guys! Think for a minute!

Pwash! Fwoosh! Pah! Mileena, Wizer, and I unleashed a one-two-three punch of Blast Ashes at the men in black rushing toward us. Polished 'em off with no problem.

But we barely had any time to catch our breath. The guys on the roof would soon be pouring inside to head us off. I was hoping to get straight to the Lavas-punching, but there was just one holdup—we had to find the guy first!

"Luke! Mileena! Do you know where the audience chamber is? Take us there!"

"The audience chamber? How come?" Luke asked suspiciously.

Heh. He still knew so little about people!

"Isn't it obvious? That's probably where Lavas is!"

Wham! When we kicked in the door, we were met with a long, narrow room flanked by lines of stone pillars. A red carpet extended ahead of us, and at the end of it...

There sat a man, not a hair out of place. He had about twenty men in black around him. It was hard to believe he'd keep any in reserve at this point, so I assumed those present represented Lavas's total local fighting force.

"Oho," the man on the throne murmured in interest. "You arrived from the front gate faster than I expected. You must have come straight here."

"We did. I knew you'd be here," I said, then took a smooth step forward.

"Oh? Do tell me, then. What gave me away?"

"What else?" I pointed straight at Lavas. "Cheap little villains like you love this kind of drama!"

My insult caused an air of hostility to flare among the men in black.

But Lavas himself simply flashed a cold smile. "Cheap villains, eh? Call me whatever you like... You know nothing about me."

"Which suits me just fine."

"Any further conversation is pointless, then." He rose from his throne and snapped his fingers. The men in black fanned out, forming a wall between us and Lavas. "I've paid my respects, so I needn't waste any more time here. I shall continue my research underground. You lot handle the rest," he said, and turned right around.

"You won't escape!" Wizer shouted, rushing after him.

With that, the battle began.

"Freeze Arrow!" Mileena, rushing into combat a second after Wizer, released a pre-chanted spell.

Several of the men in black swiftly moved to dodge, creating a slight break in their formation... which Wizer charged right through!

Swsh! His sword now drawn, he sliced through any of the men in black who hesitated, then dashed onward in pursuit of Lavas.

Dang, not bad for a middle-aged man!

Still... I felt a pang of anxiety. It was about why Lavas had holed up in the audience chamber. What was his game really? The answer was obvious if you thought about it.

He saw no further benefit in holding back against us at this point, so he wanted to concentrate as many black cloaks as possible in one spot. Within the castle, the only places fit to hold dozens of people were the courtyard, the entry hall, and here in the audience chamber. So rather than hiding away in a closet before the battle started, Lavas had decided this would be the safest place for him. That was the real reason I'd assumed he would be here. My little joke earlier was just meant to provoke him... But he hadn't taken the bait.

In other words, Lavas might've been a weird sadist, but at least he wasn't stupid—and he probably still had a few tricks up his sleeve. I wanted to go team up with Wizer... but the men in black standing in our way weren't going to let that happen.

Gourry was fighting two black cloaks simultaneously. They slashed at him in turn, but Gourry deflected both sets of attacks with speedier swordplay. There was a second clash, then a third, and one of the men suddenly lost his balance with Gourry's parry.

Gourry didn't miss the opening. With an upward slash, he cut through... I was about to say "the man in black," but instead, Gourry leaped back and swung his sword through the air next to him.

Fwish! A small sound rang out from seemingly nothing.

"Ohh?! You can cut through them, eh?" one of the men in black said from afar in an almost gleeful voice—it was Zord!

Shing! Luke blocked a strike from above with his sword. As he did...

Slash! Mileena, slicing up from below with hers, cut open the off-guard black cloak's stomach. She then channeled her momentum into a strike at another. Just as their swords collided...

"Bram Blazer!" Her spell knocked her new opponent down. In that moment, a silver flash came at her from the side.

"Dam Blas!"

Clink! Just in the nick of time, Luke's spell pulverized the silver needle streaking toward her.

"You son of a..." he hissed, glaring at Mileena's attacker—another man in black.

Silver claws grew from each of the guy's fingertips for a full set of ten. *Tink-krackle!* When they touched together, sparks danced between them. Were they metal claws enchanted with some kind of lightning spell?

"Another guy who went an' threw out his humanity, eh?" Luke whispered, then smiled boldly.

Meanwhile, my shortsword drawn, I took a defensive stance and began chanting a spell. But before I could finish it, a dark figure appeared before me. Zain again!

Shing! I just barely blocked his blade with mine, but his empty left hand continued to sail toward me. This was no ordinary punch, though. There was a magical light shining in his palm.

Not good! I thought, and in that instant, I let myself fall backward.

This seemed to catch Zain off guard. He lost his balance and had to catch himself. The stumble must have wrecked his concentration, because the magical light died in his hand as it moved through empty air.

While on my back, I kicked up at Zain's stomach! "Guh!" He let out a small groan. Forsaken humanity or not, I guess that still had to hurt!

I let my momentum roll me back across the floor. Then as I got up, I unleashed the spell I'd recited... Not at Zain, but at another man in black!

"Flare Arrow!"

"Ugh!"

He clearly never saw it coming. My spell nailed him head-on, and the dude collapsed in place. Zain then rushed at me again, quickly closing the distance between us.

I readied my blade... then thought better of it. I had no business getting into a swordfight with a guy who could give Gourry a run for his money! Instead, I pivoted on one leg right in front of his eyes and dashed off to cross swords with another man in black.

Zain, apparently not expecting me to up and skedaddle, was slow to react. By the time he actually did, I was already deep in the fray.

Vrum! Nruum! The sound of a collapsing vacuum accompanied each slice of Gourry's sword as he cut through the invisible blades Zord threw his way. And if Gourry's current sword could do that, it was proof Zord's attacks weren't magical, but physical.

"Ohh! Very impressive!" Zord shouted gleefully as he continued to hurl his invisible blades. "I thought the first one was dumb luck, but very impressive indeed!"

Vrumm! Another soft ripping sound. And then... *Fwsh!* A small cut appeared across Gourry's side.

"Yet not even you can catch them all!"

He was right. Gourry continued to counter Zord's invisible blades, but even with my dude's instincts and skill, it was impossible to deflect each and every invisible attack perfectly. Some of the blades Gourry cut through were breaking into shards that needled his arms and legs. The wounds were far from fatal and would probably heal on their own given time, but they were a serious drain on him in the heat of battle. They'd hurt for one thing, and for another, they'd be distracting. What would happen if he lost his focus and failed to intercept one of Zord's invisible blades entirely? I shouldn't even have to say it.

Seeing Gourry bloodied up and thinking it was a good opportunity, a different man in black quickly closed in on him...

"Guh!" But before he could reach Gourry, the man suddenly pitched over. One of Zord's invisible blades had speared his chest!

"Ahahahaha! What are you, stupid?! Why did you run to your death?" Zord laughed as he watched his own comrade die.

That was the reason Gourry had remained in place, swinging his sword instead of dodging. Zord was tossing invisible blades all around, not just at Gourry. It was impossible to predict where they might go.

"Gwahahaha! How long can you hold out?!" Zord's maniacal laughter echoed through the room.

Whk-krash! The spell Mileena unleashed obliterated the electrified claws on the black cloak she was facing. Luke lunged at the guy now that he was basically unarmed. Yet suddenly, the man's claws grew back to the length of swords!

Tink-krackakrackle!

Electricity raced through Luke's blade where it met the claws. It was easily enough to kill him... *if* he'd been holding his sword at the time, that is. Fortunately, Luke had released it the moment before making contact. And then...

"Dolph Strash!" he incanted, bursting the head of the clawed man in black! "Figured you'd try that. You guys are too freakin' obvious," Luke spat as he picked up his sword.

Meanwhile, Mileena unleashed the spell she'd finished casting. "Sight Frang!"

Fwsssh... Mist began to billow out from around her, filling the room. But that was all it did. Sight Frang was a nifty spell for blinding an enemy, typically to retreat, but...

"What are you doing?!" one of the men in black howled as he slashed at her.

Swsh! One slice from my shortsword took out a guy in black. Guess he'd underestimated my swordsmanship! The others quickly took their distance, swords at the ready.

Zain was coming at me from behind too. I was practically surrounded now. Time to make tracks!

"Lei Wing!" I suddenly cast my high-speed flight spell and, clad in a barrier of wind, barreled through the men-in-black blockade! I then hanged course midair, turning toward Zord, who was distracted playing with Gourry. But long before I could reach him, Zain reappeared. He was standing in my flight path, his blade leveled right at me.

Geeehhh! An old memory of a certain fishman getting filleted in exactly this way came to mind. I took desperate control of my spell and changed course again.

Huh. Wait a minute...

Struck by a crazy idea, I stuck my sword out of the wind barrier. I thought that if I cruised through some guys like this, I could take 'em all out—*bam, bam, bam*—but...

"Wugh?!" The second I held my sword out of the barrier, it was swept away by the wind! I also completely lost all balance and control, and...

Crash! I plowed into a nearby man in black. My spell instantly dissipated, sending me rolling across the ground. I thankfully managed to get up okay.

Yeah, probably shouldn't have tried that... Still, it seemed I'd mowed down three or four guys in the process.

As I got my bearings, Zain dashed at me again. This was right around the time Mileena conjured her mist.

"Guh!" A shard of an invisible blade pierced Gourry's left arm. It didn't look like a deep cut, but it wasn't shallow enough to just ignore either.

"Bwahaha! Reached your limit, eh?!" Zord's laughter rang through the room... right before everything went white, courtesy of Mileena's mist. "What?" he whispered.

Whoosh! Just then, Gourry took off at a run.

"Fool!" Zord cried, unleashing more invisiblades.

"Hyah!" Gourry swung his sword, scattering them all flawlessly. *Vwssh! Pwing!*

"What?!" Zord released more in a panic, but Gourry cut down every last one without the slightest splintering. It was as if he could see them coming now. "The mist?!"

Indeed, each invisible blade left a very visible trail in the mist, allowing Gourry to spot them. *Of course! Mileena set this up to help him!*

"Damn you!" Zord cried in panic, letting fly more blades. Gourry easily closed the gap, however. "Ngh!"

Zord reached for the sword on his belt to defend himself, but... *Fwssh!* Gourry's sword, coming faster than expected, cleaved the demon-man vertically.

"What?!" one of the black cloaks swinging at Mileena cried out in surprise.

It probably looked to him like Mileena had suddenly disappeared, but in reality, all she'd done was crouch down. The mist was causing his eyes to play tricks on him. And in his confusion... *Pssht!* Mileena's strike from below pierced his gut.

Luke struck down a second confused man in black, then locked swords with a third. The black cloaks were nothing to sneeze at skill-wise, but seeing one of their demon-fused allies felled thanks to Luke and Mileena's efforts had done a number on their morale.

"Dam Blas!"

Crash! And there went another. A man in black throwing out halfhearted attacks to keep Mileena in check ended up on the wrong end of her spell.

I was now fleeing from Zain, chanting under my breath.

"You won't escape!" he shouted after me.

When I looked back over my shoulder, I could see him in hot pursuit. Guess the grudge ran deep! He conjured a spell in his palm without an incantation and chucked it at me. Unfortunately for him, I was too far away for it to hit. I evaded the magical orb with a lithe movement. It sailed past me, disappeared into the mist, and...

Crash! I heard the sound of something breaking. It must have found one of the chamber pillars.

I continued running and ducked behind a row of the pillars lining the room. Zain was still on my tail. He was faster than me too, and quickly caught up. Magic began accumulating in his left hand again.

Now! I placed a hand to my neck and undid a small metal fastener.

Whoosh! My cape billowed off my back, and...

"?!" Zain charged right into it!

When he did, I whipped around and thrust my sword through the cape. I didn't hit anything. Moments later, I felt a presence appear behind me. He'd blinked through space—just like I expected!

"Blast Ash!" I cast the spell behind me. *Bwush!*

Blast Ash didn't require line of sight, see. You could also do things like this, reliant purely on instinct.

Clang! I heard a sword hit the ground. It was the one Zain had been holding. I turned around, and all I saw was black soot drifting in the white mist—the remains of demonoid Zain, who hadn't even let out a scream before dying.

Wham! A handful of armed guards were on the other side of the next door we kicked in. Some were leaning against the wall, some were sitting. Some were even gathered around a table playing cards. All stopped what they were doing and looked our way as we entered.

After we'd beaten the three demonoid fusions, the rest had been easy. The men in black had completely lost their morale, and we'd polished them off with swords and spells. A few had gotten away, but we were in no position to chase them around right now. We needed to find Lavas and Wizer at once!

At least, that was the plan. Problem was, we had no idea where they'd gone. We'd set out in the direction they originally ran off in, but we eventually hit a fork in the road that stopped us cold. Thus, our group of four began searching the hard way.

Lavas had said he was going "underground" for "research." I'd asked Luke about it on the way, but he didn't seem to know anything about a basement research facility. Of course, a castle like this had to be full of secret passageways and hidden dungeons. There was no doubt that's where Lavas retreated. But since Luke and Mileena didn't know how to find the one we were looking for, we were stuck with the least efficient method possible—scouring the place room by room.

"Tch. Not here either," Luke spat, and was just turning away, when…

"Hey! Hang on a minute!" one of the guards called out. "What the hell is going on here? When can we leave this room?"

He seemed more annoyed than anything, and genuinely ignorant of the situation. Judging from his and his comrades' expressions, they still saw Luke and Mileena as allies… Did that mean they weren't consciously in on Lavas's scheme, and were being deceived themselves? I couldn't be sure, but if they thought we were on the same side, we were definitely going to exploit that.

"You dunno what's goin' on at all?" Luke asked.

Another guard responded, annoyed, "Of course not. They suddenly told us to stand by until we received new orders, and that we weren't to come out no matter what. But we've been hearing all kinds of ruckus for a while now…"

"We'll explain later," I said, speaking up.

"You were Lord Lavas's dinner guest earlier, weren't you?" the guard asked.

"Yeah, but we can dish about that some other time. If you know of any kind of passage to a hidden room in the basement, tell us now! We have to find Regent Lavas before something terrible happens!"

At that, the guards shared a look. I wasn't technically lying. I'd just failed to mention that it was the lord regent *doing* the terrible things.

"Fine! We'll join you!" A middle-aged man serving as their commander grabbed his sword and stood up. The others followed suit.

Of course, we didn't really want them tagging along, but it's not like they were gonna stand down on my account. So the four of us plus about ten soldiers, their commander at the fore, ran down one hall and then another. Soon, the commander stopped at a dead end. I exchanged glances with Gourry, Luke, and Mileena, and we stepped back from the soldiers' ranks. The commander twisted a candlestick on the wall, pushed in a certain brick, and...

Clunk. The ostensible dead-end wall suddenly opened, revealing an entrance large enough for one person to pass through.

"Here it is," the commander said, turning back to face me.

Nice. Good boy!

"Sleeping!" I incanted, putting the guards to sleep on the spot.

"Lighting!" With Mileena's spell guiding the way, the four of us walked through the opening in the wall.

In short order, we found a staircase leading downward.

"Bingo!" Luke cried as he stormed down it with Mileena, Gourry, and me in tow. We hit a door at the bottom. Luke reached for the knob. "Tch! It's locked! Hang on, I'll—"

Before he could start a chant, Gourry stopped him and walked up to the door. Then... "Hyah!"

Cha-king! In a flash, the door fell to the floor in diced-up pieces. *Ha! Who needs a key when you got Gourry around?!*

The four of us stepped through, and...

"Whoa!"

I stopped and stared. Illuminated by a magical light hanging over the door was a room glittering in gold and silver. It was quite large, and filled to the brim with ornamented armor, swords, and accessories. Not just for decoration either. Anyone with an eye for sorcery could tell at a glance what they were.

"Holy crap! These're all magic items! Oho! This necklace would look beautiful on Mileena!"

"Wahoo! Can you frickin' believe it? Oho! This necklace would fetch a great price!"

"Is now really the time?" Mileena asked evenly.

Ah! Luke and I snapped back to our senses. Right. That whole Lavas thing... That said, there was no sign of him or Wizer around. And, I mean, we *had* come to the castle in the first place to swipe a magic sword.

There were enough of 'em here to make a real killing on the market. Too bad we couldn't exactly leave the inspector and the regent to their own devices while we tallied up our haul.

"Fine!" I declared firmly while filling my pockets. "We'll save the rummaging for later!"

"You're actually *going* to do it later?" Mileena whispered with a wince.

Now, if this wasn't the underground lair we were looking for, then Lavas had to have some other hidey-hole. Did this mean going back to the "search for hidden passages" game? Just the thought made me groan.

But as I was thinking that—*Crash!*—part of the wall burst inward!

Say whaaat?!

When the dust cloud settled down, we saw...

"Ah... you're all here..."

"Old man?!"

Indeed, staggering out of the dust came Wizer, the old inspector who'd ditched us to chase after Lavas. It wasn't exactly a triumphant return either. Our guy was pretty black and blue, and he was sporting some cuts that, while not fatal, were definitely serious.

"He's coming..."

His words brought our gazes to the busted-in wall... where a shifting figure was slowly approaching.

A demidemon?! It certainly looked like one at a glance, but it wasn't the lesser or brass kind I was familiar with... It had the eerily pale skin of a drowning victim and three twisted horns growing asymmetrically from its head. Its body was crooked and deformed, and emitted a choking miasma.

That said, generally speaking, the higher demons ranked, the more human they looked. Which meant, as freaky as this thing was, it probably wasn't overwhelmingly powerful. Hard to imagine how it had given the old man such a hard time...

"Oh, there you all are. Looks like you came to the wrong underground room," came Lavas's voice from behind the demon. Then, with unhurried steps, he showed himself.

"You! Still not dead, huh?!" Luke scoffed, drawing his sword. "You think that one little demon can do anything against us?!"

"Hmm..." Lavas stared pensively at the demon for a time. "He *has* been asleep in lifewater this whole time. He was a failed experiment, you see, like the ones slumbering beneath the facility where Zain lured you two."

A failed experiment?!

"Wait a minute! Are you saying those chimeras were all originally people you kidnapped too?!" I shouted.

"Yes," Lavas responded indifferently, still peering up at the demon's face.

The bastard!

"This demon is a rather special case, though. I carelessly piled on the abilities... and it put a tremendous strain on the body. That's why he looks the way he does. He's unstable and imbalanced, although he has a great deal of power to make up for it." He paused for a moment, then turned to face us again. "Allow me to introduce... Half-Demon Experiment Mk. 1, Veisam Fritz Langmeier. The lord's *true* heir."

The four of us gasped. Now it made sense... I guess Wizer couldn't attack the demon once he knew its true identity.

"This is Lord Langmeier's castle and territory. There were plenty of people to stand in the way of my ambitions here. 'Eliminate all obstacles' is always good policy... But while it would have been easy enough to murder these particular obstacles, hiding the aftermath of a massacre can be difficult. So, I thought, why not use them as guinea pigs instead? They're out of the way, it forwards my research, and once they're no longer human, they can no longer denounce me. Logical, no?"

"No, not logical. Inhuman," I whispered angrily.

But Lavas replied with perfect calm, "Cutting-edge pragmatists are never appreciated in their own time."

"I don't quite get what's going on, but..." Gourry drew his sword and took a step forward. "I don't think I can let you get away with it."

"What he said," I seconded, drawing my sword as well.

A smile appeared on Lavas's face. "I see. If you insist... It's not as if I intend to let you live either way. Go, Veisam."

"Hraaagh!" The half-demon Veisam roared in response to Lavas's command. Lavas seemed to have him completely in his thrall.

"Icicle Lance!" It was Mileena who cast abruptly at Lavas. Her projectile sailed by Veisam for Lavas, but...

Crash! A second before it hit him, Veisam raised his right hand and dispersed Mileena's magic. Without missing a beat, he then charged right for us!

The rest of us quickly moved to dodge, but Gourry alone remained in place. He leveled his sword at Veisam and...

No way! He can't just kill the guy!

"Hahhh!" He ducked under Veisam's arm and lashed out with his sword! *Swsh!*

"I cut his heel cord!" Gourry informed us while turning his gaze cautiously between Veisam and Lavas. "That should keep him—"

Before he could finish... "Hraaagh!" With a howl, Veisam rushed him.

"What?!"

Crash! Gourry swiftly jumped aside, plunging into the mountain of treasure.

"Really now, try not to wreck the place," Lavas laughed. "I told you, I gave him a variety of abilities. He can regenerate instantly from most anything you throw at him. Short of decapitation or lopping off a limb, he'll just keep moving."

He was right. As Veisam came to a stop and looked around as if evaluating his prey, we could see the back of his left heel stained red. It was where Gourry had severed a tendon, and it had healed almost instantly.

"Now, Veisam, get it together and finish them off," Lavas ordered.

"Hraaagh!" Veisam again howled in response. A dozen arrows of flame appeared in front of him. They were aimed at Luke and Mileena... And Wizer!

Not good! The other two would be fine, but Wizer was in no condition to dodge a spell.

Ka-bwoobwoobwoosh! The flaming arrows rained down and...

"Wind Strike!" Luke swung his sword through the air, producing a shockwave to disperse the fiery volley.

"A magical sword?!" Lavas cried from the sidelines in admiration.

Indeed, the nameless magic sword Luke wielded could produce an effect similar to Diem Wind on command with a slash and some willpower.

After buffeting the arrows, Luke made a beeline for Veisam! "Nothin' personal!" he called.

Slash! A swing of his sword sent Veisam's right arm flying, and Luke kept up the momentum to charge at Lavas behind him. He had the right idea—if we could defeat Lavas, there would be no one left to control Veisam. That probably wouldn't pacify the poor guy, though...

Luke took a swing at Lavas and—*Shiiing!*—with a piercing metallic screech, his sword shattered!

What?! Lavas didn't appear to be holding a weapon. He'd merely deflected Luke's blade with a bat of his hand. *No way...*

"Ngh!" Luke quickly leaped back. *Crack!* The armor on his right shoulder also broke into pieces.

"I see. You decided to go after me first, did you? A sensible plan. However—"

"Raaaaaaaagh!" A cry from Veisam interrupted Lavas. The skin around the arm that Luke had severed had begun to turn black and melt, the effect spreading quickly to the rest of his body.

"Hmm... The imbalance is even worse than I thought," Lavas muttered calmly as Veisam's screams continued to resonate. "Enough damage and his self-regeneration goes completely haywire."

Soon, the howling turned to whimpering. Then came silence as Veisam's melting body collapsed into a black puddle in the middle of the floor.

"Less useful than I expected, I suppose. Though this does save me the trouble of disposing of him."

"How dare you..." Gourry whispered.

He readied his sword, but that was all. He must've realized the same thing I had. Given that she hadn't tried anything, Mileena had picked up on it too. While we stood there, frozen in place, Lavas slowly turned his gaze on us.

"For an army's leader to take to the field personally... is the worst of all possible strategies. Yet you've left me with little other alternative." A glint appeared in his eyes. Was it a flicker of madness, or... "I need you all to die."

"Dam Blas!" In that instant, I released the spell I'd been reciting.

But—*Fwish!*—Lavas raised a hand and dispersed it. No ordinary human could perform such a feat. This made his true nature all too obvious.

"Lavas," I said to the man still smiling confidently despite the loss of all his pawns. "You're also a demonoid fusion."

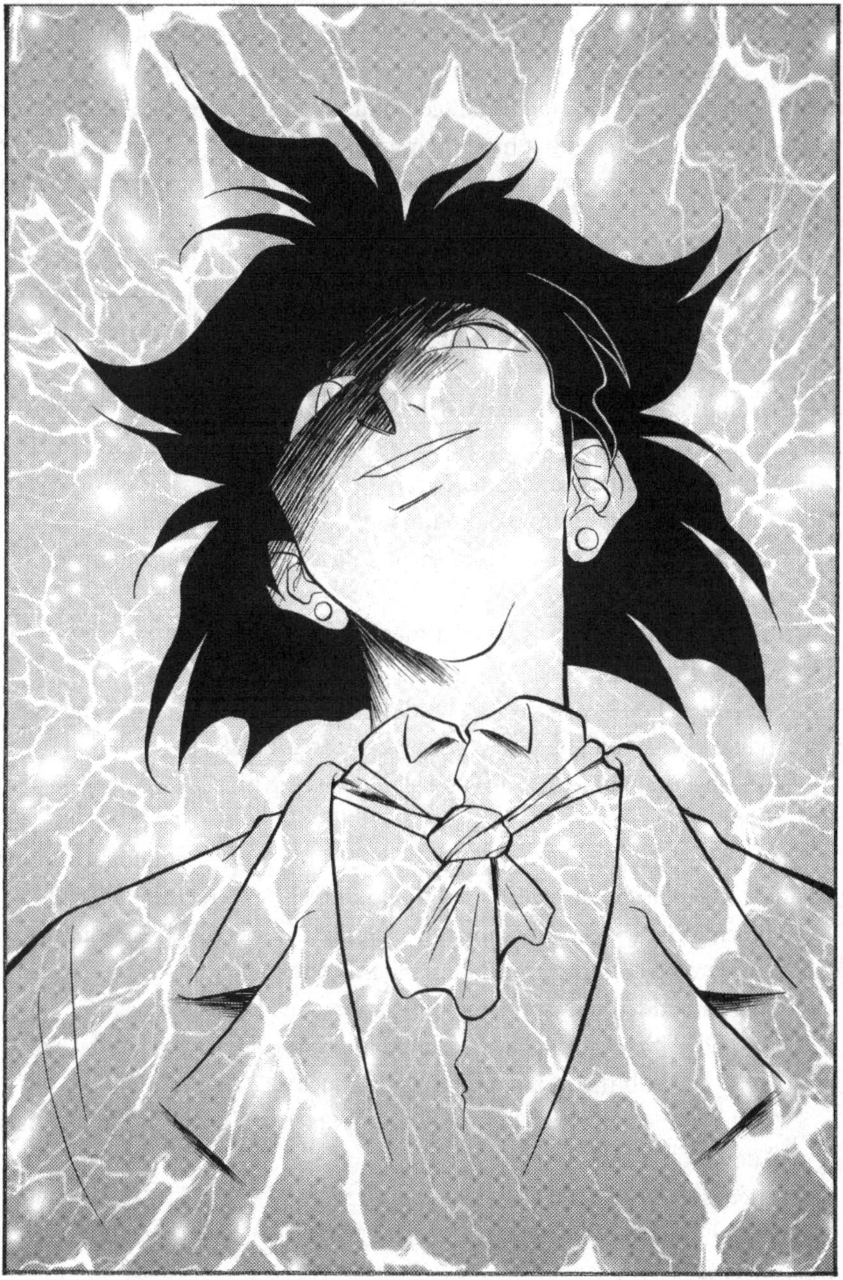

"Demonoid, eh? What an amusing description." Slowly, Lavas approached us. Luke took a hurried step back, awed by the hostile aura radiating out from him. "It's rather difficult to fit such power into a human form, I'll have you know. I only recently mastered the technique. You see, I needed to empower my underlings, but I couldn't have them using their given powers against me. And the best way to prevent that? Simple. To make myself stronger than they were."

Damn. I'd taken Lavas for a third-rate villain who always delegated to his goons. But the way that the mere mention of *him* had cowed even Sir Zord the Reckless... That wasn't the behavior of a man afraid of displeasing his boss. It was fear of a far more powerful being's wrath.

"I'm a novice in both the martial and magical arts, so this will be my first field test... of how strong I am!" As he spoke, Lavas's left hand flashed. Two magical blades flew at me and Gourry!

"Rgh!" Gourry and I groaned in unison, quickly drawing back.

Fraaaaaaaash! The blades tore through the trove of magic items on the opposite side of the room.

Brr... I shuddered when I saw a magical helmet roll out in front of me, sliced in half like butter.

"Not bad, if I do say so myself! Or did I make myself *too* strong, perhaps? Bwahahaha!" With that, he threw his next attack at Luke.

Dude just managed to dodge and arm himself with a sword he picked up off the floor.

"Now, now! That's not yours!" Lavas flicked his finger, producing another invisible blade of a shockwave. *Shing!* It hit Luke's new sword and snapped it.

"Mileena! Get the old guy topside!" I shouted. It was too dangerous for an injured man to be hanging around during this fight.

Mileena nodded in response and began leading the man upstairs.

"Now, now! No running away!" Lavas made a seal with his hands. "Void!"

What?! In the blink of an eye, Lavas disappeared. Then...

"Wagh!" Mileena cried out, and moments later, both she and Wizer toppled down the stairs.

"Mileena?!" Luke cried as he ran over to them.

"I'm... I'm okay." She managed to pick herself up, then pulled back with both Luke and Wizer.

"Hmm… was that one too weak?" Descending the staircase leisurely as he muttered to himself was… Do I even have to say it? It was Lavas, who'd phased through thin air.

"Elemekia Lance!"

"Futile!" Lavas shattered my spell with a magic bullet he'd unleashed. At the same time, Gourry dashed at him, sword drawn. "I told you it was futile!"

But with speed greater than Lavas had anticipated, Gourry closed in and took a swing!

"Ugh!"

Clatter! Dang, Gourry almost had him! Lavas had unfortunately managed to move right in the nick of time to break the sword. But… *Fwsht!* Lavas trembled slightly.

Gourry had another blade in his left hand—one he'd probably swiped up from off the trove on the floor. The instant his first sword broke, he'd drawn the second and thrust it into Lavas's stomach.

Did he do it?! As I wondered that, Gourry released the sword and leaped back. *Tink!* An invisible blade cut cleanly through his shoulder guard.

"Impressive indeed!" Despite being run through, Lavas's confident tone didn't waver. "If only you'd been kind enough to assume I was defeated and let your guard down!" He pulled the sword out of his abdomen. Not a single drop of blood spilled from the wound.

It didn't work?!

"Now, I'll start with…" Lavas slowly turned toward Mileena and Wizer.

"Ruby-Eye Blade!" Howling, Luke charged at him. He'd picked up another sword that was now aglow with red light. Lavas looked over his shoulder, and… *Vrum!*

"Gwuh!" It was Luke who fell to the ground with a grunt.

Multiple somethings—lances or tentacles, it was hard to describe them—had erupted from Lavas's back, piercing Luke's shoulder and left thigh.

Holy crap! This guy really had sold out his humanity!

"Blast Ash!" Mileena threw a spell at him, but…

"Void!" Lavas, blinking again, appeared right next to her. "That was far too predictable!"

Wham!

"Hgn!" Mileena moaned when Lavas kicked her hard in the trunk. He raised his hand aloft, and...

"Blast Ash!" Then my summoned darkness started to envelop him from his left side. *Bwom!*

I wasn't sure why myself, but on instinct, I leaped to the side. When I did...

Vwum! A pair of magical blades ripped through where I'd just been standing.

Pwssssh! With the sound of air being let out of a balloon, the blackness of my Blast Ash swirled and disappeared.

"Graaaaaaaagh!" From within it, Lavas appeared with a scream.

This was a spell that could take out a brass demon in one hit, and he'd no-sold it with his magic power alone?! The way he howled in pain as the skin on his face turned a dusky ash color suggested it had done *something*... but for him to survive put him on a level above most pure demons!

After one of the blades Lavas unleashed passed me by, it had crashed into the stone floor and smashed the various magical items strewn about it... No. Amidst all the shredded remains, a single glint of silver lingered. The intact blade of a magic sword freed from its sheath?!

"Gourry! That sword!"

"Right!" Gourry leaped in response. Lavas threw an invisible blade after him.

He can't dodge that! I thought, but a split second later—*Swsh!*—Gourry slashed aside the shockwave with the sword.

"Tch!" The slightest hint of panic crossed Lavas's face. He leaped to the wall and grabbed a magic sword for himself.

Gourry dove straight at him. Lavas held the sword in his right hand and threw an invisible blade from his left. But one slash from Gourry's sword rent it asunder!

"Rgh!" Lavas quickly readied the sword in his right hand.

It was probably a magical blade on par with the one Gourry had picked up. Lavas most likely meant to block Gourry's attack with it, pinning him in place, and then hit him close-range with an invisible blade attack from his other hand. But if their swords were equals, this would come down to a contest of skill!

Clink! Gourry slashed through Lavas's magic sword, hand and all—and kept going through his waist! But...

"Guh?!" Gourry, having sped past Lavas in his attack, quickly whipped around to dodge something. Lavas had unleashed spears from his back that sailed through the air just beside him! "You...!" Gourry took his distance and assumed a fighting stance once more.

For, even cleaved in two through his midsection... Lavas hadn't fallen. At least, not completely. I wasn't sure how he was doing it, but Lavas's body was now gone from the waist down and the rest of him—his upper half—was floating in the air.

"How... How dare you ruin my body?!" The cross-section of his severed right hand was now swarming with tentacle-like growths.

Holy crap! How was this guy still alive and kicking?! Had he forced some powerful demon to fuse with him in his lust for power? Lavas turned back and tried to skewer Gourry with his right-hand tentacles. I could see the glint of Gourry's sword as it moved, and though it looked like he'd sliced through the tentacles... they wriggled around his blade's reach. Then—*Crackle-krak!*—they unleashed a shower of electricity on the big lug!

"...Khhh!" Gourry collapsed without a word.

He was clearly trying to get up again, but the hit seemed to leave him numb. All he could do was twitch. I wanted to throw an attack spell to help him out, except I hadn't finished my chant yet. Lavas laid eyes on the fallen Gourry, and...

"Dynast Blas!" *Crackle-krak!*

Lightning appeared from thin air to encase Lavas's body! As for who'd cast the spell... it was the heretofore silent Wizer! Lavas contorted in pain, his mouth gaping in a soundless scream.

We'd done it! Dynast Blas was easily enough to fry most pure demons. With a hit like that—

"Graaah!" Lavas howled, and the lightning burst away from him!

No freakin' way!

"Annoying fool!" he hissed, swiping with his left hand. *Fwoosh!*

"Gwah!" shouted Gourry, Luke, Mileena, and Wizer as the shockwave blasted them all back into the piles of treasure.

"Tch! Not as strong as I'd hoped," Lavas spat, gazing at his left hand. And then, slowly, he turned toward me.

I found myself dropping my chant in progress. I just stood there. The spell I'd been drumming up… It was the same one Lavas had just shaken off.

This was nuts. Even knowing he was either host to or fused with a demon for power, Lavas's endurance was unreal. His attacks themselves weren't so different from any low-tier pure demon's… But no low-tier pure demon could just shrug off a Dynast Blas like that. And yet…

"Ah…" A sound of surprise escaped my throat as realization dawned on me. I peered hard at Lavas. "I see… I get it now. That's why you're so tough to kill…"

"Ohh?" Lavas narrowed his eyes in amusement.

"The clothing and accessories you're wearing… They're all magic items, right? For defense and recovery."

That would explain everything. I'd been wondering why, with all these magic items lying around, he wasn't using any himself. Why would a person (okay, not technically a person anymore) this self-obsessed not deck himself out in armor?

"Finally figured it out, did you? You're exactly right," Lavas admitted readily. It wasn't his own magic power that had allowed him to resist a Blast Ash or sweep aside a Dynast Blas, but the power of the magical protection he was wearing. "So, what's the plan now that you know?"

Geh… I didn't actually know what to say to that.

"There isn't one, is there? Your allies have fallen, leaving you all alone. What do you think you can possibly do?"

He was right in that my little eureka moment didn't change my predicament. A Dragon Slave would take him out, but that wasn't a realistic option in a place like this. That left me the option of amplifying a spell like Dynast Blas, which could defeat a pure demon at standard strength… But I had a feeling he'd just dodge it if I tried.

Either way, I still had to try! I started working on the chant.

"Futile!" In response, Lavas fired an invisible blade from his left hand.

His aim was poor and I saw it coming, so I speedily leaped aside. He seemed weaker now. Even with his magic protection in place, tanking an attack spell with only half a body was bound to bring some cracks to the surface.

Lavas next lashed out at me with his tentacle arm. Was he going for another electric shock?! I kicked a sword lying at my feet, sheath and all, at the tentacles. *Crackle!* The blade shorted the electricity from the tentacles. I followed up by kicking a nearby globe at Lavas. These were pretty petty attacks—childish, even—but I didn't know how else to buy time. It's not like you can just bring a sword to a tentacle fight.

"Ngh!" Seeming frustrated by my persistence, Lavas used his tentacles to smack down everything I kicked his way. "Enough!" He then raised his left hand and released an area-of-effect shockwave. It was weak but covered a wide range, making it impossible to dodge.

In that case... I took a big leap back. Just as I touched off the ground— *Crash!*—the shockwave hit me.

Even jumping back to ride the momentum rather than fight it, I really felt that one. Still, I managed to endure the pain and land upright, kicking aside some more scattered treasure in the process. Then I finished my spell!

"Dynast Blas!"

"Void!"

My voice and Lavas's rang out in unison. He instantly vanished.

Knew it! He freakin' dodged! The electricity I unleashed zapped empty air. As it did, I felt something behind me. Of course, I'd known this was coming... I simply leaped to the side as the invisible blade whizzed past me. Then I turned and leaped back. Lavas and I squared off from a distance again.

Damn it. This confirmed my worst fear. He'd always blink away the second I incanted words of power. If he were warping around at random, I could chant on the run and strike wherever he appeared, but... either Lavas realized that or he was just a little jerk, because he always reappeared behind me. If only there was a way to exploit that...

Casting a Dynast Blas over my shoulder was out, of course. I'd end up caught in the blast. Maybe if I could use the brief time lag between when Lavas disappeared and when he appeared to get around into his blind spot... No, he'd have a plan for dealing with that already.

Wait a minute... Yeah, that *would work!*

I pulled farther away from Lavas and began reciting a spell. This was Ragna Blade, a black magic number that called upon the power of void, capable of tearing apart even the kinds of pure demons that could soak a Dragon Slave. No amount of protection from magical items could save him from getting nailed with this baby. Its main drawbacks were its short duration and range, but it was my only ticket to victory right now!

"Curse you!"

Maybe he didn't want any repeats of our earlier clashes, because Lavas was now avoiding lightning tentacle attacks and wide-range shockwaves. He continued to fire the smaller invisible blades, however, each strike scattering more and more treasure. The room glinted with flashes of silver and gold. I dodged every attack that came my way... then released my spell!

"Ragna Blade!"

"Void!"

As expected, Lavas phased away at the first hint of my words of power. But I now had my dark blade in my hands, and I made my move.

Lavas reappeared right behind where I'd been standing. He wasted no time throwing a shockwave in front of him and shooting tentacles from both his arm and his back. But I was nowhere to be seen.

He paused, alarmed by losing track of me. And in that instant, without warning...

My blade of darkness cleaved Lavas through.

Splut... Sluph... His left half hit the floor, followed by his right.

My dark blade vanished, and I looked over my shoulder to see Lavas's further bisected upper body lying behind me. It was crumbling into white sand before my eyes. So ended Lavas, the mad king who'd made a demon of himself.

After determining that he was gone for good, I stood up.

Lavas had probably died unaware of how he was beaten, but the idea behind it was quite simple. The moment he'd blinked through space, I'd stretched my arms out and fallen backward. Lavas had then appeared right above me, oblivious as to where I'd gone. See, the loss of his lower half gave him a new blind spot—below him. I'd only had to flex my abdominal muscles and sit up to finish him.

"Guess it's all over now," I whispered to myself.

"Not… quite…" Gourry responded. With everyone else unconscious, he was the one of my allies who rolled over to face me. "Would you mind… patching us up?"

"Anyway, I s'pose I should thank ya," Luke admitted somewhat bashfully as we sat around the table.

It was now the day after our fight beneath the castle, and everyone had had a chance to recover. Fortunately, none of them had proven especially hard to heal. A little Recovery spell and a good dose of bed rest worked wonders. Of course, the latter also meant it was noon before the others could join me at the table, leaving us to enjoy a meal that wasn't quite breakfast and wasn't quite lunch.

"Thank me? For what?" I asked in response, stopping with a piece of bread halfway to my mouth.

"Well, we'd be dead now if you hadn't beaten that bastard. So… I figured I oughta say thanks."

"You can say it with a thousand gold coins!"

Bfft! Perhaps realizing I was serious, Mileena, who was silently sitting beside Luke, expressionlessly spat out her soup.

Luke tried to change the subject. "But all joking aside—"

"Not joking," I interjected calmly.

"—Who do you reckon's gonna take over here?" Luke continued, gazing into the distance as he tried to force the change of subject.

"That'll be a grand, please," I insisted, forcing it back.

"Think they'll appoint another lord?"

"I'll accept 999!"

Sweat began to trickle down Luke's face. *Aha! Almost got 'im!*

"I'll bet the guys in black are still around here an' there, but I wonder if they'll keep doin' their thing, what with their boss dead an' all."

"Fine, you got me. Nine-ninety."

"Argh! Shut up already!"

It was Luke who caved first. *Heh. Simpleton.*

"Anyway! Judgin' by the look of things, I'd say we helped you out too! And you probably swiped a ton of treasure from that room! Includin' that sword!" he barked, pointing with his fork at the new sword on Gourry's belt.

He had me there. It was indeed the very blade that had survived Lavas's attack and cut the guy in two. I didn't know what its magical deal was, but it seemed like a pretty special item. Man... first the pauldrons I'd bought a little while back, and now this unknown sword. We were winding up with a lot of mystery equipment lately. But that was neither here nor there.

"I'll admit plenty of trinkets from that trove found their way into my pockets." I nodded in agreement to Luke's observation. "However, my dear Luke, that has no bearing on this. Human greed knows no bounds!"

"Oh, c'mon! If you want money so bad, just head back to the castle and take whatever else you want from the basement!"

"Hey, that's not a bad idea!"

"Not that it's any of my business... but perhaps you should refrain from discussing crimes in front of an inspector," Wizer interjected, a hot sandwich in one hand.

"We'll save that for later, then. So, what are you two gonna do next?" I asked.

Luke and Mileena shared a glance. "Same as always, right?" Mileena responded.

"S'right. We're gonna travel the world in search of treasure. Me and Mileena's romantic journey continues!"

"He's correct... aside from the 'romantic' part."

"Excuse me, but aren't you forgetting something?" The one who objected was Wizer. "There's still cleanup to be done here, remember? All most folks know boils down to, 'Something happened at the castle yesterday, and now Regent Lavas is gone.' If no one steps in to clear things up, you'll be taken for murderers!"

"Oh..." we all sighed in the same breath.

Dude was right, though. The castle guards *had* seen us searching out the hidden basement chamber and all. They probably knew our names too...

"Now, I can handle most of it myself, but I still need each of you to give a formal statement. First, I'll ask the sorcerers' council to get in touch with the relevant offices. Then we'll hold an inquest and inspect the scene. It'll probably take about a month. Sorry, but you made this bed… It's time to lie in it," Wizer informed us, a slightly nasty grin on his face.

Ugh…

And so we put Solaria City behind us… wasn't something I'd get to say for a while.

Afterword

Scene: Author + L

Au: That's another reprint come and gone! This was volume 10, *"Conspiracy in Solaria"*!

L: Isn't Solaria the name of the hotel you were staying at when you had to name it?

Au: Yes! I think I mentioned this somewhere before, but I was staying at a hotel for an event at the time, and my editor needed me to settle on a title for publicity reasons. So I just used the hotel name. Er... Well, not *just*. The place wasn't called the Conspiracy in Solaria Hotel or anything.

L: I think that went without saying! Still, how could you just nick a name like that? You should've at least tweaked it a little.

Au: Well, I do tweak names now and then. But if I go too far, I can end up duplicating the name of a character I've used before or altering something into obscurity.

L: I seem to recall a short story where something about a nine-tail fox became something about an obnoxious couple.

Au: Sometimes I put *G*ndam* parodies in the short stories too. There was also a time I included a Northern Song Dynasty (Hokusou) vase that I tweaked by making Hokusou into "fox owl" (fokkusu ouru). It had a fox and an owl crest. Stuff like that.

L: I imagine nobody figured that one out.

Au: Yeah. I thought people might not, so I dropped a couple of hints, but no one recognized the origin of the vase.

L: It kinda feels like... maybe you should own up to it.

Au: Well, when I'm playing games on my own time, I prioritize clarity for myself. I frequently give my characters obvious names. For instance—I don't use this one anymore—but before I debuted as an author, I'd have a mage named Lina. An RPG I played a few years ago had so many character classes that I couldn't keep them straight, so I just named my characters after them. The warrior guy was Battler, and the warrior lady was Figh from "fighter." I'd also give my female units cute-sounding names with "lin" at the end. For example, I'd have a star mage called Starlin.

L: That's awful! There's nothing feminine or cute about that! I hope your allies throw you into line! I can't even tell if those are tweaks or cop-outs!

Au: But compared to that, naming Solaria after a hotel is nothing!

L: Honestly... I know you're probably just messing with me, but anything would sound better after those horrible examples. I have a feeling that Sherra's a victim of your terrible naming sense too, isn't she?

Au: At first it was just a joke, but later on I had a Q&A with fans that went kind of like this...

Q: *"Dynast's four subordinates aren't named Dai, Nast, Grau, and Sherra, are they?"*

Me: *"That's awesome! I'm stealing it!"*

Au: That's how it happened!

L: Don't outright steal things! And now I feel bad for Dynast's subordinates!

Au: Ha! No worries. I'll tweak them a little so it's like... Dae and Nosst and Grao and...

L: Don't just tweak them *that little*! Hey! I was wondering, but... You didn't name *me* irresponsibly like that, did you?!

Au: That would be funny, but sadly, no.

L: Sadly?! I'm starting to wonder... Did my self-imposed moratorium on slaughter in afterwords to improve my image give you the mistaken impression that you could get smart with me?

Au: Wait, that was a PR thing?!

L: Yeah. And I'd say the jig is up. Fortunately, I happen to have one of those Author Destructo Lasers that the karaoke place was giving out to celebrate the grand opening of their new location near the station.

Au: What?! Wait! How did you get such a tailor-made— *Zzzzzt! Fwsh.*

L: The author has now been reduced to his component particles. But as long as darkness remains in men's hearts, cheap and overly obvious naming schemes will continue to plague the world. They're the worst for those who must bear them, so when you lovely readers have kids, make sure not to give them weird names! And with that warning to all of humanity... So long, everyone! See you next volume!

Afterword: Over.

By Hajime Kanzaka
Illustrations by Rui Araizumi

CONTENTS

Chapter 1: Insurrection?! The World's a Dangerous Place These Days...

"C'mon, lady. Why don'cha give us all you got while we're still bein' nice?"

"If ya don't—"

It was a pleasant morning on the main road. The handful of bandits who'd popped out from the trees were interrupted in the middle of their usual cliches... by my attack spell!

Or, at least, that's how this would usually go. What had *actually* quieted them this time was the sudden appearance of a presence deep in the woods. Hatred, sorrow, rage, hostility... It was like a mix of every negative emotion humans possessed. Miasma.

"Wh-What the...?"

It popped up so abruptly that even the bandits, a notoriously slow-witted lot, hushed up as they began scanning the area around them. And while they were doing that, I was quietly reciting a spell.

"You... You think our ears're playin' tricks on us?"

"No... There's something there! An' it's close!"

The bandits whispered to each other in tones bordering on shrill as the presence drew nearer. Then came a rustle of underbrush, and...

"Hraa—"

"Blast Ash!"

Fwwsh! Before it could even finish its roar, the brass demon diving out of the forest was reduced to dust... by my attack spell.

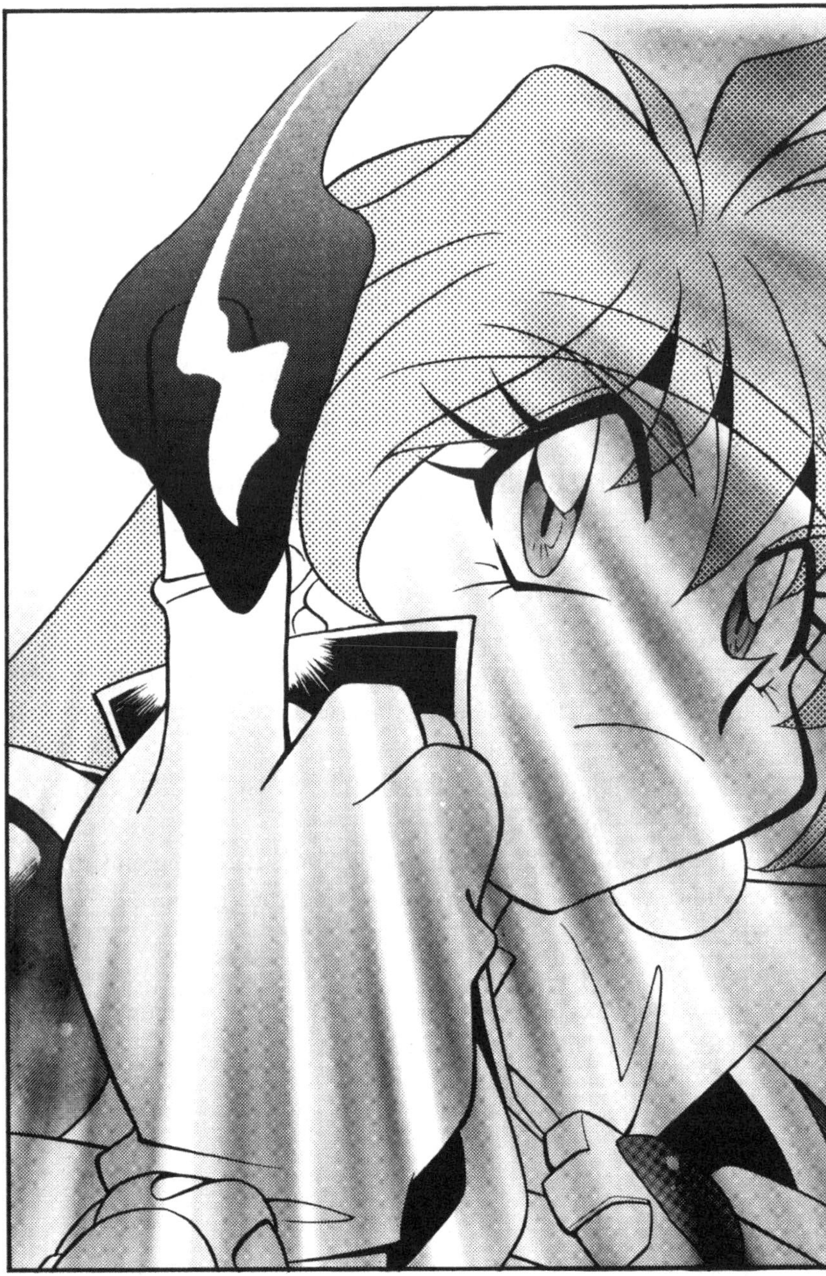

"Boy, this stuff keeps happening lately, huh?" my companion Gourry pondered aloud as he gazed up at the clear blue sky overhead.

After blasting that brass demon, I'd blasted the cowering bandits (natch) and helped myself to their spoils of the day. We'd since continued down the narrow road through the forest.

"You mean the demon I blew up?" I asked.

"Yeah. That stuff," Gourry replied, glancing over his shoulder. I looked back as well, but the spot where we'd fought the demon was well out of sight by now.

"I guess it is happening a heck of a lot more than it used to..." I whispered with a sigh, unable to hide my gloom at the thought.

Lesser demons, brass demons... They were bottom of the barrel as far as demon species went, and I'd beaten that last one lickety-split, but that didn't mean they should be taken lightly. Any demon at all was a major threat to even your run-of-the-mill swordsman or sorcerer. And yeah, in isolation, they were easy pickings for someone of my prowess... But even I might end up in real trouble if they caught me off guard or swarmed me.

You used to be able to count on the fact that they rarely appeared in large numbers—operative phrase being *used to*. For the past half year or so, it was just as Gourry had said. They seemed to show up wherever we went, wreaking their particular brand of havoc.

For instance, we'd be staying at an inn, they'd suddenly attack, I'd kill them all with a spell, and then I'd end up having to pay for the damage to surrounding buildings. Or I'd go to raid a bandit base for fun and funds, only to find it already ravaged by a roving demon horde, thus forcing me to huck a Dragon Slave at a nearby mountain to vent my rage about the lost income, only to end up dealing with complaints from the locals. Just all kinds of terrifying attacks.

And for some reason, this was all happening more and more often. I still didn't know why. But...

A kind of nebulous anxiety—*Something's happening out there*—was taking root in people's hearts.

"Huh... Guess something's up," I remarked, stopping just as I was about to pass through the town gate.

We'd arrived at Telmodd City on the border of Lyzeille. It was a pretty big place and had been developed in a planned manner... which sounds nice and all, except that "planned" basically equates to "boring." About the only distinctive feature Telmodd had going for it was the fact that it was totally walled off, which wasn't especially remarkable as cities went. But, eh, enough of my thoughts on urban planning.

"What's wrong, Lina? Why'd you stop?" Gourry asked, puzzled.

"Look."

I pointed at the rightmost stone gatepost, which was affixed with a sign that read: *"Attention, all traveling sorcerers. If you have no other urgent business, please report to the local sorcerers' council immediately."* It was signed by the sorcerers' council at large.

"What's that mean?" he asked, still baffled despite the simplicity of the message.

I'll concede that, on the face of it, it just sounded like a request for visiting sorcerers to check in. But what got my attention was the wording. It wasn't asking for us to stop by the *Telmodd City* council, but the *local* council. That suggested this was a mass-distributed request. In other words, they were in the market for a *lot* of traveling sorcerers. Plus, the message didn't contain so much as a hint about the reason for the request, which told me it was serious enough that the council didn't want the general population to know about it. In fact, I'd seen a similar notice once before...

"I guess we'll just have to go check it out," I said, passing through the gate.

Gourry and I got the lowdown at the sorcerers' council, enjoyed a light lunch at a local eatery, and were just setting out for our new destination when...

"Excuse me... Might you be Lina Inverse?" called a voice from behind us as we walked down the main drag.

"I might be. Why?" I responded.

I turned to see a girl standing there. Well, I say "girl," but she was probably my age. Maybe even a little older. She had short, blond hair and green eyes, and was really quite beautiful... though her charm was somewhat dampened by the black hat and cape she wore, marking her as a sorcerer, as well as the troubled expression on her face.

"Um... I overheard your name at the council. You're *the* Lina Inverse everyone talks about, aren't you?"

"Depends on what they're saying. Uh, not that I'm about to ask for quotes."

"Well, just a lot of rumors that... I'm not sure I could exactly define as complimentary."

Twitch.

"That's probably me, then, yes..." A vein in my forehead throbbed as I processed that unflattering choice of words, but I managed to respond quite calmly.

"I need a favor from you! Please, take me to Crimson!"

"Hey!" I squawked, seizing her hand and pulling her into a nearby alley. I lowered my voice so that no one else could hear us. "Keep it down! If you're asking for an escort to Crimson, you must know what's going down there, yeah?"

"Yes, of course," she responded firmly, trying to hide the desperation in her eyes.

So, what's going down in Crimson Town, you ask? Attempted insurrection by a branch of the sorcerers' council.

When I said I'd seen a notice similar to the one at the front gate before, I wasn't kidding. That was when a sorcerer, serving as a minister in a small kingdom called Lagd, staged a rebellion using the local sorcerers' council. I'd helped put that to bed with a fellow sorcerer, and together we'd saved the king. The minister was punished, and the whole thing came to an end without much harm done, but...

This time insurrection was brewing in Crimson at the edge of the Empire of Lyzeille. The chief conspirator was the head of the local sorcerers' council, a position without much political power at all. Apparently, however, he'd killed the local lord and seized control of the city. When news of this reached the capital, the emperor had dispatched his army to quash the rebellion.

Now, in practical terms, it was really only a matter of time before they put the whole thing down. But in a show of good faith and in the interest of reinforcing trust between institutions, the sorcerers' council was hoping to handle it first.

Thus they were instructing all battle-ready sorcerers to make for Crimson. Except, with all the unpleasant rumors swirling around these days, they'd asked that we go in secret so as not to raise any alarm. Clean things up quietly and make an official announcement after the fact—that was both the council's and the empire's preferred policy.

In other words, this was definitely *not* something we should be talking about while standing in the middle of the city's main thoroughfare. The way this girl was looking at me, though, suggested she definitely had her reasons.

"Okay, well... let's hear your story. First, what's your name?"

"Aria Ashford..." It wasn't she who responded, but a cracked, aged male voice from nearby.

I turned in surprise to see a shadowy figure standing deeper down the alley. He was dressed in unadorned black, with a dark cape and hood pulled so low over his eyes that it was difficult to make out his face. He was short—shorter than me, even—possibly owing to his hunched posture.

"Who... are you?" Aria asked uncertainly.

"I see," the old man said, ignoring her. "So this is one of the assassins you're hiring... to destroy Lord Kailus."

"Wait a minute. Are you...?!"

"You may call me Zonagein. Now... show me what you can do."

Fwee... A sharp whistle echoed through the sunless alley. I couldn't parse all the details of the situation in the here and now, but there was one thing I was damn sure of—that sound was this old man's declaration of war.

I began to recite a quiet spell, Gourry drew his sword, and then...

"What?!" Gourry and Aria shouted in unison, stunned.

The darkness was... writhing. It was an unsettling sight. The umbra of the alley seemed to pulse and shiver around Zonagein. No, wait, it was...

When Aria realized it herself, she let out a soft shriek, for what had looked like writhing darkness was actually dozens of rats pouring into the shadows! There was no way they'd been there the whole time. They must have responded to the old man's whistle.

"Does that mean... this guy's a beastmaster?!"

Still, it wasn't like a bunch of rats—not even a whole dang mess of 'em—could be any threat to me in this situa—

Krik. Interrupting my train of thought was a soft sound from the back of the alleyway, like a door straining on its hinges. Beside me, Gourry, who was about to charge forward, stopped in his tracks. And then... *Crack! Krika-crack!*

"Ah..." Aria quietly groaned as the sound grew louder and louder.

It was coming from the dozens of rats gathering around Zonagein. Although... was it really fair to call them rats anymore? The no-longer-really-rats were transforming before our eyes. Their flesh and bones snapped and burst, forming new ones in their stead. Creatures once small enough to hold in my hand were now the size of my arm span and growing.

To be honest, I was pretty curious about what they were gonna turn into, but this clearly wasn't the time for idle speculation. Instead...

"Freeze Arrow!" I swapped targets, taking the spell I'd meant for Zonagein and unleashing it on the transforming rats. A dozen or so icy bolts froze the creatures one after another.

At least, that was the plan. But—*Fwifwifwish!*—every one of my frigid projectiles dissipated anticlimactically on impact!

"No way!" I shouted, shocked.

What kind of creature could brush off Freeze Arrows like this? I only knew one answer. Demons.

"Heh heh... What do you think? A rare and beautiful sight, hmm?" Zonagein said, as if to confirm my suspicions. He smiled at me confidently, surrounded by the lesser demons he'd forged from the rats.

Krakoom! There was a sudden burst of fire and explosions, followed a second later by the screams of bystanders.

Gourry, Aria, and I had just leaped out and to the side of the alleyway as a hail of Flare Arrows (courtesy of the lesser demons) shot out into the main avenue. Fortunately, collateral damage was kept to a minimum, as—maybe due to the time of day—there weren't many people around.

"Everyone run!"

No sooner had I yelled that than the lesser demons emerged onto the street. This started a new wave of screams, and the few passersby still present quickly took off in panic.

Okay! Now that we were out in the open, we could fight!

"Gourry! Back me up!" I began reciting a spell.

"Right!" Gourry charged, sword drawn, at the lesser demon horde.

"Hraaagh!" Seeming to realize the incoming threat, one of the lesser demons let out a howl that conjured a dozen Flare Arrows. But before it could fire them...

Swsh! Gourry leaped in, slicing his sword through the creature's stomach!

"Graaagh!" The demon cried its last and fell, its flaming arrows dissipating into nothing.

One down!

"Amazing!" Aria remarked from the sidelines, marveling at Gourry's swordsmanship.

But this was no time for wide-eyed spectating! There were plenty of lesser demons to go. In fact, they were still spilling out onto the street.

Gourry cut through a second, and by the time he felled a third, I'd finished my spell.

"Bram Blazer!"

This was a spell that sent a blue light piercing through its target. It felt like a shockwave to living things, while dealing some serious damage to the undead and demons alike. It'd normally put the latter in a whole world of hurt, but this baby was amplified. The blue light I shot forth flew through several demons poking their heads out of the alley and...

"Graaaaagh!" They collapsed with a scream. This little stunt caught the attention of several other demons that had previously been focused on Gourry.

"Aria! Get away!" With that, I drew the shortsword from my hip and sprang forward while chanting quietly.

"Hragh!" howled a lesser demon in my path, producing a volley of Flare Arrows that rained down on me in a shower.

I dodged them with a light leap to the side, and... "Elemekia Lance!" I released the spell I'd been working on. While watching out of the corner of my eye to make sure it met its target, I turned and began my next incantation.

Lesser demons were strong and tough with magical power to spare, but teamwork was beyond them and they were pretty stupid, so their attacks were fairly rote. Gourry and I always had to stay on our toes against a swarm of 'em, but on the flip side, they weren't too scary as long as we were cautious.

Soon enough... "Assher Dist!"

Kra-pash! My spell vaporized the final lesser demon. That just left that Zonagein guy!

"Oho... You made quick work of those lesser demons. Impressive indeed," came a voice from above.

Surprised, I looked up to see the petite black figure perched on top of a nearby roof. He must have used Levitation or something to get up there while we were cleaning up the demons.

"Why not stop watching and come on down?" I called. "You wanted to test us, right? If the lesser demons didn't do the trick, doesn't that mean it's time for you to fight us yourself? Or did you climb up there because you're scared?!"

"No, no... I merely seek great heights. You know what they say about smoke and fools." He brushed off my provocation leisurely enough, even throwing a little self-deprecation into the mix.

Dang... I guess age really does come with experience.

While I was staring up at the old man, Gourry took a smooth step forward. "Then why don't we come up there and join you?"

"Don't do it," I said, my eyes still locked on Zonagein. Gourry seemed to think he was just small potatoes... but I saw him differently.

Lesser and brass demons were created by summoning low-tier demons from the astral plane into mindless small animals, transforming them in the process. Earlier, Zonagein had called the local rat population to him first—fodder for an instant swarm of lesser demons. Even your average "pretty good" summoner could only muster up a handful of demons at a time, which suggested exceptional skill on Zonagein's part.

It would be easy enough for us to fly up to the roof, but our actions would be limited severely while we were in the air. Zonagein potentially had talents beyond just summoning, and he'd no doubt want to use them while we were compromised. That was why I'd hoped to bait him down, but he wasn't biting. In that case...

"Well? Not coming?" he taunted.

"No," I said flatly.

"Hmm... I see. What a pity. Well, it makes little difference to me," he said with his usual leisure. "But are you sure you can say the same for yourselves? If I wished, I could turn all the rats, cats, and dogs in this city into demons."

"Oh yeah? Well, whatever floats your boat. No skin off my nose."

My casual reply finally seemed to rattle Zonagein. "Eh? You think I'm bluffing, do you? Or do you think you can handle thousands of lesser demons at once?"

"Neither!" I declared, raising a finger decisively. "What I'm saying is that we're just gonna ignore whatever you do and walk away!"

"What?!" Gourry, Aria, and Zonagein all cried in unison.

"W-Wait a minute now! What in the world..." the old man on the roof fretted.

But, true to my word, I turned away and launched into a brisk walk. "C'mon, Gourry, Aria. Let's get outta here. While the old man's playing up on the roof, we'll head to Crimson and beat that wicked council chairman."

"Hey, come back here! If you won't, I... hrm... I'll destroy the whole city!"

"I think he's trying to tell us something..." muttered Gourry.

"Oh, just ignore him. Standard old guy ranting."

"You sure about that?"

"But... he said he would destroy the city," Aria objected.

"Don't worry about that, Aria. Dude just likes the sound of his own voice," I said without turning back.

Truth is, I wasn't bluffing either. I had my reasons for thinking this way.

The fact that he'd brushed off my earlier attempts at provocation suggested that Zonagein wasn't the type of guy to lose his cool and act rashly. Plus, at the very start, he'd said that he wanted to see what we could do. That meant his real goal here was to take our measure. He wouldn't destroy a city in a fit of pique.

"W-Wait! Come back here, I say! You can't really be so irresponsible! Young people these days..."

Without another glance at the griping old man on the roof, the three of us left Telmodd City in the dust.

"Okay, Aria. What's the deal, exactly?" I asked.

"Well, I'm happy to explain, but... why here?" Aria quietly asked in return.

Just outside the city limits, we'd departed the main road and entered a forest of moderate size nearby. I hadn't stopped to ask questions until we were fairly deep inside it.

"Why else? It seemed pretty obvious that that Zonagein guy was gonna come after us once he got off the roof. His most likely course of action would be to search the road from Telmodd to Crimson, meaning he'd eventually catch up to us if we'd stayed on said road. Of course, we're still going to Crimson... We're just gonna hide out here for a bit first and chat, and then go at our own pace once he's breezed by," I explained, spreading my cape out on a patch of grass and taking a seat.

"Ah... I see," Aria said agreeably.

By contrast, Gourry was skeptical. "But Lina, if that old man *doesn't* come after us, aren't we just wasting time?"

"Let me put it to you this way, Gourry. Would you prefer to head straight for Crimson and risk ending up with lesser demons a-go-go?"

"Well, no..."

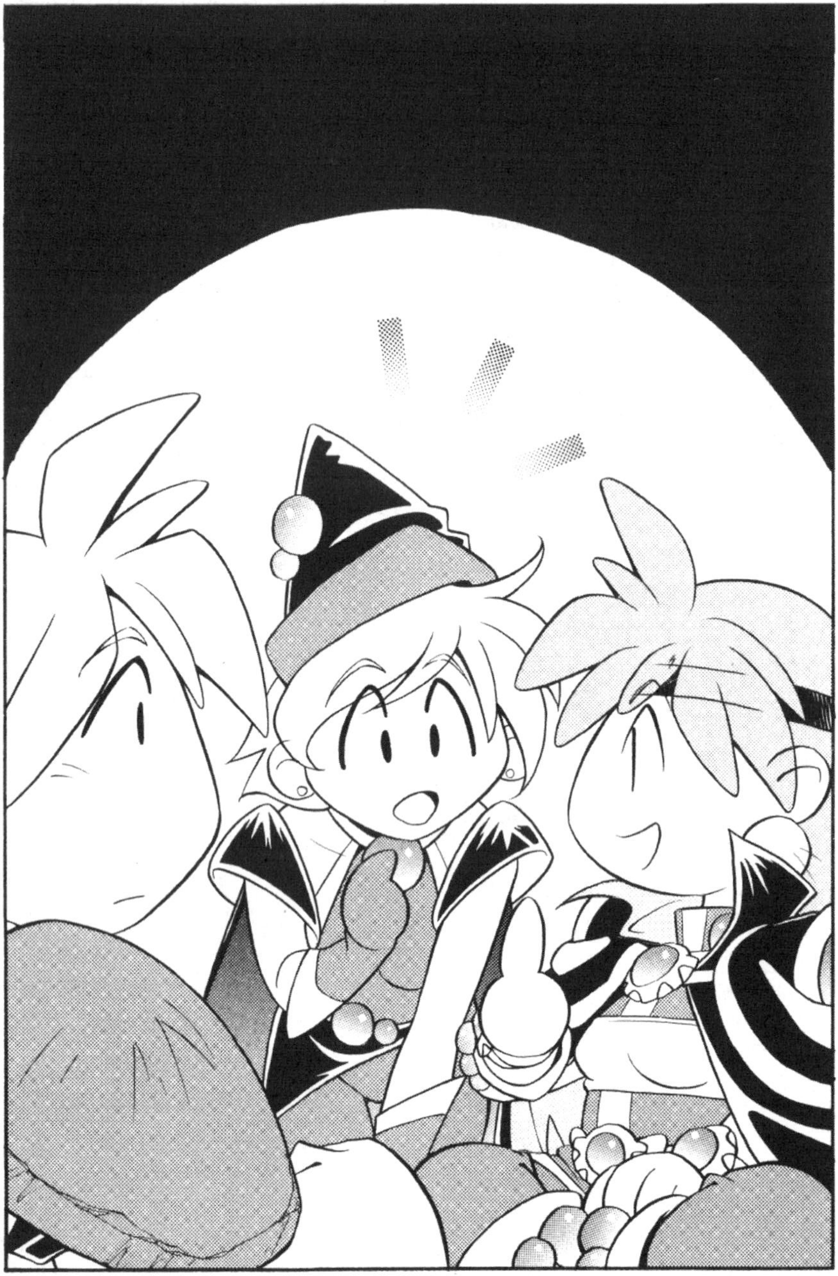

"Right? So here we are. You ready to dish, Aria? Why are you itching to get to Crimson, and why is that Zonagein guy after you?"

"Well…" She spread out her cape and took a seat herself. She looked down for a while, deep in thought, and when she finally looked up again, she spoke very frankly. "I need to save my big sister."

Her sister's name, she said, was Bell. She was a kind, beautiful woman that Aria was proud to call family. Bell had met a man and fallen in love. If this were a fairy tale, they'd have gotten married and lived happily ever after… but unfortunately, reality rarely played by the rules.

One day, Kailus, the once-married head of the Crimson sorcerers' council, fell in love with Bell on sight. Kailus had a great deal of influence, and his management of the council and abilities as a sorcerer were indeed prodigious. But he was considered lacking in what some would call the human graces. Despite his prestige in sorcery circles, he wasn't especially well-liked. There was a reason his wife had left him.

On top of all this, Bell was nineteen while Kailus was well over forty. Nobody thought he stood a chance at wooing her, yet Kailus pursued her nonetheless. Bell refused him because she was engaged… but it wasn't long after that her fiancé died under mysterious circumstances.

Rumors spread that Kailus had killed the man to take Bell for himself, all while making it look like an accident. Nobody knew who started the rumors, but people assumed that Bell would never find it in her to care for a man with such suspicions hanging over him. Except…

"Shortly thereafter, my sister married Kailus," Aria whispered, her eyes cast downward. She spoke without detail, haltingly, as if not particularly pleased to be sharing this information. "I asked her why, but she wouldn't tell me… She only gave me a troubled look. And soon after, she stopped seeing me. But from what I've heard, she's not happy in the slightest."

Go figure, I thought to myself as I listened to her story. I had no idea why Bell would have agreed to marry this Kailus person. Sure, you couldn't rule out that she might've fallen in love with him somehow, but… From what Aria'd said, Kailus seemed like *that* kind of guy. You know, the type that makes a grab at whatever strikes his fancy but loses interest the minute he gets his mitts on it. Whatever Bell's motives for marrying the guy might have been, I couldn't imagine her prospects for happiness were good.

"I've been doing research at the Crimson council," Aria continued, "and one day on my way there, a messenger stopped me. He said that my sister wanted to see me. She'd never contacted me like that before, so I quickly went to meet her. That's when she told me..."

"That Kailus was plotting an insurrection?" I asked.

Aria nodded firmly. "Probably with the intent of getting the council involved. She told me to go and alert another council office. Sairaag used to be home to the largest council closest to Crimson... but it was mysteriously destroyed two years ago."

"Bwuh?!" Gourry and I found ourselves shouting.

Aria cocked her head to the side. "What is it?"

"Oh, er. Nothing, nothing..."

In truth, me and Gourry had maybe-sorta-kinda been involved in the destruction of Sairaag... *Actually, I never actually reported all that to the sorcerers' council, did I? O-Of course, I'll totally get around to it... sometime...*

"So your next best bet was Telmodd City?" I urged Aria on, sweeping the part about Sairaag under the rug.

"Yes... It's possible there were others closer by, but Telmodd was the only city I was certain had a council branch and that I knew I could reach."

"I see..."

I could imagine it'd be pretty dispiriting, under the circumstances, to head to a city you didn't know well and get lost on the way, or to arrive only to find it didn't have what you were looking for.

"But... Kailus seems to have made his move before I was able to spread the word. I managed to make it here and report to the council... But the very next day, I heard that Kailus had assassinated the local lord and that the emperor's army had mobilized." She let out a soft sigh. "It seems the town is fully under Kailus's control now. I don't know what forces he's mustered, but if the imperial army is taking action, it's only a matter of time before the city is retaken. And if that happens, my sister might be drawn into it..."

"I think I follow. You want to beat the army to Crimson and do something about Kailus?"

"Yes... Of course, I'd handle it myself if I could, but while I can use some attack magic... it's really only at a 'better than nothing' level. I have no proper combat experience either."

Her story checked out. During our tussle with the lesser demons, she'd just dithered around, unsure of what to do. Jumping into a fight took a degree of experience, guts, and abandon... that Aria just didn't seem to have.

"So you were waiting for someone to take you back to Crimson... and that's when we showed up?"

"I know I'm asking a lot. I know that I'll be a burden and that things might not work out even if we make it there, but..." she started, then stopped.

"But... you still want to save your sister?" I asked.

Aria nodded silently.

Hmm... I see...

I had my own big sister back home... although she was way stronger than me, frankly. Even if trouble found her, she'd break her own way out with a smile. That made it kind of hard for me to relate to Aria's concern for her older sis.

"Well, I will say," I began, scratching my head, "hearing your story does make me wanna sock this Kailus guy one, but..."

"But what?" Aria looked at me nervously.

I shot her a wink in reply. "But I dunno what he looks like, so I'll need someone to point him out to me."

"You mean...?!"

"We're going to Crimson. Together."

"Thank you so much, Mistress Lina!"

"Just call me Lina. Now, let's camp out here for a bit and then head back out."

"Of course!" she agreed with a smile.

I had to wonder if she realized that I hadn't pressed her about why Zonagein was after her.

Kailus likely knew that Aria had left town, but he shouldn't have known that she was in Telmodd. Nevertheless, Zonagein had found her here. It was possible that Kailus had simply sent a lackey to every city in the area... The part that struck me, though, was that Zonagein wasn't there to capture or kill Aria, but rather to test the mettle of the sorcerers she'd hired—

in other words, me. This was further evidenced by the fact that the lesser demons hadn't even spared her a glance during our throwdown in the city.

There had to be more to this than met the eye.

At first, our journey went smoother than expected. From what we heard in the villages we stopped by, old Zonagein had indeed passed through ahead of us, just like I'd hoped.

Ha! Sucker! I thought smugly to myself.

At least, I wished I could just be smug about it... The truth was, we couldn't put off a fight with Zonagein forever. We might even end up facing him in Crimson Town, where he'd have plenty of buddies to back him up.

There was another kink in my tricky little scheme too. According to intel we'd picked up on the road two days after leaving Telmodd, the imperial army's vanguard had also moved through not long ago. It was only a unit of two hundred soldiers, so they probably wouldn't attack Crimson outright, but it was a sure sign we needed to hustle.

And then, on the fourth day of our journey...

"It can't all be smooth sailing, I guess..." Gourry said, coming to a stop on the forest road we were traveling.

"Huh?" Aria likewise halted and gave Gourry a questioning look.

"He's saying we've got company," I said dryly. "Company that's not great at hiding its presence."

"...Well, I don't exactly make a habit of this kind of thing," came the voice I expected from the woods. With the rustling of brush, the same black-clad figure that we'd met in Telmodd emerged.

"Hey, Master Zonagein. Super tracking skills you got there. Funny how you didn't notice us taking a break in the forest after leaving Telmodd."

"Now, now. I found you in the end, so let's let sleeping dogs lie," he said, easily brushing off my mockery once more.

He really did seem like a pretty smart guy. His strategic choice of location suggested good judgment too. The forest was great for ambushes, what with all the cover around. But it played to Zonagein's strengths in a more specific way... The thick greenery. The sprawling wild. Woodlands teemed with small animals, each one a potential vessel for Zonagein's demonic summoning powers.

That said, I wasn't exactly helpless here.

"I guess you have so little faith in your own abilities that you're gonna sic your lesser demons on us again?" I asked, trying to bait him once more.

I figured he'd brush this off too and move right to the summoning. Then I'd use the time I'd bought to whip up a big spell of my own! However...

"Oh, not at all. Sorry to disappoint if that's what you were counting on," Zonagein replied, casually quashing my plan. "Having witnessed your fight in the city, I know that lesser demons would be nothing more than a nuisance to you. Not that I mind that, of course... My companion informed me that they would get in the way of his fight anyway."

"Your companion?" I asked with a frown.

"Oh, yes. Allow me to introduce him. You hear that? Stop hiding and come out, Graymore," the old man called.

A chilling hostile presence rose up behind us.

What?! I quickly turned back and saw... more of the forest? No. There was definitely something moving in the shadows of the canopy. Soon enough... a figure stepped out from the trees and into the afternoon sunlight.

"A lizardman?!" Aria shouted in shock.

It was an adequate description. He was covered in scales the color of dead leaves and had a long tail, both typical traits of lizardfolk. But there had to be more to this Graymore guy. Zonagein was putting more faith in him than the dozen or so lesser demons he could summon, after all. Plus, apparently Graymore had been hiding behind us this whole time—and we hadn't sensed him.

"Now then, Graymore... Which would you prefer?" Zonagein asked.

"The swordsman," Graymore replied simply.

Then—*Fwsh!*—the claws on both of his hands extended. Ten in all... and pretty long. The longest one was the length of a full sword, the shortest that of a dagger. Were those his weapons of choice? I slowly turned back to Zonagein.

"I see," he said. "Then I'll be fighting you, little miss."

"Looks that way. But y'know, if we're gonna chat like this, you should have the decency to show your face."

"Oh? I didn't realize I was hiding it," Zonagein replied, unceremoniously raising his lowered face.

"Huh…" I murmured when I caught a peek of the visage beneath the hood. He was a white-bearded old man who might've even been pretty good-looking in his younger years. "You look pretty normal."

"Were you expecting something monstrous?" He gave me a wincing smile.

"Well, kinda…"

"I'm very sorry to disappoint you. Not that I came here to please you, of course…"

"Yeah, fair point."

"But we could talk for ages like this if we wanted… Shall we begin?"

"Sure thing!" I said, drawing the shortsword from my belt, reciting a spell under my breath, and charging straight for Zonagein.

In that instant, he turned around and retreated into the forest. His hands were still hidden under his cape and he showed no sign of brandishing a weapon, but I couldn't let my guard down. There was always a chance he could produce a knife from its folds to throw at me.

Zonagein kept his back to me and maintained some distance as he fled. But I wasn't gonna run this game of tag forever!

"Freeze Arrow!" I released my completed spell at Zonagein.

It wasn't a one-hit-kill number, but it would be quite disabling if I nailed him. Even a glancing blow should slow him down some. As my frigid bolts rained down, Zonagein easily dodged them by taking cover behind a tree.

Hmm… Figured that would happen.

In a forest full of obstacles, I knew it would be hard to land a decent hit with projectiles. Frankly, I'd have considered it a lucky break if a single arrow had found its target. My *real* plan was to fire off a few simple Freeze Arrow barrages and get Zonagein to write me off as the win-through-force type. Then I'd spring a Van Layl, which conjured tendrils of ice along the walls and ground, to freeze him over before finishing him off with a bigger spell! So to keep up the ruse, I began chanting another Freeze Arrow, when just then…

"Van Layl!" It wasn't my voice that echoed through the trees, but Zonagein's.

What?!

Frosty vines spread out in all directions from Zonagein's current location, letting out an icy crackle as they went. And, of course, "all directions" included toward me!

Crap! He got the drop on me! I sprang back, but the tendrils continued to spread.

Darn it! I cursed to myself as I thrust my shortsword into the ground. Zonagein's icy vines crawled up its blade. That bought me a little time, which I used to do an about face and flee the scene.

I emerged from the forest, arriving back where we'd started. Gourry and Graymore were already locked in combat.

Shing! Cling! Clang! The striking of metal against metal rang out over and over. It seemed like Gourry was the one on the defensive!

From what I could tell, Gourry had the superior skills... but Graymore had ten claws of varying lengths on his side. His movements seemed sporadic at a glance, but they came in nonstop waves. It was all Gourry could do to keep dodging him. He wasn't getting a chance to turn the tables. Every time he tried to put distance between them, Graymore would close in to keep the upper hand.

We believed Gourry's new blade to be a powerful magic one, though I didn't know exactly what it did. Between it and his skills, though, Gourry easily should've been able to cut through Graymore's sword-claws. But...

Graymore took a step forward and—*Zwee!*—something whistled through the air. It was his tail! Graymore lashed at Gourry's feet! Thankfully, Gourry leaped back at just the right time. That left Graymore off-balance and immobile. Gourry's sword flashed!

Ting! Ta-ting! Ting! Several of Graymore's claws moved to block it, snapped, and went flying!

Now's your chance! I thought, but instead, Gourry took another step back.

Fwsh! The broken-off claws returned to their former length.

Aha... Definitely a tricky opponent. I would've liked to offer a little spell-based support, but anything I fired off ran the risk of hitting Gourry. More importantly, I doubted Zonagein was gonna give me the leeway. I could feel his presence just behind me even now!

Okay then!

"Van Layl!" Without stopping, I placed a hand on a nearby tree to unleash my spell and kept running. The spreading vines of ice froze their way down the trunk to the ground, then the grass...

But when I looked back, I saw no sign of Zonagein. Nevertheless, I could sense his presence looming nearby.

Where is he?! I quickly scanned the area and... "Above?!" I looked up and saw a figure hovering high between the trees.

"Freeze Arrow!" It was now Zonagein's turn to rain down icy bolts.

"Fireball!"

Fwoosh! A flaming globe met the icy arrows and burst into a shower of red fire.

As for who'd cast it, that honor went to... Aria?! The burst of flames scorched the treetops and Zonagein among them.

"Harrgh!" came a pained voice beyond the fire.

Okay! Now!

I quickly chanted a spell... "Bram Blazer!"

And I fired it into the flames! I couldn't see Zonagein amidst the blaze, but I didn't see any escape for him either! My blue bullet pierced the inferno... but yielded no sign of a hit. Had I missed?!

"Freeze Arrow!" Zonagein's voice came at me from another direction.

When did he— I reflexively ducked behind a nearby tree. But...

"Augh!" Aria cried out.

Damn! I could see Aria crouching on the ground some distance away. She'd taken a direct hit from the Freeze Arrow, leaving her left leg iced over from the shin down.

Zonagein was standing not too far off, at the edge of the forest. How had he gotten over there? A Levitation spell wouldn't have moved him that quickly...

"A Fireball in the middle of the forest? How reckless," he remarked, slowly approaching Aria. The quiet muttering that followed was definitely a chant.

Oh crap! Is he going for Aria?! I had to save her, but my spell wasn't gonna make it in time! And the sword I might have used to slow him down was currently frozen in the forest! In that case...

"Bram Blazer!"

Bwoosh! Suddenly, with no warning at all, a shockwave of blue light sent Zonagein flying. He fell dramatically to the ground, but managed to get up again. He glared in the direction of the spell's caster...

"Now, now, old man. It's a man's duty to be kind to beautiful ladies."

Our new arrival was an unfamiliar face. He struck a rather pretentious pose as he stared down Zonagein.

"Ngh...!" The old sorcerer looked between me and the new guy and, perhaps realizing he was now at a disadvantage, cried out to his companion. "Graymore! We're leaving!"

Shing! Claw and blade clashed.

"Guh!" Gourry toppled, either overpowered or off-balance, in a way that exposed his back to his opponent. Graymore raised his claws. But at that exact moment...

"Graymore! We're leaving!" Zonagein's cry echoed from the forest.

This gave Graymore the tiniest bit of pause, which Gourry used to twist around and strike at him with the sword in his right hand! *Clink!* Graymore was unfazed. Gourry's slash, executed from an unstable position, was easily swept aside by the lizardman's claws. However...

Following the momentum of his slice, Gourry kept twisting. A streak of light flew from his left hand!

"Gah!" Graymore let out a quiet cry, then fell onto his back and lay motionless. A razor-sharp *something* was stuck deep between his eyes.

What was it, you ask? It was one of the claws that Gourry had snapped off earlier. He must have scooped it up when he toppled over, and then used that feint with his sword to create an opportunity for the deadly throw.

Was that planned or improvised, man? Either way...

Upon seeing Graymore fall, Zonagein silently retreated into the forest and disappeared. I'd have preferred to finish him too, but incautious pursuit was the root of all injury. Besides, I was way more worried about Aria at the moment. I ran over to her and inspected her frozen leg. Fortunately, her boots and pants offered a degree of protection, but we still had to do something about it, and fast.

"First, we need to warm up your leg."

"Hey, is she okay?" the unfamiliar man asked in concern.

I turned to him and replied, "Treatment first. Introductions later."

"My name's Dilarr," the man said as he dumped some sticks onto the fire we'd started to warm Aria up, right around the time the adrenaline of the fight was wearing off.

This Dilarr fellow looked a little over twenty. Black hair, black clothing, a little on the scrawny side... If he put a little more effort into grooming, he might pass for handsome, but his scraggly facial hair and dirty clothes put the kibosh on that.

"Ah... thank you for saving us," Aria said, bowing her head to him as she warmed her leg by the fire.

He waved his hand dismissively. "Hey, it's nothing. It's a man's duty to save a beautiful woman in distress," he replied lightly. "By the way, may I have your name?"

"I'm Aria."

"Are these your assistants?"

"Hey," I barked with a glare.

"More or less," she replied.

"Hey!"

"I was just kidding," Aria said, waving her hands defensively as I turned my glare on her. "But they are helping me. I'm on my way to Crimson."

"Crimson?!" Dilarr's eyes opened wide. "Then... you're also answering the council's call for aid?"

"'Also'? Is that what you're doing too, then?" I interrupted.

He cast a sidelong glance my way. "Just so you know... when highly attractive men and women are talking, it's not polite for the ugly to butt in."

"Excuse me?!"

"Ahh, Lina! Calm down!" Gourry quickly held me back before my rage could pick up steam.

"Oh, let me introduce them. This is Mistress Lina Inverse and Master Gourry," Aria said with a smile, when just then...

Steppa-steppa-step! Dilarr scuttled back dramatically, gazing at me in terror. "L-Lina... Inverse? Er, I mean... Mistress Lina Inverse?"

"Yeah?"

"*The* Mistress Lina Inverse?"

"I'm not sure how I feel about that definite article right there... but yeah, I'm probably the gal you've heard stories about," I answered with a glare.

"Yeeeeek!" Dilarr suddenly prostrated himself on the ground. "Please forgive me! I didn't know! I meant no offense! Forgive me! Don't kill me! I'll give you all the money I have!"

"Hang on now!"

Just what kind of stories are people spreading about me?!

"Er... Master Dilarr, there's no need to be frightened. She's not as bad as the rumors suggest," Aria said with a wince. Unfortunately, that didn't make me feel a whole lot better.

Dilarr quickly scrabbled up to Aria, seized her shoulders, and whispered earnestly into her ear, "It's not worth it, Aria! I don't know what circumstances brought you to them, but keeping such company... Aren't you afraid you'll catch the Lina Inverse?"

"I'm not a disease!"

"Ack! She heard me!" Dilarr quickly scuttled away again.

What's with this dude?

"C'mon, don't worry so much. I've been traveling with her for a while and..." Gourry began cheerfully enough, then petered into silence. After a lengthy pause, he scratched his head and concluded, "Actually, I got nothin'."

"Don't sound so hopeless! You're acting like nothing good has happened to you since we started traveling together!"

"But Lina... *has* anything good happened to me since we started traveling together?"

Guh... Well... okay, maybe not, but...

"A-Anyhoo..." I turn away from him and back toward the other two. "Aria has to get to Crimson. For reasons."

"Reasons?" Dilarr inquired.

"Yes..." Aria launched into her halting explanation again.

"Hmm... I see." Once Aria finished her story, Dilarr (who had returned to the fireside) scratched his chin with his thumb and said, "But Aria, if you're headed for Crimson, let me give you a warning. Don't take the main road there."

"What? Why not?"

"Well... as you can probably imagine, I'm a fellow sorcerer. I'm heading to Crimson myself at the council's request. The reward's a pittance, but I'm low on cash and it's usually best to do what the council says. There's just one problem... The imperial army's squatting a half a day's walk down the road. Seems they've been held up by guerrilla attacks from lesser and brass demons."

Demons?! I found myself scowling at this news. I would've assumed the attacks to be Zonagein's handiwork, but as far as I knew, he'd been out looking for us. That meant Kailus had another summoner of his caliber working for him... which in turn meant that the imperial army might not have such an easy time taking the city back after all.

But while I was contemplating all this, Dilarr went on. "As a counter against demons, they've been drafting every sorcerer that passes by. In a 'volunteer capacity,' if you know what I mean. They almost got me too, but like hell I'm going to take orders from some military hard-head. So I went on the run, and that's how I bumped into you guys. If you want to get ahead of the army, you'll have to go around them."

Aha... Makes perfect sense.

"Still... taking the scenic route is really going to set us back. It'll be days before we hit Crimson," I mused, folding my arms thoughtfully.

A detour to avoid being drafted might mean we arrived after the whole thing was over.

"I wonder..." After a brief pause, Aria whispered, "I think there might be a way."

Chapter 2: Forward Ho! Destination, the Sorcerers' Council!

I'd never been to Crimson Town myself before, but I'd heard about it. It was a series of small islands in the middle of a large lake, connected by bridges, that had eventually grown into a city. It was crisscrossed by canals, and most travel there was done by boat. It was a pretty popular tourist destination too. But they said that all of the buildings there were painted white, which left me with one nagging question about the place. Namely, why call it *Crimson*? However...

"Aha... so that's where the name comes from."

All my doubts were dispelled the moment I gazed down upon the city from the mountaintop. Evening was just breaking, with the sun starting to sink behind the mountains. The water in the canals glimmered red in its waning light, and the buildings took on a burning scarlet hue.

Yeah, okay, "Crimson Town" makes sense now...

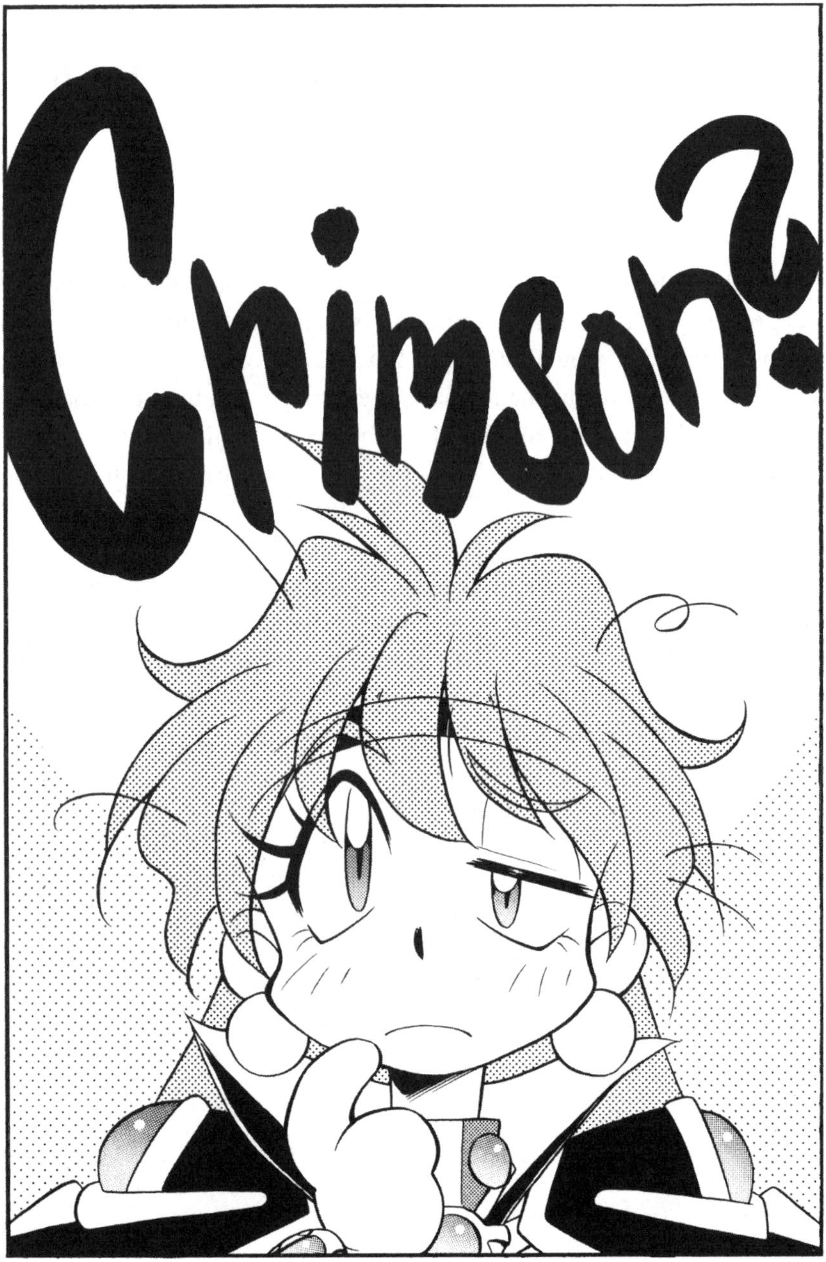
Crimson?

"It should be just down this way," Aria announced as she emerged from the brush behind me.

Her suggestion to reach Crimson while avoiding the imperial army had been to get off on a side road, scale an unassuming nearby mountain to reach the lakewater's source, and then follow the river down. Frankly, it seemed unlikely that the imperial army and Kailus's men hadn't thought of the idea of getting into town via its waterways, but somehow, we hadn't run into either on the way here.

See, Crimson sat upon a lake fed by several rivers, the largest of which cut through these mountains. Aria said that when she was little, she'd frequently explored her way to its headwaters with her big sister. To think those childhood adventures would prove useful at a time like this... Was that a good or ill omen for us?

"Well... we'd better get a move on," Dilarr said, putting a presumptuous arm around Aria's shoulders.

Yeah, this guy'd ended up tagging along too. He couldn't simply walk away from the sorcerers' council mission, after all, but he also couldn't get past the imperial army on the main road on his own. This was pretty much his only recourse. That was his excuse, anyway... but in practice, he mainly seemed to want to hit on Aria.

"E-Excuse me, Master Dilarr..." she stammered.

"Hmm? Oh... Heh. You scared, Aria?"

"She doesn't want your mitts on her, you jerk!" *Crack!* I introduced Dilarr's face to my bootheel. "Come on, Aria. You need to be firm with these guys, or they'll just keep escalating."

"R-Right..." she responded vaguely to my friendly warning.

"Ow, ow... Y'know, I think maybe you're a little *too* firm..."

"All part of my charm!" I quipped.

Dilarr fell silent, grimacing.

"Anyhoo... Take us to the river, Aria."

"All right," she agreed, leading us through the brush.

After some more walking, I began to hear the sound of rushing water.

"Here we are," she said, at last coming to a stop.

"Here?" Gourry looked around uncomfortably. "This looks like... a waterfall to me."

"It is," Aria replied confidently.

Indeed, a massive stream of water was roaring down the cliffside. We'd come out on a ledge about halfway up the fall, and you could've fit a two-story building between where we stood and the river below... Actually, what lay below was less a river and more of a gorge. Vast quantities of emerald water gushed between its banks.

"You're not gonna tell us to jump in, are you?" Gourry asked cautiously.

Aria winced while waving her hands. "Oh, of course not! There are two or three more waterfalls up ahead. We'd die if we did that."

Aha... That explained why the imperial army and Kailus's goons weren't poking around here.

"We just have to make it down one way or another, and then we'll be in Crimson."

Right. So we just have to...

. ...

"Hey, wait a minute!" I slinked over to Aria. "'One way or another'? You mean you haven't even thought about how we're going to get there?!"

"N-No, I have! I simply meant that there are several ways to go about it. We could travel along the water with Levitation, or we could follow the valley down the mountain road... The mountain road won't exactly be easy going, but I could handle it even as a child, so I don't think you'll find it excessively difficult."

"Those are out, unfortunately," I said easily.

"What?"

"Either method would get us found by Kailus's forces. You and Kailus are both Crimson locals. If you know these routes, then he does too. The road you mentioned isn't meant for large groups, so even if the imperial army's aware of it, they won't use it. That's why it might *seem* like Kailus doesn't have anyone posted along the route... But as we get closer to town, I bet there'll be lookouts, at the very least. Even if we travel at night, whether we're floating by with Levitation or creeping through the brush, they're bound to spot us. Then they sound the alarm and... I won't say the game's over, but it definitely gets harder."

"B-But... we can't turn back. Finding another route now would take much too long."

"Hmm..." I muttered, glancing at the viridescent water splashing noisily downward. "Say, Aria... this river's pretty deep, right?"

"What? Why, yes. It would be deep enough for boats to travel if it weren't for the waterfalls."

"Okay. Then I know what to do."

"What's that?" she asked.

I pointed to the plunge pool at the bottom. "We go *in* the water."

Ssshooossssssssh... For a time, the only sound to be heard was the rushing of the fall.

Then...

"Whaaaaaaaat?!" Gourry, Aria, and Dilarr all cried out in unison.

"Hang on a minute, Lina! You're not asking us to swim, are you?!"

"We can't do that! I told you there are more waterfalls downstream!"

"I'd rather take my chances with the enemy forces!"

"I never said we were swimming, damn it!" I shouted over the three whiners. "I mean, duh! We'd die! I'm talking about using a Lei Wing spell to go underwater in a *protective wind barrier*! That'll ensure us an air supply, and if the water's deep, we can dive low enough that we're not visible from the surface."

Of course, a typical Lei Wing could never carry four people, caster included... But an amplified Lei Wing courtesy of the talismans I'd gotten from a certain someone should do the trick.

"Oh, that's perfect!" Aria exclaimed.

"No arguments here, then," Dilarr agreed readily.

"You sure? That seems pretty darn reckless too..." Gourry was the lone remaining voice of dissent.

I ignored him, of course. Granted, his response was actually the most rational one of the three... But rather than admitting that, I simply smiled and said, "Then it's decided. Let's head out. We'll tether ourselves together. Be careful not to drop any of your gear in the water."

And with that, I started on my own preparations. Needless to say, I'd retrieved the shortsword that Zonagein had briefly frozen back in the forest. It wasn't the best sword by any stretch of the imagination, but I wasn't interested in paying for a replacement. To make sure I didn't lose it in the water, I tied the hilt to the sheath, then looped the string around my belt to hold the whole thing in place. I attached the tether around my belt too. By the time I was done, the others looked more or less ready to go.

"Okay... everyone ready?" I asked them.

They nodded. I nodded back and began reciting a spell under my breath. When it was ready...

"Lei Wing!"

Wreathed in a barrier of wind, we plunged into the river.

"You tricked me! Mistress Lina, you tricked meeeee!"

"Don't talk, Aria! You'll bite your tongue!"

Her and Dilarr's shrieking echoed through the wind barrier. Of course, I understood the impulse to scream.

Traveling underwater in a bubble *sounded* easy enough, but this was no gentle cruise. For one thing, the bottom of the river wasn't flat and smooth. It was filled with rocks and trenches that churned the water, making it impossible to predict the speed and direction the turbulent current would take us at any given moment.

So that's how we were sailing... Although I suppose it would be more accurate to say "swept along." I could slow our descent a bit when we went over a waterfall, but other than that, we were basically at the river's mercy. I probably don't need to tell you how that felt for the passengers.

So, like I said, I understood the impulse to scream given our precarious situation... but I didn't appreciate the accusations of trickery. I'd said this trip was doable, not that it was comfortable or safe!

In contrast to the screamy twins, Gourry remained silent. Every time I glanced back at him, he seemed to have an expression on his face like, "Ah, my lot in life." After all, he had no choice but to ride this out until we reached Crimson.

We'd passed through—rather, fallen down—what felt like three waterfalls so far. Based on Aria's earlier description, I figured we had to be closing in on town by now, but I couldn't even poke my head out of the water to look around. I'd have to bring the whole bubble topside to do so, which would draw the attention of any nearby enemies. That left me to infer our position from the state of the water around us.

Once we hit the city, the current should dissipate and we should be able to see signs of life up above. The sun was almost completely down now, so visibility wasn't great, but with the strong moonlight that night, it was still possible to make out anything close enough.

Speaking of, it does kinda feel like we've slowed down a bit. I scanned the area around us while keeping control of my spell and...

When I glanced right, I fell silent.

"Mistress Lina?" Aria noticed the change in my demeanor, followed my gaze, and...

She, too, went silent when she saw it. The... eye.

In the water right outside the wind barrier, a single eye was watching us. It was about the size of a fist, and it was keeping pace like it was tailing us. To be honest, it was pretty dang freaky... In fact, it was terrifying. I couldn't make out what it was attached to, but I could tell that—whatever it was—it was floating in the water behind the eye, and it was big.

"Um..." Aria turned toward me, both her smile and her voice strained. "It's probably... a fish?"

It didn't look like a fish to me, though I didn't say that aloud. Instead, I picked up speed. We quickly put some distance between us and the eye, but...

"Gwah!"

I heard a strange splashing sound as Dilarr cried out. I looked to see numerous green tentacles breaking through the wind barrier from behind, wriggling around as if searching for us.

"What the...?!" Gourry drew his sword (no mean feat in the cramped space of the barrier) and sliced through one of the tentacles.

Stupid me! It's a city on the water! Of course they'd have aquatic sentries!

"They've found us! I'm going up!" I yelled.

Staying underwater now was all con and no pro, so my goal was to shoot us to the surface. But as soon as we began to rise—*Wham!*—the whole wind barrier jolted like we'd hit something.

"Mistress Lina! Above us!" Aria cried.

I looked up to see two strange figures looming large over our bubble. With the surface to their backs, I could say for certain now that they weren't fish. They flitted around, darting through the water and...

Fwsh! Two blade-like fins cut into the top of the barrier.

"No!" Gourry quickly parried them, but even with his incredible swordsmanship, the unstable footing in the bubble made it hard for him to make full use of his talents.

One of the deflected fins began to withdraw as if cowed, but then plunged at us again.

"Aria! Cast Freeze Arrow!" I called.

"Huh? But that would—" She hesitated, bewildered.

Dilarr, however, began chanting. "Freeze Arrow!"

Dilarr's arrows manifested *outside* our bubble. In other words, out where the looming figures were. Of course, I didn't know if the spell would work on them or not... But at the very least, it should freeze the water around them. And sure enough, the Freeze Arrows began emanating ice to snare our attackers and hold them in place. So trapped, their fins dislodged from our barrier as we sped away.

Okay, now up we go! I focused my mental energy on propelling the wind barrier, shooting us up through the depths and into the night. The sky was bright and starry. Moonbeams glittered on the water's surface. I could see winged creatures overhead, and houses cloaked in darkness below. We were well within Crimson Town now.

Wait... Winged creatures?! I quickly looked around again.

Now, "winged creatures at night" calls to mind images of bats and owls and such, but what was currently hovering in the skies over Crimson wasn't any of those. Its wings were bat-like, to be sure. But the creature resembling an unpainted life-sized doll carrying a spear was decidedly *not* a bat. Said creature was looking right at us with its eyeless, mouthless, noseless face and leading a flock of a dozen or so other creatures that resembled lesser demons with wings.

Oh hell! A navy and an air force?!

Still, I didn't have freedom of movement right now. I piloted us down to a nearby street and dismissed my flight spell. As I did...

Sploosh! Multiple figures popped out of the water. They were covered in scales that glittered wet in the moonlight, and seemed to be a combination of fish and lesser demons. They had arms and legs with protruding fins much the same shape as the ones that had cut into our barrier earlier.

"Tch!" When he laid eyes on the fishy figures, Gourry drew his sword and charged.

"Wait, Gourry—"

Wha-bam! Before I could finish, Gourry and I both toppled over.

I sprang back up immediately. "We're tethered together, remember?!"

"S-Sorry!" Gourry quickly got to his feet, severed the rope with the sword, and took off again.

I freed my sword from its sheath and got to work cutting myself free from the others too.

Swsh! Gourry's blade glinted in the moonlight as it cut down one of the fishlike demons.

"Hrooooo!" Another of its kind a bit further away made a sound like it was howling at the moon. When it did, dozens of cold arrows appeared before it!

These are...!

"Gourry! Time to make tracks!" I called, turning around and doing just that.

Our current array of foes consisted of a handful of fish demons, a dozen or so flying demons, and that winged doll thing. We could beat 'em, of course, but it would take time we didn't have. Reinforcements would surely arrive before we could finish the job. For now, we needed to regroup.

"H-Hey! Lina!" Gourry quickly took off after me. Aria and Dilarr, naturally, followed suit.

Fwoosh! As we ran, I heard the sound of wings tearing through the air. Sensing hostility approaching from behind us, I ducked into an alley while chanting a spell.

I looked up to see multiple flying creatures against the sky visible between the buildings. As I'd suspected, their wingspans didn't let them enter narrow alleyways... But that didn't necessarily mean that we were safe. They could always attack from above!

"Hrooooo!" The demons howled overhead.

At the same time, I released my own spell! I put my hands on the alley wall and... "Blast Wave!"

Bwam! A giant hole opened into the house on the other side.

"This way!" I cried as I leaped through it, followed by the other three.

"But isn't this someone's—"

Before Aria could voice her objections—*Crababababash!*—dust billowed up in the alley. The airborne demons had probably fired down a volley of some attack spell or other. Obviously, I'd anticipated that, which was why I'd barged into the building beside us.

Aria was worried about the house's owners, but the place seemed abandoned to me. There weren't any lights on in the windows, after all. It was too early to retire at this hour, but too dark out to putter around inside without any light. And, in further support of my suspicions, the room we'd jumped into was completely desolate. Not one scrap of furniture to be seen. It was hard to say if the owners had skipped town when the chaos had started or if the building had been uninhabited for longer than that, though.

At any rate, the big question now was what to do next. The enemy knew we were here. They'd probably come after us soon. They'd bust in, overwhelming us with their numbers...

Or, more likely...

I softly began to chant a spell.

Some time later, the demons unleashed their magical assault on the building.

Thunk... Whumpa-whump...

"Called it," I whispered softly in the dark while listening to the muffled commotion.

"Called what?" Aria asked.

"That they'd try to blow up the whole house with us in it," I replied, though our current circumstances weren't conducive to casual conversation. I quietly chanted a spell, and... "Lighting!"

Poff! A small magical light appeared in my hand. I could finally see for myself that we'd all escaped unscathed.

"Say, Lina... can you get us a little more space?" Gourry asked. "Kinda cramped in here."

"I was flying by the seat of my pants, man. I mean, I can open things up... but not too much. We're underground, after all."

After we'd leaped into the empty house, I'd realized the demons were going to nuke the place, so I'd used the tunnel-digging spell Bepheth Bring to open a hole in the floor and escape underground. I could open the hole as wide as a room, but digging a tunnel that big with no supports was more likely to cause a collapse. Still, wriggling around together in uncomfortably close quarters did feel stupid. We weren't worms, y'know?

I recited the cant under my breath and... "Bepheth Bring!"

Swaths of earth were carved away at my command. I had to wonder... where exactly did all that dirt go? Not that this was really the time for philosophical questions. Anyhoo, we soon had enough space for everyone to sit in a circle.

"Sheesh... what a mess." I spoke up first, naturally. "I figured Kailus would have his home turf well guarded, but I wasn't expecting a full sampler platter of demons."

"Demons? You mean those piscine and avian monsters?" Dilarr asked, his brow furrowed.

I nodded. "Not sure about that flying doll-looking thing... but the other winged monsters and their fishy counterparts are probably lesser demon bastardizations. Or maybe genuine lesser demons of an unusual pedigree. One of the fish guys earlier cast Freeze Arrow with a howl, just like lesser demons do."

This was pure speculation on my part, but I could imagine that Zonagein had created lesser demons to serve as a navy and an air force by having them possess fish and birds the same way he had with rats in Telmodd.

Dilarr scratched his chin with his thumb. "Boy, this is a fine situation we're in... I might've been better off getting bossed around by the imperial army."

"I'm sorry... for dragging you into this," Aria said despondently.

Dilarr responded quickly, "No, I'm not blaming you, Aria! It's just, you know, sensitive people like you and me aren't cut out for this kind of thing. That's all."

"Oh yeah?" I interjected.

"I wonder what that's supposed to mean..." Gourry mused with me.

"Er, wait! I wasn't saying you're *in*sensitive!" Dilarr backpedaled.

This guy was gonna talk his way into serious trouble someday...

"At any rate, the first order of business now is figuring out how to proceed from here," I said. "Honestly, with all these demons roaming around, it might be easiest just to blow up the whole city..."

"Please, Mistress Lina! Don't! There are still innocent people here!" Aria pleaded fervently.

"Sh-She's right! It's not worth it! Reconsider! Please!" Dilarr begged with equal intensity.

"I was just joking, you goons!"

"Sounded pretty serious to me…"

"Get off my back, Gourry! Anyway… if we want to infiltrate the enemy's base and just take out Kailus, we need to figure out how to get there. Aria, do you know where we are in relation to where Kailus might be?"

"Kailus is most likely at the sorcerers' council. But as for where we are… I don't know the entire city by heart, and I couldn't even get a general idea in the dark like this."

"So you got nothing."

"I'm sorry I'm so useless," she said, slumping over.

"Hey, no big. But that does mean our top priority is getting our bearings. Therefore…" I began chanting a spell.

"Hang on, Lina. You sure it's safe to poke our heads topside?" Gourry asked in a rare bout of insight.

"Fair point. The demons could still be hanging around, but there's no guarantee we won't be greeted by a swarm of them even if we wait around a while. And I don't think we have much time to waste in the first place."

The entrance to the hole we'd made had likely been sealed when the demons leveled the house. We could asphyxiate if we stayed down here too long. And even if we didn't, the demons might be cautious enough to dig into the rubble to make sure we were dead. If they found the entrance to our little hidey-hole… They'd flood us out, no question. Either way, it seemed to me that staying put would only turn up the danger, so I began whispering a spell.

"Bepheth Bring!"

Whum! As I touched the earthen wall, soil shaved away to create a long tunnel stretching out ahead of us.

"How's about we keep digging, go a ways, then come up somewhere else?"

The group nodded in firm agreement.

It was too bad...

"Bepheth Bring!"

...the work was so monotonous...

"Bepheth Bring!"

...that it was getting kind of annoying.

"And another Bepheth Bring!"

Just chanting and chanting...

I couldn't say how far we'd made it before the earth we were tunneling through began to turn muddy. I held up my light and, as expected, found the ground below us soaked through. (Incidentally, my light source was a Lighting spell cast on the tip of my drawn shortsword. Typically, magical lights can't be extinguished until their timer runs out... but this way, if I needed darkness, I could just sheath my sword.)

"We're hitting water..." I grumbled.

"We are under a lake, after all. There are canals running overhead too. Oh... and we really don't want to hit one of those, so perhaps we should dig deeper," Aria proposed.

"Right. Got it." I used my next Bepheth Bring to tunnel us in a more downward direction as we kept crawling through the mud.

"Boy, this is seriously rough going..." Dilarr complained from behind me. "My clothing's sopping. I feel gross."

"Buck up, Dilarr. Aria and I aren't whining, are we?"

"Yeah, I guess not... But there's gotta be an easier way."

"We can do this above ground if you want, but if the enemy finds us, you're on your own."

"Well, that's not exactly appealing either... I get it! Just shut up and keep crawling, right?"

"Yep," I replied, then began to chant my umpteenth spell.

"By the way, Lina," Gourry piped up as I started incanting, "there's something that's been bothering me these last few minutes... Hey, are you listening?"

Of course I was. But I couldn't respond mid-chant.

"The ground feels a little different..."

Oh, come on...

"Bepheth Bring!" I cast my spell, carving out a new section of tunnel, and replied while I was groping along, "Of course it does. It's basically all mud now."

"That's not exactly what I meant..."

"Then what did you—"

No sooner had I said that than—*Splut!*— my right hand sank into the ground.

...Huh?

And then...

Sploosh! Water flooded up from below.

"Glug... Glurk..." I groaned and blinked a few times. The first thing I saw was a blanket of luminescent moss overhead.

I looked myself over and picked myself up. Fortunately, I was still intact. Gourry, meanwhile, was laid out beside me.

I glanced around and could see we were surrounded by water. It was a lake, dotted with islands barely large enough to build a one-room hut on. Gourry and I had washed up on one of them, and Aria and Dilarr on yet another nearby. Above us, the whole ceiling was scattered with softly glowing moss.

"...An underground lake?" It wasn't me who murmured that, but Aria, who was also apparently just coming to.

Yup. We'd found ourselves in a subterranean pool beneath Crimson. This was the first I'd ever heard of such a thing existing, mind you.

"Oww... Hey, what is all of this?" Dilarr asked as he, too, sat up.

I cast a glance his way and replied, "I suspect there's an underground river feeding this thing. We must've been passing over it when..."

"When the floor gave way?"

"You got it. Hey, Gourry, wake up already!"

"Mm..." As I shook him, Gourry stirred and let out a moan. Then he sat up with a start. He looked all around, and his eyes stopped on me. "What I was gonna say is that it felt like we were walking on a really thin board."

"I... I see..." I scratched my head, wincing.

"I didn't know there was an underground lake here either..." Aria whispered in awe as she looked around. I'd just used a Levitation spell to reunite us on the same island.

The light from the luminescent moss wasn't especially bright, and the stone pillars around us holding up the ceiling impeded our vision significantly. But even so, the fact that we couldn't see the edges of the lake… Was it bigger than the town of Crimson itself? I could understand why a lifetime resident of the city like Aria was so surprised to find out such a place existed. As for the more pressing matter at hand…

"So I guess you can't tell where we are in relation to the city above, huh?" I asked.

"I'm afraid not. I'm sorry," she replied.

"Like I said, no big. None of us are badly hurt, which means we weren't swept very far, for sure. But we don't have much other choice now… We'll just have to open another hole."

Sst! It was then I felt a presence appear far behind us. I reflexively whipped around to see… the surface of the lake perfectly undisturbed.

"What is it?" Aria asked.

In lieu of response, I began chanting a spell. The presence I felt… I knew it wasn't just my imagination. Gourry, who had the instincts (and smarts) of a wild animal, seemed to sense it too. He drew his sword and gazed penetratingly into the water. Then…

I caught sight of a figure flitting beneath the surface. A lot of figures, in fact! *Is it them?!*

I didn't have to wonder long, for—*Splash!*—more of those fish demons burst out of the still water! Their scales glimmered in the glow of the luminescent moss. And the second they appeared…

"Freeze Bullid!" The subzero bullet I fired froze over a part of the lake. Some of the demons landed on the glacial surface, while others were trapped in the ice.

"Raaaaagh!" Gourry dashed at our incoming foes, light on his feet in spite of the slick terrain.

But the demons weren't going to sit there and be slain. "Hrooooo…!" Their howling echoed through the dimly lit lake cavern, and before them appeared countless arrows of cold!

No, those are—

Nroom! The projectiles whistled through the air as they sped toward us. Gourry pressed his charge and cut down several of them. When he did—*Bloop!*—they scattered to the ground in sparkling droplets.

"Water?!" Dilarr shouted from behind me.

Indeed, the arrows the demons had conjured were made out of water, not ice. That was no reason to underestimate them, however!

Vreeeoom! One liquid bolt whizzed right by me, tearing a hole in my cape. Fired at high speed under high pressure, water was still nasty as heck!

"Aria! Dilarr! Freeze the lake and give us some legroom!" I shouted without even a glance behind me.

"R-Right!"

"Understood!"

I then began chanting a spell.

While this was all going down, Gourry had sliced through two more demons. He was heading for a third when, all of a sudden, he stopped in his tracks and leaped to the right. At almost that same time...

Crash! Countless watery arrows broke up through the ice, shredding the area where Gourry had just been standing. It was a barrage from more enemies below. I couldn't see anything at the bottom of the lake, which meant I had no idea how many there were... so for now, I'd just have to beat the ones I could see!

"Dynast Breath!" I fired a spell at one of the silhouettes lurking in the water. I cast a glance at Gourry and saw he'd already polished off most of the demons on the ice.

Okay! Time to retreat back to a single island and lure the demons onto land! I was about to share my plan with Gourry, when just then...

"Eek!"

"Aria!"

I heard Aria shriek, Dilarr cry out for her, and then a loud splash of water! I turned and saw a panicked Dilarr staring at a fragmented patch of ice floating on the water's surface. Aria was nowhere to be seen.

No way...

"She fell in!" he shouted, his anguished scream echoing through the cave. "Can't... Can't we do something?!"

If the water were safe for diving, I could have used a Lei Wing to dive in, find Aria, and save her. But that would mean releasing my wind barrier to grab her and swim back up to the surface... and our enemies wouldn't just sit idly by while I did that. In fact, what were the odds they'd ignored Aria when she fell in? In all likelihood, she was already…

"Where's the girl?!" Gourry asked as he returned to us.

Dilarr and I could do naught but stand there in silence. The demons' attacks had been quelled for now, but…

Bloosh! I heard a splashing to my right. All three of us whipped around in surprise.

On an island not far away… stood someone I'd never seen before. If I had to describe him, I'd say he looked like a drowning victim with an aqua hue. But this was no drowning victim, nor was it a zombie… His body was swollen as if waterlogged, but large fins grew from his feet, and there was webbing between the fingers of his taloned hands. Where a human would have a nose and a mouth, he had a mess of green tentacles. I guessed those were what had wriggled into our wind barrier on the way into Crimson Town… Pretty gross, honestly.

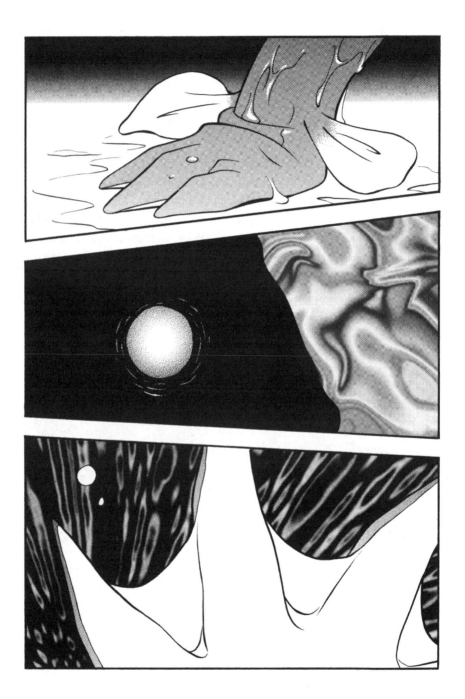

In most cases, I would've greeted this guy with an attack spell on sight, but in this case, I had to show restraint...

He had Aria in his arms.

"She's still alive... for now," came a wet, muffled voice. It sounded like someone talking with their mouth full.

"Mm..." As if to confirm the claim, Aria stirred and slowly opened her eyes. "Ah... Wh-What?! No!"

Waking to the gravity of her situation, she struggled desperately, but the arm around her refused to budge. The creature clamped its free hand over her mouth to keep her from chanting a spell.

"Gotta say... I'm impressed you knew we were here," I threw out there.

"My name is Narov. Do not underestimate me. After I attacked you in the canals above, I doubted you'd try to use them to reach Lord Kailus again. But I didn't think you'd be willing to go walking around the city either. Which meant you had only one path left..."

Oh?

"Hmm... So you're Narov, huh? You may be in charge of the underwater security here in Crimson, but you're not as smart as you think you are."

"What was that?" he asked, his expression unreadable.

I puffed out my chest. "You said we only had *one path left*... meaning this is the way to the sorcerers' council! It was very kind of you to volunteer that information!"

"What? Are you telling me... you didn't know?"

"That's right! We just stumbled here through blind luck!"

"I'm not sure that's worth bragging about..." Gourry commented quietly from behind me. I ignored him, of course.

"I see..." Narov's expression remained unchanged. Not that I'd be able to tell if it *did* change. "Then I only need to finish you here. Don't bother resisting, by the way. I assume you know what will happen to this woman if you do."

Splish! As Narov threatened us, about a dozen fish demons surfaced to surround the island we were standing on. It wouldn't be too hard to beat them... if they didn't have Aria hostage, anyway.

Time for some good old-fashioned fast-talking!

"Heh. Please," I scoffed. "So, fill me in. If we don't resist, what guarantee do we have that you'll release Aria unharmed?"

"I give you my word. Once you're defeated... this one woman will pose little threat to Lord Kailus," Narov claimed brazenly.

I raised my voice a little. "Gimme a break! How stupid would I have to be to take a hostage-taker at his word? You may think Aria's not much of a threat... but you'd have nothing to lose by breaking your promise and killing her to be sure! Besides, I've got a policy about aqua-colored guys with face tentacles..." As I spoke, I took a small step to the side. At that exact moment...

"Freeze Arrow!"

Dilarr unleashed a volley of frigid bolts that froze the water from our island to Narov's in an icy bridge. Gourry immediately dashed across it.

"What?!" Narov shouted in shock right before Gourry leaped at him and—*Swsh!*—bisected his head.

While I was talking to Narov, I'd realized that Gourry and Dilarr were whispering behind me. I'd then heard Dilarr chanting a spell. That's why I'd intentionally raised my voice to draw Narov's attention. Then, when I heard Dilarr finish his incantation, I'd simply moved aside to let him do his thing.

Narov reeled back and began to collapse without as much as a scream. Gourry freed Aria from his arms.

Pwaaash! When Narov's body hit the water, the demons around us howled in chorus. "Hroooooooo!"

Liquid arrows were pointing at me and Dilarr from all sides! Had the loss of their commander led the demons to attack indiscriminately?! Fortunately, I'd guessed something like this might happen!

I ran over to Dilarr and placed my hands on the ground. Just as the demons unleashed their watery barrage...

"Bepheth Bring!" I cast the spell I'd chanted at my own feet!

Whush! The ground beneath us instantly disappeared, and Dilarr and I tumbled down a short ways. I'd carved out a trench that spiraled outward like a snail's shell. It put us low enough that the arrows passed harmlessly over our heads.

Okay... Now things are looking up!

I quietly chanted a spell, and then... "Blast Ash!"

Vwum! I peeked my head up out of the trench to fire, turning one of the fish demons to powder.

The battle was moving in our favor. We were all holed up in my makeshift bunker, popping up here and there to fire off spells. Any demons that dared to charge in close were swiftly cut down by Gourry's blade. The same scene repeated over and over again as we steadily thinned the enemy's numbers.

After all, the water surrounding the island had been frozen solid, and we were currently in a crater below ground level. In order to hit us with an attack, the demons had to get closer. And in order to do that, they had to crawl over the ice. We just had to nail 'em once they were in our range. As long as we didn't let our guard down, we had this in the bag. If Narov were still alive, he might've been able to think up a plan, but right now, all the demons could do was mindlessly press their offensive. Before long...

"It's gotten quiet," Aria said. We'd killed more demons than I could count at this point.

"Yeah," I responded, poking my head up to scan the battlefield. There wasn't a demon in sight. "Looks pretty safe..."

"Did we get them all?" Dilarr sighed as he stood up.

"Don't get ahead of yourself. I don't see any more, but they could be in hiding," I said, standing up with him to take a proper look around.

There was neither hide nor hair of demons anywhere. We could assume for now that we'd vanquished the enemy. In which case...

I turned back to the group. "If what Mr. Greeny-Blue said was true, there's a way to get to the sorcerers' council from here somehow. How do you guys feel about searching it out and busting in?"

"But Lina, how would we even go about finding it?" Gourry asked, looking around uncertainly.

Dude had a point. The underground lake was massive. We didn't know what said way looked like, and locating it wouldn't be easy... Under normal circumstances, that is.

"Besides... there'll be enemies guarding it too, don't you think?"

"Of course, Dilarr. But let me ask you this... Would you prefer to return to the surface and look for the council building while fending off dive-bombing demons?"

"No, that's... a little too dangerous for my tastes."

"Right? So we're doing things my way. I've got a plan. Aria, Dilarr, you can both use wind barriers and Levitation and stuff, right?"

"Ah… I think so."

"Sure, of course."

"Okay. I'm gonna cast a Levitation to get us all off the ground while you two each cast a wind barrier around us."

"Why bother with that? Isn't Levitation enough?" Dilarr grumped.

"You'll see. Let's go," I said, taking hands with Gourry and Aria as I chanted. Dilarr then took Aria's hand and… "Levitation!"

I cast my amplified Levitation spell and the four of us lifted off. Aria and Dilarr then finished their own chants to complete a double-layer barrier around us.

Okay. All ready!

I started carrying us through the air. Visibility wasn't great. The luminescent moss wasn't universally present along the roof of the cave, and some of the patches without it looked like tremendous black holes. We normally wouldn't have stood a chance of finding an entrance when we didn't have the faintest clue what it looked like, but…

"Listen… I know I'm playing along and all, but are you sure you can find the way like this?" Dilarr started complaining not long after we took off.

"C'mon, we'll be fine. Just don't whine so much that you get distracted from maintaining your wind barrier."

"Didn't plan on it… But are you really, *really* sure about this? If we wander around for a while only for you to concede it was a wild goose chase, that'll be quite a bit of egg on your face."

"I know—"

Wham! At that exact moment, a jolt shook our wind barrier.

"Lina! Behind us!" Gourry shouted.

"On it!" I cried. I then shifted the spell to turn us around and descend.

Not far back was one of the lake's small islands… one with a stone pillar stretching all the way to the ceiling. That was where the attack had originated! *Wham! Wham!* Countless water arrows continued to rock the barrier.

There! I strained my eyes and saw a few creatures swarming around one spot on the water's surface. I made a beeline for them.

"Hey! Hey! What are you doing?!"

"Mistress Lina! This is much too reckless!"

"Quiet! Hold the barrier steady!"

We were rapidly closing in on the island. As we approached, I could see the enemy more clearly. *Two fish demons and... What the heck?*

A single streak of red light appeared beyond the arrows of water flying at us. A foreboding chill ran up my spine. I quickly changed course, and no sooner had I done that than the red light made contact!

Thrum! It easily broke through our two-layer barrier. *Not good!*

But just before it struck me, Gourry cut down the red light!

"Lina! Let me down there first!"

"L-Let you down?"

"Just do it!"

"F-Fine! Dilarr, Aria! On my signal, drop the barrier! Then cast a blast of either Flare Arrows or Freeze Arrows at the enemy! Got it?"

"B-But..."

"You sure about this?!"

"Just do it! Gourry, you ready?"

"Yeah, anytime!"

I glanced over at the enemy. Another volley of watery arrows splattered against our wind barrier, and another red light appeared beyond them.

"Now!"

The barrier vanished. The red light closed in. I shoved Gourry toward the pillar, and the recoil got us both moving as the red light streaked through the place we had been. Gourry sailed through the air and...

Krrk! He impaled his sword into the pillar! Dragging it through the stone to reduce the speed of his descent, he slid down the pillar... straight toward the mess of demons! Naturally, they weren't about to ignore that. They looked up at Gourry and...

"Freeze Arrow!" Aria and Dilarr both finished their spells in the nick of time.

Their frigid volley rained down on the demons locked on Gourry. Obviously, a spell like that wouldn't hurt them... but it was sure as heck enough to distract them from the descending swordsman!

"Dilarr, another wind barrier! Aria, Levitation!"

"Right!"

"...What?"

Dilarr and Aria quickly began chanting—the former without hesitation, and the latter only after a moment of uncertainty. Meanwhile, all but one of the demons seemed confused. The lone holdout still had its eyes locked on Gourry. It screeched, and arrows of water manifested around it.

Not good!

The demon fired at Gourry, but—*Skreek!*—he suddenly changed the course of his descent, dodging the projectiles with ease.

Of course! He could alter his angle of approach by shifting the position of his sword in the stone pillar. *You're pretty clever from time to time, Gourry! Even if that might've just been instinct kicking in...*

Gourry successfully landed smack in the middle of the enemy swarm. But we weren't just sitting on our hands here either!

"Windy Shield!"

"Levitation!"

"Concentrate on keeping those up no matter what, you hear me?" I warned Dilarr and Aria as they cast their spells. Then I dismissed my own Levitation and began chanting my next spell.

Battle had broken out between Gourry and the demons below. With his skills, he could easily prevail over two demons, but he seemed to be struggling against our singular non-demon opponent.

Sheesh... Better help the big lug fast!

"Fireball!" I unleashed my slightly altered Fireball.

The typical version of this spell created a ball of light between your palms that would explode when it hit something, scattering flame everywhere. But this one... The ball of light appeared a bit behind us, outside the wind barrier.

Okay, let's go!

"Break!" I snapped my fingers, and—*Fwooooosh!*—red flame engulfed our wind barrier!

"Gwah!"

"Raaagh!"

Aria and Dilarr's screaming swirled around in the wind barrier, which was now—propelled by the blast—streaking toward the battlefield at explosive speed. *Kra-pwash!* We smashed into the water near the island. Unsurprisingly, this got the demons' attention.

Dilarr dismissed his wind barrier, and when he did…

"Blast Ash!"

Vwum! I pulverized one of the demons. Obviously, I'd been chanting the whole time we were falling.

"Aria! Abort the Levitation!" I now called.

"Ah… Right!" She quickly did as she was told.

We splashed down into knee-high water. I figured the remaining demon would charge us, but it seemed to be retreating instead. I slowly waded over to the island, accompanied by Aria and Dilarr.

Gourry was still glaring at the non-fish-demon creature. It truly was a strange sight. The best way I could describe it is a massive lump of swollen, pale flesh… Like a melting ball quite a bit larger than a human is tall. The flesh itself wasn't quite transparent, just unhealthily pallid. And right around where a human's chest would be protruded a curiously out-of-place relief—the face of a young man with golden hair, so handsome it looked like a carving. But as if to prove it was more than just a decoration, the mouth on the young man's face opened.

"A pleasure to meet you. You may call me Aileus." It was an unabashedly human voice. "I'm aware of most of the situation. I must say, Narov proved more fragile than I expected. He was quite strong, so he really should have just faced you head-on rather than resorting to cowardly hostage tactics." He spoke casually, as if we were having some pleasant chat. "Still, it would be a shame to let him just go like that. I think I'd like to get more use out of him."

"What in the world do you mean by that?" Dilarr asked.

"This, of course." A bright smile appeared on Aileus's face.

Brble… The flesh next to the man's face began to swell.

"Urgh!" Aria let out a noise of disgust.

For beside the countenance of young Aileus… grew the still-bisected head of Narov!

Chapter 3: Showdown in the City of Crimson Water

"Graaaaaaaah!" Narov's vertically split head cried out. The tentacles around his mouth squirmed and writhed.

Hang on… Did this guy absorb Narov's dead body?!

I wasn't sure how powerful Narov had been when he was alive, but at the very least, this development had given his creepiness a real shot in the arm. Nevertheless, I had no obligation to let him show off what he could do! I began a quiet chant, but before either Aileus or I could make a move…

"Elemekia Lance!" Dilarr let fly a spell from behind me—one capable of dealing damage directly to the spirit and taking out a lesser demon in one hit.

Aileus was basically a lump of flesh growing out of the ground, so he had no way to dodge it. Dilarr's spear of light hit him dead-on… but the young man's face didn't bat an eye, and Narov's face just kept howling and waving its tentacles.

Then—*Fwsh*—the section of flesh hit by the Elemekia Lance flaked off like a scab, and…

"Graaaaaaaah!" Narov's head let out another cry. Countless points of light appeared around him, causing the air itself to creak!

Guh!

"Dodge!" I called to my crew, aborting my spell and quickly taking some distance myself.

As I ran, our opponent unleashed his light in all directions! I managed to dodge the first few points streaking toward me and—*Vrm!*—then came a sudden, powerful vibration hard enough to hurt my ears. It was followed by a wave of heat and steam.

"Everyone okay?!" I called out.

From beyond the haze, I could hear each of my allies reply...

"I'm fine!"

"Think so..."

"I'm alive, at least!"

It seemed everyone had managed to survive, but that was a hell of a spell Aileus had just fired off... That had to be a Blast Bomb. It was a real doozy, basically like firing off multiple powered-up Fireballs at once. The balls of light had burst against the water's surface, creating the surge of steam.

Thanks to that, we now couldn't see our enemy at all. Of course, he was in the same predicament... or so I hoped, but it wasn't wise to make assumptions about a guy who'd already surrendered his humanity. Plus, that wasn't the only thing working against us. Because I'd been using my shortsword like a torch with Lighting cast on it back in the tunnel, I'd lost it when we were swept away by the underground channel. It wasn't a fatal blow to me or anything, but it was always nice to have a blade on hand to deflect attacks or distract opponents. But, welp, no use crying over spilled swords!

I began to chant a spell...

...!

And suddenly, inexplicably, I felt a chill run up my spine. I moved to the left on instinct. No sooner had I than—*Skrch!*—I felt something lash out of the mist, brushing by my pauldron.

"Guh!"

"Wuh?!"

I could hear Gourry and Dilarr yelp through the fog at almost that same moment. Was Aileus using it as a smoke screen after all?! I wasn't about to let him have it that easy!

"Diem Wind!"

Fwoosh! My powerful blast of wind blew the misty haze away, and once I could see again, I beheld the bizarre form that Aileus had taken. The lump of flesh was still rooted to the ground, with the face of the young man and Narov bulging out of it as before... But now a few dozen arms had sprouted from it. Well, I call them arms, but of course, they weren't *human* arms. They were more like the branches of a dead tree, unusually long and multi-jointed.

Of course... So that's *what came out of the mist.*

Now, when the fog cleared completely...

"Fireball!"

Whoom! Dilarr's spell scorched Aileus. Gourry charged him at the same time, and Aileus reached out as he approached.

"Hng!" Gourry sliced at him with his sword! I expected to see Aileus's severed arm go spinning through the air, but instead...

Zing! There was a hard sound as it was merely deflected to the side. Apparently this guy was tougher than he looked.

Moreover, the part of Aileus's body that was burned by Dilarr's Fireball earlier just flaked off, allowing new flesh(?) to swell up in its place. It was exactly what had happened with the Elemekia Lance earlier. His entire body was probably similar to a lizard's tail, capable of being shed and regrown at will. But if that was the case, there had to be a critical part of him that couldn't regenerate... And *that* would be his weak point.

"Graaaaaaaah!" Narov's head screamed once more.

It was like a mindless howl to human ears, but I figured it for a spell chant. The writhing of his mouth-tentacles was probably the formation of spell sigils. At any rate, now that I knew he had hella magic up his sleeve, I couldn't let him finish that chant!

"Hell Blast!" Aria cried.

"Zellas Bullid!" I did the same.

We launched our spells simultaneously. Hers broke through Aileus's arms to hit the young man's face. Meanwhile, mine swerved around the arms to pulverize Narov's head!

Bullseye! That should interrupt his spellcasting!

But Aileus himself showed no sign of slowing down. He was using five or six of his arms to keep Gourry in check while the rest continued to sporadically attack me, Aria, and Dilarr. Fortunately, Aileus's control of the arms seemed imprecise. Their aim was poor and their movements predictable such that even Aria the greenhorn could dodge them. Nevertheless, this wouldn't actually end until we took the dude down.

Aileus's face where Aria had hit him flaked off, but more flesh swelled into place immediately to reform his visage. "It's pointless, you know..." it whispered.

"I don't believe it!" Aria cried out hopelessly.

Hmm... She really isn't used to fighting at all, is she?

I'll concede that this guy's face just *felt* like it was screaming, "Hey! Got your weak point right here!" But a regenerator type like him wouldn't leave an obvious weak point so exposed. His face was probably a decoy meant to draw our fire.

Meanwhile, Narov's head was still in the middle of regenerating from my hit... Maybe it was slower to recover since it wasn't originally a part of Aileus's body. Still, it was clearly going to come back and start chanting new spells. I was really hoping to finish this before then, but...

Aileus's real weak point was likely somewhere deep inside his body. If we just kept hitting him with standard magical attacks, he was just gonna keep on sloughing off the damaged flesh.

Wait, in that case...

While dodging swipes from his arms, I quietly chanted an amplified spell. "Bram Blazer!"

Whom! A blast of pale light capable of killing even a lesser demon plowed through Aileus's body!

"H... Hraaaagh!" A death rattle echoed through the dim underground cavern.

His branch-like arms let out a dry rustle and began to droop limply over the island. I'd figured a piercing spell might be able to hit his weak point, and it looked like I was on the money. Aileus's body began to crumble like baked clay.

"I think we did it," Gourry sighed in relief.

"Looks like." I nodded in response. "So, anyway... the way forward is probably somewhere on this island."

"Wait a minute," Dilarr piped up, glaring at me. "When you said you had a plan to find the way... did you mean *this*?"

"Yep," I admitted casually.

In short, there were bound to be enemies protecting the path to our destination. So if we made ourselves obvious enough, they were bound to come for us. Essentially, my plan had been to wander around, wait for enemies to attack, and figure wherever they were camped out for the way forward.

"Are you crazy?! You could have gotten us killed!" Dilarr shouted.

"But I didn't, so really, what's the harm?" I countered sweetly.

Fists shaking, Dilarr was about to argue more. "You... You little..."

But he was interrupted when Aria called from right behind the pillar in the center of the island, "Mistress Lina! Could this be it?"

I went to look and found her pointing to a hole at the base of the pillar. But...

"It's pretty small," Gourry whispered, frowning.

My guy had a point. The hole seemed to go pretty deep, but it was only barely wide enough for me to crawl through if I took my pauldrons off. Even if this led somewhere, Gourry and Dilarr wouldn't be able to use it.

"I don't... think this is it. That Narov guy said it was a path, so I'd expect it to be big enough for him to pass through it, at least," Dilarr said perceptively. And he was right. There was no way Narov or those fish demons could shimmy through this narrow passage.

But... Wait a minute. Could it be...?

I quietly chanted a spell—"Lighting!"—and tossed the magical ball of light I produced into the water.

Pwsh! Visible below the island, in the now-illuminated depths, yawned a large underwater cave.

Plip... plip... I could hear the sound of water dripping around us. The air was damp.

We'd entered the waterlogged cave via a Lei Wing, traveling through it that way until we finally reached air. At that point, I'd dismissed the spell and we'd started walking.

If this really was the path to the sorcerers' council, it was reasonable to expect an enemy ambush up ahead. The fish demon that had disappeared during our battle with Aileus had probably fled here... or more likely, returned to base to report our raid. If all we cared about was speed, flying would have been better than walking, but walking seemed the safer choice given the likelihood of enemy attack.

Incidentally, there was luminescent moss on the ceiling and walls down here too, so we didn't need to prepare a light. That said...

"Boy... it sure is a long way," Gourry sighed after we'd been walking for quite a while.

The path was slippery, making it hard to pick up the pace, and the monotony of the scenery added to the feeling that we'd been walking forever. But even then, this path was freaking long. I wondered if it had taken us even lower than the underground lake.

"But I sure hope that, after all this walking, we don't find out we took the wrong cave," Dilarr said, sounding exhausted.

I couldn't blame him for feeling beat. We'd entered Crimson Town around sunset, and it was probably past midnight by now. In other words, apart from the time we'd spent unconscious after our impromptu little trip on the underground river, we'd been going pretty much nonstop. I'd question the humanity of anyone who *wasn't* exhausted at this point.

Aria was seeming pretty spent herself. She hadn't said a word since we entered the cave. Still, we had no time to rest at the moment. We needed to infiltrate the enemy base and clear things up as soon as possible. To be honest, I'd started to mull over the idea of just blowing up the sorcerers' council building with a Dragon Slave the minute we got there... But then again, Aria's sister could be inside. Well, I'd cross that bridge when I came to it.

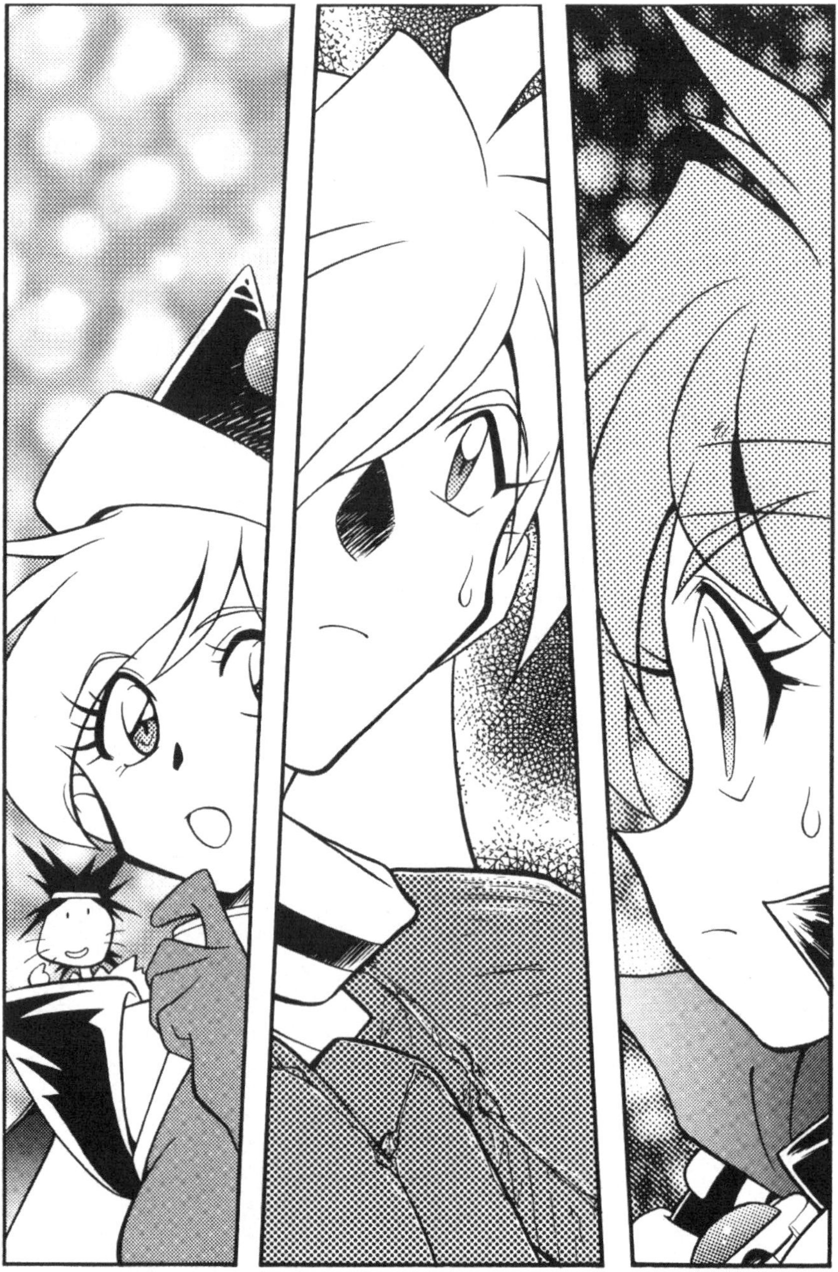

"This looks like the right way to me," I offered.

"What makes you say that?" Dilarr asked.

"Well, duh... They made a path."

"A path? You mean this thing we're walking right now?" Gourry asked in Dilarr's stead.

"Exactly. See those stalactites on the ceiling? They should have corresponding stalagmites beneath them, but the ground here is flat. That means someone cleared them out for better passage. Speaking of, I think we're close to our destination too..." With that, I turned my eyes up ahead. Both sides of the passageway were lined with jars of various sizes. "The place is obviously used for storage, meaning there's gotta be someone nearby doing the storing. Say, Aria, you were part of the Crimson council, right? Did you ever hear anything about an underground pathway?"

"Well... I'd heard there was an underground storehouse... but there was a dedicated group to manage it... so I never went there personally..." she responded haltingly, sounding tired indeed.

Hmm... A place like this connected to the council basement surely would have generated at least a little talk, right? Or was there something about this underground passage that necessitated keeping it a secret? We'd just have to keep going and find out.

I pressed onward as I thought this all over, and the number of containers and other tools whose purpose I couldn't identify gradually increased in number as we went. Finally...

"I'd say that's a jackpot," I remarked as I came to a stop.

I was standing in front of a metal door which looked completely out of place in the ongoing stone tunnel into which it was built. Had someone been expanding their basement, happened to hit this cave, and just slapped a door there? Yeah, right. Despite its slapdash placement, the door was reinforced with stone. I couldn't sense any enemy presences behind it... but there could always be someone capable of cloaking themselves.

"All right... Moment of truth. We're going in," I said.

Someone gulped. Gourry silently drew his sword, preparing for a surprise attack. Dilarr whispered a spell under his breath. I put my hand on the door, pushed, and...

"Oh, go figure. It's locked."

"Hey!" Dilarr roared, interrupting his spell just to yell at me.

But c'mon. Of course a door in the middle of a cave system was gonna be locked.

"Hmm, hang on. I think it's a simple latch. In which case..."

After a little inspection, I took a slim knife I'd stored in my pauldron and slid it between the door and the frame. I then dragged it upward and... I felt movement accompanied by a small clink. Seemed I'd undone the lock.

Okay!

"*Now* here we go," I said as I gave it a push.

A heavy, metallic creaking resounded as the door slowly opened inward. It looked like there wasn't an ambush waiting for us, at least. But...

"Seems pretty small for the council's basement, huh?" Dilarr whispered as he looked around.

"There are definite signs of life here too..." Gourry added. When I looked to see, he was indicating various cooking and cleaning implements strewn about.

They were right... This place was only a little larger than a room in any standard home. There was a single unlit lamp hanging from the ceiling, and more than half of the things lying around were obviously for household use.

What in the world...?

I chanted a spell. "Lighting!"

I tossed my magical light up toward the ceiling, and when it was in place, I could see clearly... that this was the basement of a private dwelling. There was a stairway further inside.

"I can't help feeling like we're in the wrong place..." Gourry observed.

"W-Well... we should probably go upstairs and see what's up, at any rate." After laughing him off, I made a beeline for the staircase in the back. The other three quietly followed me.

The stairway was steep and narrow. There was a simple lock on the door at the top, but I pulled a pin out of my pocket, stuck it into the hole, and opened the thing with ease. After making sure there were no signs of life on the other side... *Creak...*

Beyond the door was a hallway. I walked out into it, followed by Gourry, Aria, and then Dilarr.

"This isn't the council hall..." Aria whispered with a glassy-eyed expression.

Yeah... Knew it. It was a rather large mansion with excellent stonework, but it was still a private residence.

"Ugh... Hell, was I wrong, then?" I muttered.

"Should we try to go further down the tunnel instead?" Gourry asked.

"Yeah, guess we probably should," I conceded.

We turned to head back down the stairs when...

"This is... Kailus's mansion."

Aria's trance-like words stopped us in our tracks.

"Are... Are you sure?!" I asked.

"I'm certain. I only came here once—before the insurrection, when my sister called me here—but I'm sure of it. I recognize this place," Aria responded with confidence, then swiftly set off.

"H-Hang on! Aria! Where are you going?!"

"My sister's room," she replied without turning back or slowing down. In fact, she picked up the pace. With no other choice, we followed after her.

All right... So we'd mistakenly assumed the "path" meant the "path to the sorcerers' council," but it actually turned out to be a path to Kailus's mansion. Narov must have realized the misunderstanding... but he'd been under no obligation to correct it, of course.

Aria proceeded without fear despite the likelihood that enemies were near. She only stopped when she reached a door. She took in a deep breath, reached for the handle, and before we could even try to stop her, she yanked it open! And then...

"Sister..." There was a tremble in her faint voice.

It was a large room, furnished with a canopy bed and a nightstand, illuminated by nothing but the moonlight streaming in from the terrace windows. Beside the bed sat a rocking chair, and standing next to that was a girl who looked very much like Aria. Her long, silver hair glimmered in the moonbeams.

"A... Aria?" she asked.

"Bell!" Aria cried, running to throw herself into her sister's arms.

"Aria... what are you doing here?"

"I came to save you! The imperial army is coming to stop Kailus's rebellion. Just the thought of this city becoming a battlefield with you here, I… I came to save you!" she gushed, her voice choked with tears. Her reunion with her sister seemed to have released all her pent-up emotion.

Bell stroked Aria's hair gently, then turned her gaze to us. "Who are these people?"

"Her bodyguards… more or less," I replied. "But introductions later. For now, let's clear out. There's no telling when the goon squad might show."

At my words, Aria suddenly looked up. "Th-That's right… Sister, you must come with us."

"I'm afraid that won't be happening…" a new voice cut in, echoing through the room. A familiar one.

"Zonagein?!" I shouted, whipping around to see the familiar diminutive figure standing there in his hooded cloak.

Next to him was a man of about forty with raven hair. He wore a high-collared cape embroidered with silver thread along with various jeweled amulets dotting his outfit—which didn't much suit his cheap villain mug.

Given the timing, I had a guess as to his identity. "You wouldn't be Kailus, by chance, would you?"

"I would. I praise you for making it this far… but it's the end of the line for you. Prepare to meet your doom."

"Pfft!"

Kailus frowned in annoyance at my abrupt laughter. "What's so funny?"

"I just knew you'd say something like that!" I took a wide stance and pointed boldly at Kailus. "You look like a third-rate villain, and you talk like one too! Even a kid would find you hilarious!"

Kailus's brows arched even higher, but perhaps fearing another reprisal from me, he desperately held back his anger. "Fair… Fair enough, girl. But cliche or not, you will still die here."

"Well, well! We'll see about that!" I said as I drew up against the wall. Just then…

"Fireball!" Dilarr, who'd been chanting behind me, unleashed a blazing globe!

Fwoosh! The burst of flames to follow licked the corridor. We hid behind the open door to ride out the heat. This was the same distract-and-strike tactic we'd used against Narov underground. And there was nowhere to escape the attack in this narrow, straight corridor. But...

Zing! Crash!

An arrow of light streaked through the still-swirling smoke to pulverize the door we were using as a shield! I flew back from it and began chanting a spell. As the smoke dissipated, far down the hall, I could see Zonagein and Kailus.

They got that far that quickly?! Just as I was thinking that, I heard a strange rustling sound, and suddenly... Zonagein was right in front of me! With that same bizarre speed, he'd come all the way back down the hallway. I reached instinctively for my missing sword...

Wham! I heard a heavy impact from right above my head. Gourry had come running to block something black lashing down at me.

Is that...?

It looked like a spider's leg. A giant one. And I could see a number more growing from the old sorcerer's back.

"Impressive... But then, you did defeat Graymore," Zonagein said, his spider legs skittering him backward.

Even though he'd sold out his humanity, he apparently still wanted to avoid a close-quarters fight with Gourry. In that case...

I released my incanted spell. "Bram Blazer!"

I turned and shot the blue light at a new hostile presence behind me! It hit a woman in green who'd appeared down the hall at some point, but just as it made contact—*Vrm!*—she unleashed a blue light of her own that filled the corridor!

"Guh!" As it did, a shockwave racked my body. Its power was on the low side, but that was a Bram Blazer for sure! Had she reflected my spell back in a dispersed form?!

After the light receded, the woman in green— No. When I looked at her again, I realized my mistake. She wasn't *wearing* green. Her face, her torso, her hair, her limbs... Her entire body was translucent like an emerald.

With this new addition to Kailus's side, we were definitely in a fix. I'd been hoping to bump the guy off here and skip straight to the denouement... but things were shaping up to be a little trickier than that.

"Back into the room!" I said, retreating back to the sisters. "Aria! Bell! We're getting out of here!" I shouted before starting a chant.

Once Bell was out of the mansion, I could bring out the big guns and level the whole thing!

"Don't let them escape! Get them! Zonagein! Mycale!" Kailus's voice, coming from the hallway, stopped Aria in her tracks.

"Did... he just say..." she muttered.

"What're you doing, Aria? Get moving!" Dilarr shouted, kicking open the terrace window.

"I..." Aria swiftly began running again.

Gourry stood off against Zonagein when he appeared in the door and... "Wait! Don't go!"

By the time he shouted that, Aria, Bell, and Dilarr were already on the terrace. Just as the three of them halted—*Whunk!*—a large scythe-like object speared through Dilarr's chest from above. Slowly, he collapsed to the ground.

"Master Dilarr?!" Aria screamed, sounding pained.

Gourry and I dashed for the terrace ourselves. The minute we stepped out onto it—*Whoosh!*—something sliced through the night wind, but Gourry's sword knocked it away. I supported the collapsed Dilarr with one arm while taking Aria's hand with my other. I checked to make sure Gourry was holding on to my shoulder, and then unleashed the amplified spell I'd been chanting!

"Lei Wing!"

At the very least, I thought we'd be able to use it to get us out of there. But just as my spell activated...

"Eek!" Bell shrieked. I looked and saw something like a dead tree branch grabbing her leg.

Wait, isn't that...

"Sister!" Aria cried. Bell's hand had slipped from her grasp!

"Flee!" That was all Bell could say as she fell from my completed wind barrier.

The four of us took off into the air, leaving her behind.

"Please—!" Aria just managed to hold back a full-throated scream. She probably meant to ask me to go back and save her sister... but she probably also realized that Dilarr needed treatment.

Except... I could already feel the warmth leaving his body. I knew what it felt like when someone was dying.

In the abandoned building, there was only darkness, musty air, and silence. Nobody tried to speak. Not me. Not Gourry. Not Aria.

After taking flight, it had taken us a while to shake off the pursuing air force and find shelter in this vacant old house. Dilarr was already dead by then. I'd used magic to dig a hole in the basement, given him a simple funeral, and then...

The three of us just sat there in the darkness. I couldn't say for how long.

Eventually, Aria whispered, "I... What should I do?" There was no emotion whatsoever in her voice. "I couldn't save my sister. I let Master Dilarr die..."

"It's not your fault—"

"It *is* my fault!" she insisted—or rather screamed—interrupting me. "I... If I'd held on more tightly, I could have saved her! If I hadn't wanted to come to Crimson, Master Dilarr... Master Dilarr might not be...!"

"I think I'm more responsible for Dilarr. I didn't realize *he* would be out there, so my plan was all wrong," I whispered with a self-reproaching smile.

"'He'? You mean you know who did this?" I heard Gourry ask in the darkness.

I nodded, even knowing he couldn't see me. "I think... it was Aileus. The guy we fought on the island in the underground lake."

"You mean... he survived?" Aria whispered.

"It's less that he survived, and more... I think the version of him we defeated underground was just one part of him. When we Lei Winged it out of Kailus's manor, I glanced back and the whole place was covered in vines with these round lumps stuck here and there..."

"You mean...?!" Gourry gasped.

I nodded again. "Yeah. I think Aileus is really flora rather than fauna. His above-ground and underground bodies are connected somewhere..."

The fact that he'd entwined the whole mansion meant that his presence was dispersed, which was why Gourry and I hadn't sensed it right away. It was potentially possible that whatever was covering the house was just someone else with abilities like Aileus's, but that scythe-like thing that hit Dilarr... It was the same shape as the fish demons' fins. And given that we had one fish demon underground unaccounted for, it seemed more likely to me that Aileus had absorbed it rather than there being a discrete but similar entity hanging around.

If I was right about all that... then Aileus was a truly dangerous foe. I had no idea where his weak point could be either. We could probably eliminate the problem by blowing the whole mansion away—operative word being *probably*. You could kill an animal by crushing its head, but some plants could regenerate from their roots or even a single leftover branch. If Aileus had plantlike properties, he might be able to regenerate completely from any scrap we left behind.

"They're sure a tough bunch to deal with," I muttered. "I don't know how formidable Kailus himself is, but there's Aileus, plus that flying puppet with its winged demons, and then Zonagein and that Mycale person..."

"Actually, about that..." Aria interjected as I was listing off our enemies. "When I joined the council... there was another girl who joined at the same time. We were assigned many of the same projects and we became friends. Her name was... Elydia Mycale."

"Huh?" I breathed.

"And... I just remembered... that one of the people who ran the underground storehouse... was named Aileus."

"Wait, you don't mean...!"

Aria's only response was silence.

"Can I ask... if Mycale and Aileus were supporters of Kailus?" I ventured.

"Well... I only knew Aileus by name, so I'm not terribly familiar with him... But Elydia openly hated Kailus."

"Hey, where exactly is this going?" Gourry asked.

I let out a small sigh. "It's shaping up... like Kailus turned the members of the council into chimeras under his control."

"But... is he even capable of such a thing?" Aria questioned. "Kailus was a jack-of-all-trades. He was familiar with attack and healing spells as well as curses, magic item artificing, and chimera creation... but at the same time, he wasn't especially knowledgeable about any of them. I wouldn't think him capable of making chimeras that advanced."

"So there's someone else running things, you think?"

"It's... possible. But I don't know Kailus particularly well myself... It's also possible he knows a lot about chimeras and I simply wasn't aware of it."

"I see," I responded vaguely.

Still, I wouldn't have pegged Kailus for a serious chimera researcher based on what I'd seen of his mansion. They tended to be the kind of folk who kept big laboratories in their basements—and I'm not just saying that. Creating chimeras required a lot of space, and your average sorcerers' council wouldn't let anybody take up that large a share of their communal facilities. Besides, sharing space with others in the same field usually resulted in stolen theories and techniques. That's why chimera researchers with the funds to make it happen preferred to build their own dedicated facilities somewhere in their own houses, typically a sequestered basement.

Of course, it's not like I'd seen every corner of Kailus's mansion for myself. It was possible there was a secret basement apart from the one we'd come through, or maybe a lab on the second floor, as unusual as that would be. But even if that were the case, I felt like there should've been signs... And there was certainly no way he'd been using council facilities to turn everyone there into chimeras.

"Mistress Lina, about Elydia... I mean, Mycale... Is there no way... to return her to normal?" Aria asked.

I didn't have an answer. I knew another guy who'd been turned into a chimera and was searching for a way to restore his humanity. I didn't know how he was doing now, but he'd had one hell of a struggle with it in the time I'd known him. In the words of another acquaintance, just because you knew how to make a juice cocktail didn't mean you could extract the orange juice from it once it was mixed.

In Mycale's case, it also seemed pretty clear that she was being controlled. If it was just the work of a Marionette spell, defeating Kailus should solve that problem. But if her mind had been overwritten using brainwashing or a similar technique, then...

"Ah... I suppose not." Aria's sad voice resonated in the darkness.

"I personally don't know much about chimeras, so I can't give you a definitive answer... but if it is possible, it won't be easy."

"I... I see." There, she fell silent.

"Say, we should probably get some rest," Gourry offered, as if waiting for his chance. "We can't do anything until we recharge our stamina. We're gonna finish this tomorrow, right?"

"Yeah... right." I nodded in response. "Let's get some sleep for now, Aria. Tomorrow, we'll... We'll get Bell back and make Kailus pay."

Evening arrived the next day. The light streaming in through the abandoned building's windows had just turned red with the setting sun when we decided to make our move. Our destination? Kailus's mansion.

"How do we get there?" Gourry asked.

"We'll take the waterway," I answered. "If we go on land, we risk the air force spotting us, and underground, we risk getting lost and running into the same issues as last night. But that Narov guy is gone and there should be fewer fish demons in the canals now. Granted, our enemy might be expecting that much from us, but it still seems safer than going by land. We'll dig a tunnel from here, link up to a canal, then use a Lei Wing to head for Kailus's mansion underwater. Aria, please show us the way."

"I will," she said firmly with a nod.

I nodded back and began to chant my spell.

"Incoming!" Gourry cried out as we neared Kailus's mansion.

I could see something approaching through the crimson-tinted water. It was Aileus's tentacles!

Vroosh! Several scythe-like objects pierced my wind barrier to get to us. *Zing!* While grabbing me with his left hand, Gourry swung the sword in his right to deflect the attack. And then…

"Freeze Bullid!" Aria conjured her spell outside the barrier! It froze the surrounding water solid, trapping the tentacles in place. It was the same spell Dilarr had used on the fish demons the day before, and it was impressive how quickly she'd learned to use it! "We're almost there, Mistress Lina!"

"Okay! Going up!" I directed my barrier to ascend out of the water and into the air.

Indeed, we were right next to Kailus's estate. As before, the whole building was tangled in Aileus's vines, and we could see the air force scattered in the skies above it. I ignored them and made a beeline for the mansion! The air force pursued us, and Aileus's scythe-tentacles darted out to block our way. I'd been hoping we could just bust in through the terrace, but oh well!

"Fireball!" Aria incanted. Her spell appeared behind us, rushing our way, and…

Bwoom! It burst when it made contact with the wind barrier!

"Whaaaaa?!"

The explosive force accelerated us forward—right through the tentacles and the terrace window, throttling us into the mansion!

Whew, I know I used the same tactic yesterday, but… Aria really must be pissed!

At any rate, I dismissed my spell and landed us on the floor inside.

"Hey, Aria…" Gourry said with a troubled expression, putting a hand on her shoulder. "Just so you know, learning from bad role models can really set you down the wrong path in life."

"What's that supposed to mean, Gourry?" I asked sharply.

"Oh, nothing… Anyway, let's get going."

Don't ignore meee! I wanted to object, but Gourry was right; we didn't have time for petty squabbling right now.

We'd intentionally come in through Bell's room, but she wasn't anywhere to be seen. They'd probably moved her elsewhere.

"Here we go!" I proclaimed, kicking open the door and moving into the hallway. We needed to find out where they'd taken Bell. "Aria! Do you know where they might have put your sister?"

"I don't!"

"Okay, then we'll just have to search everywhere!"

Purely on instinct, I picked a hall and ran down it. Aria and Gourry followed. We kicked in every door we came across until the three of us reached the entrance hall. And there…

"My, my… A bit reckless, aren't you?" asked Zonagein, who'd arrived silently on the legs growing from his back.

I then heard the creak of floorboards. When I turned to look, I spotted Kailus slowly descending the stairway that encircled the great hall, accompanied by the silent Mycale.

"Aha… so you've returned," he said. "And you're down one member."

"Where is my sister?!" Aria shouted angrily, apparently aggravated by his words.

"Bell, you mean? She's in the mansion. That's all I'll say, but I must ask… Do you think you can do something with that knowledge?"

"Oh, I'm gonna do something all right," I informed him, striding forward a step. "Aria, stay calm. Don't let this hack get your goat."

"You…!" Kailus began to shriek in rage.

"If he's such a hack," Zonagein interrupted quietly, "how did he kill one of your allies?"

Aria was about to protest, but I raised a hand to stop her. "A war of provocation is a waste of time for all of us."

"You're right. In that case... Let's get to it!" Zonagein began to scuttle across the floor.

Gourry moved to meet him, sword at the ready. Just as Gourry was about to strike, Zonagein leaped upward! He spun once midair, and...

"Bram Blazer!" He released the spell he'd chanted! His target was... Mycale?!

Shah! Mycale's entire body shone with light. Its power was low, but a shockwave erupted in time with the light, hitting me, Gourry, and Aria!

Hey! That kinda hurt!

Zonagein landed behind the temporarily stunned Gourry, and without turning back, swung two of his legs down at him! But Gourry sensed the attack coming. He reflexively leaped straight forward to dodge, then dashed ahead toward Kailus! Mycale interposed herself. And then...

"Icicle Lance!" Kailus released a spell at Mycale's back.

Bwoosh!

"Guh!" The spell, scattered by Mycale's body, turned into a blizzard that caused Gourry to back off fast.

She can even disperse that kind of spell?!

Kailus using the spell-scattering Mycale as a shield while he sat back and watched... That was a tricky strategy to counter. If I hit him with an attack spell, Mycale would block it and reflect it back at us. But if we moved into melee range, Kailus would cast a spell for her to spray us with.

Granted, that didn't mean we were helpless. I was confident Mycale couldn't disperse every single spell. If we hit her with something big enough, it would destroy her for sure. The real question was, exactly how big was "big enough"? If I slapped her with a Dragon Slave, there was no way she'd be able to withstand it, but I couldn't drop a bomb like that indoors. And if I used a slightly weaker Dynast Blas or a Zellas Bullid, and she happened to refract it back on us...

I mean, those were spells that could wipe out a pure demon in one hit, so even a dispersed version would probably do us in. And after hearing that

Mycale was a former friend of Aria's, I wasn't eager to just kill her. That meant our smartest move now was to attack Kailus from several angles at once.

Okay! In that case...

"Gourry! Keep Zonagein occupied!"

"Got it!" he responded, then spun around to face the old man.

My eyes remained locked on Kailus and Mycale as I began chanting my next spell.

"Got time for me after all, eh?" Zonagein said as he moved several legs to block Gourry's sword strike. Appendage and blade clashed, and both parties held for a split second before...

Fwee! There came a sound like a whistle, and a thread shot from Zonagein's mouth wrapped around Gourry's sword hand!

"Ngh!" Gourry groaned, and just then...

"Icicle Lance!" Aria fired a spell at Zonagein's flank!

He quickly leaped up off the floor with his spider legs, sending him over Gourry's head with the string still wrapped around his hilt. Gourry, his movements restrained, was at the disadvantage, but...

Now! I dashed straight for the place I predicted Zonagein would land. Zonagein realized what I was doing and hesitated for a brief instant. He was trying to decide if he should attack Gourry or deal with me first! And in that time...

"Flare Lance!" I launched the spell I'd been chanting as I ran, then took a deep breath and held it.

Mycale quickly moved to intercept the spell and disperse it back at me. I closed my eyes and—*Fwoom!*—powerful heat surrounded me. Me and Zonagein both!

"Gah!" he cried.

Indeed, that spell wasn't meant to be a surprise attack on Kailus, but rather an attempt to hit Zonagein. Flare Lance typically had the power to roast an opponent in one hit, but I'd purposefully dialed it back some. Combined with the effect of Mycale's dispersal, it was just hot enough to toast your skin a bit.

But what happened when you *inhaled* heat like that? Unlike me, who'd closed my eyes and held my breath, Zonagein had seared his own lungs. His expression was one of agony.

Whunk! Behind him, having escaped the blast of heat, Gourry ran the old sorcerer through.

"Ghhk!" He let out a near silent scream as the spider legs on his back clawed at the air. And then...

"Dam Blas!" Aria, who'd also been outside the dispersal zone, unleashed a spell of her own.

There was no surviving all that. Zonagein's back legs spasmed repeatedly, then fell still.

"One down, two to go," I said, shooting a bold smile at Kailus.

"Hng!" he grunted. His face twisted with hatred, but it was also marred by panic.

I glanced around, maintaining a grin. "You're in a pretty sticky sitch, yet I don't see the flying guys or Aileus rushing to your aid... I'm guessing they're stuck outside, huh? That means all you've got here to protect you is Mycale, the one-trick dispersal pony... I hope you're ready for pain, Master Kailus," I said with absolute confidence.

I was sure a threat like that would drive Kailus outside to seek the aid of Aileus and his winged minions. I was counting on it, in fact. Once Kailus was outside, I could use a big area-of-effect spell to finish him off for good! And once I'd beaten Kailus, there'd be no need for us to fight Mycale or Aileus. But...

"Ha... haha..." Kailus let out a pregnant laugh and slowly walked up to Mycale's side. "I see... But this... This is my dream, and the likes of you will never ruin it!"

With that, he grabbed Mycale by the back of the head.

What's he—

A hard cracking sound rang out. Green fragments shot through the air.

"Elydia!" Aria screamed.

Kailus had shattered Mycale's head with his hand.

What the?!

"Haha... ha..." Kailus embraced Mycale's body from behind as it slumped over, headless.

"What are you doing?!"

"Isn't it obvious? Haha… I won't know what to do if I don't…" Kailus replied, his very answer mad. The glint in his eyes told me his sanity was gone. I didn't know what he was planning, but…

The first one to notice was Gourry, who cried out, "Their bodies!"

I turned his way for a moment, not understanding. He was looking straight at Kailus. I turned back again… and saw it for myself. Slowly, Mycale's body was sinking into Kailus's.

Is he… absorbing her?!

It seemed Kailus was no longer human himself. Soon, he'd completely swallowed Mycale.

"Bwahahahahaha!" Kailus's crazed laughter echoed through the room.

Chapter 4: Crimson, When the Marionettes' Feast Ends

"Freeze Arrow!" Aria fired a flurry of frigid projectiles to interrupt the mad laughter reverberating around us.

Hey, hang on!

Rather than dodging the arrows, Kailus just tanked them! Then—*Whoosh!*—a freezing wind assaulted us, exactly like the one Mycale had refracted. Except, actually, this was more "chilly" than "freezing"...

"Just as I thought..." Aria breathed.

Of course! She'd dialed back the power of her Freeze Arrow in an experiment to see if Kailus had absorbed Mycale's power.

"Bwahahaha! That won't work! Don't you see? Mycale's power is mine now! Your spells can't harm me!" he cackled, apparently failing to realize that it was just a test.

Sheesh, what a hack...

Yet while Kailus was third-rate in the brains department, he still wasn't to be trifled with. We had no way of knowing if Mycale was the first person he'd absorbed... In fact, it was safest to assume he'd gone on an absorb-a-thon before this and had a host of weird powers to choose from.

But then...

A doubt flashed through my mind for the briefest of moments, but I didn't have time to dwell on it. Our priority now was figuring out how to beat Kailus.

"Just so you know, I have more than just Mycale's abilities! Allow me to demonstrate!" he bellowed, then let out a bestial howl. A dozen icy bolts appeared in the air around him.

A lesser demon's power?!

Kailus launched the arrows... straight at himself!

Not good! The ensuing wave of biting cold rushed over us even as we leaped away.

"Guh!" Gourry groaned slightly, but readied his sword and dashed at Kailus. However…

"Hraaagh!" Kailus howled again, retreating backward. Another blast of cold followed.

Sheesh, this guy really knows how to use his abilities! Had he just fired the Freeze Arrows on their own, Gourry would've been able to knock the icy projectiles aside with his sword or dodge them. But there was no deflecting sheer cold. Naturally, the diffusing of the blizzard meant that it barely did any real damage, but repeated blasts would eventually lower Gourry's body temperature enough that he'd be too numb to move properly. Not even the big lug could dodge a Freeze Arrow when he could barely feel his legs.

Kailus certainly talked like a washed-up villain, but he made the grade in terms of skill. That meant we'd have to counter with some schemes of our own.

"Gourry! Aria! This way!" I cried, then darted down one of the corridors that branched off of the entry hall. "Lend me a hand, Aria!" I called. I explained what I needed from her, and we began chanting spells together.

"Think you can escape?! Think again!" Kailus shouted excitedly as he gave chase. On cue…

"Dam Blas!" I fired—not at Kailus, but the ceiling right above him!

Crash! It collapsed with a ruckus, raining down rubble of all sizes.

"Tch! A cheap trick!" Kailus backed up to avoid the falling debris, then climbed over it in the still-roiling dust to continue his pursuit. And when he did…

"Dam Blas!" On my signal, Aria fired a second spell at the ceiling. Dust now filled the hallway.

"More petty tricks!" Kailus leaped back again, cursing all the while.

Meanwhile, our team fled further down the hall. As we went…

"Dam Blas!" Aria slung another blast at the ceiling.

"Would you stop it already?!" Kailus bellowed, again pulling back to avoid the collapse, then clambered over the rubble to press his chase.

That was the moment I'd been waiting for.

"Ragna Blade!" Responding to my words of power, a black blade appeared in my hands. No way could he disperse *this* attack!

"What the—?!" Kailus shouted in surprise when he heard my voice in much closer proximity than he'd expected. "Hraaaaagh!" He quickly raised a war cry, sending an arrow of light he'd conjured straight into himself.

Shahh! Kailus's whole body gleamed, and the light he dispersed shot up and down the hallway. When it did, I leaped and brought my black blade down on him... from directly above!

"What?!" Kailus finally caught on, but it was too late! The sword of darkness soundlessly cleaved him through.

See, after I'd signaled Aria to fire a Dam Blas on the ceiling, I'd cast the Levitation spell I'd been chanting and used the dust as a smoke screen to rise up through the hole she'd made. The second floor was laid out like first, so I'd kept pace with Aria and Gourry's retreat down the corridor below while chanting my Ragna Blade. Aria's next Dam Blas had opened a hole in the floor below me, and I'd leaped through it while cutting down at Kailus.

"Guh!" Kailus's whole body instantly turned black. And then...

Clu-pow! It burst. When the dust settled, the only people in sight were Gourry and Aria.

"Did we do it?" she asked.

I nodded firmly. "As far as Kailus goes, yeah."

"Then..."

"The question is... what will the remaining enemies—the ones Kailus was controlling—do now?"

There was still Aileus tangled around the mansion, the winged doll, and the flying lesser demons—and those were just the ones we'd met so far. I was hoping Kailus's death had released his servants from their curse or mind control or whatever it was. If it hadn't, they'd probably be coming for revenge, and I shouldn't need to explain what a pain in the neck that would be.

"We'd better check before we go save Bell. It wouldn't be a great look if we picked her up only to face a full-on assault on the way out. Speaking of which, can Bell use attack spells?"

"No, none..."

"No offensive magic whatsoever?"

"She can't use any magic at all as far as I know. I was interested in it when I was younger, so I joined the sorcerers' council. But my parents ran a small tavern and my sister usually helped out there instead... I think she preferred cooking to sorcery."

"I see. All the more reason to get a handle on things outside first. Let's see what we can from the windows there," I said as I opened the door to a nearby room.

It looked like a guest suite, about the same as the one we'd found Bell in before. I had a look out the window facing the terrace. There were no signs of any enemies... or of any hostile presences at all.

"What do you think, Gourry?"

"Not sure how anything could be out there... I'll step outside, just to be sure. You guys stay here."

"Got it. Be careful."

Gourry opened the window to the terrace, sword in hand. He scanned around for any signs of life, and shortly thereafter, set foot on the terrace. He then turned back to face the mansion, and...

"Whoa..." he breathed with a mix of surprise and confusion.

"What is it?!"

"Well, it's... Just come out, okay?"

Aria and I shared a look, then cautiously stepped out onto the terrace ourselves. We turned our eyes toward where Gourry was looking.

"Huh?"

"What in the..." The two of us breathed in equal bewilderment.

Aileus's vines coating the mansion, along with the lumps of flesh scattered here and there among them... were all now completely withered. The lumps looked like large, dead flowers rustling dryly in the wind, while the... vines, tentacles, whatever they were... had turned brown, desiccated, and lifeless.

"Is he dead?" Gourry whispered.

A deafening silence fell over us.

"You don't think...!"

A thought struck me. I swiftly cut back inside and across the room to reenter the corridor. Gourry and Aria followed.

"What is it, Mistress Lina?!"

"Just checking something!"

I ducked into the room we'd flown in through earlier tonight—Bell's former room. I ran up to the broken window, exited to the terrace... and after a gasp, I just stood there in silence.

Out on the lawn lay the winged doll that had once commanded the winged demons, looking like a marionette with its strings cut. The flying demons, previously everywhere, were now nowhere to be seen.

"What's going on here?" Gourry whispered from behind me. But of course, I didn't have an answer for him.

"Is this... because Kailus is dead?" Aria whispered uncertainly.

Given the timing, that was likely the trigger. Yet while it was certainly possible to create chimeras whose lives would expire when a certain person died, you'd have to really jump through some hoops to get there.

"But why would Kailus set it up like this?" I asked.

"Well..." Aria thought a minute. "Perhaps he didn't like the idea of his subordinates outliving him... Oh, or maybe he programmed them that way as an incentive for them to protect him! I'm sure that's it!"

"Hmm..." I hummed thoughtfully at Aria's theory. It would definitely explain a few things, but... Something just didn't add up.

"Hey! Wait a minute!" I wasn't sure if he'd heard us or not, but Gourry's voice suddenly took on a serious tension. "If Kailus wanted to take everyone with him, then... isn't your sister..."

Aria and I looked at each other, aghast, then booked it into the corridor.

"Sister! Sister!"

"Mistress Bell? Answer if you hear us!"

"Hey! If you're there, say something!"

The three of us called for Bell as we scoured every room we could find. You'd think a place this size would have a servant or two around, but it was totally deserted. Our cries echoed through the empty mansion. After a good search, we concluded that, at the very least, Bell was nowhere on the first floor.

"You don't think she's..."

"Aria, don't lose heart! There's still the second floor!"

"R-Right..."

I ascended the stairs and threw open the door to a nearby room with an audible slam.

For a while, we just stood there. There was a wide-open window on the other side of the room, its lace curtains billowing in the breeze. A white rocking chair sat facing the night. Sitting in it...

"Aria?" Bell turned to look at her sister. There was a smile on her face that seemed somehow melancholy.

"Sister!" Aria cried as she ran up to her, and Bell stood up to embrace her gently. "Sister... Sister."

"It's... over, isn't it?" Bell asked quietly, sweetly stroking Aria's head.

"Yes... We beat Kailus. Now the city can be peaceful once more, and we can be together again..."

Bell simply gazed into the distance silently. It was like she was staring at something in the distant past, now gone forever.

"Is there anyone left in the mansion?" I asked.

"No. They've all been gone. Since the day the insurrection started," Bell responded, her gaze still faraway.

I knew it was a big damper on the sisters' reunion, but there was something I had to know. "By the way, are you okay, Mistress Bell? Kailus seemed to have made everyone else into a chimera, including himself..."

Aria looked up in realization. "That's right... Sister, are you all right? Did Kailus... He didn't do anything to you, did he?!"

Bell just smiled softly again. "I'm all right, Aria. After all, it wasn't Kailus who changed them. It was me."

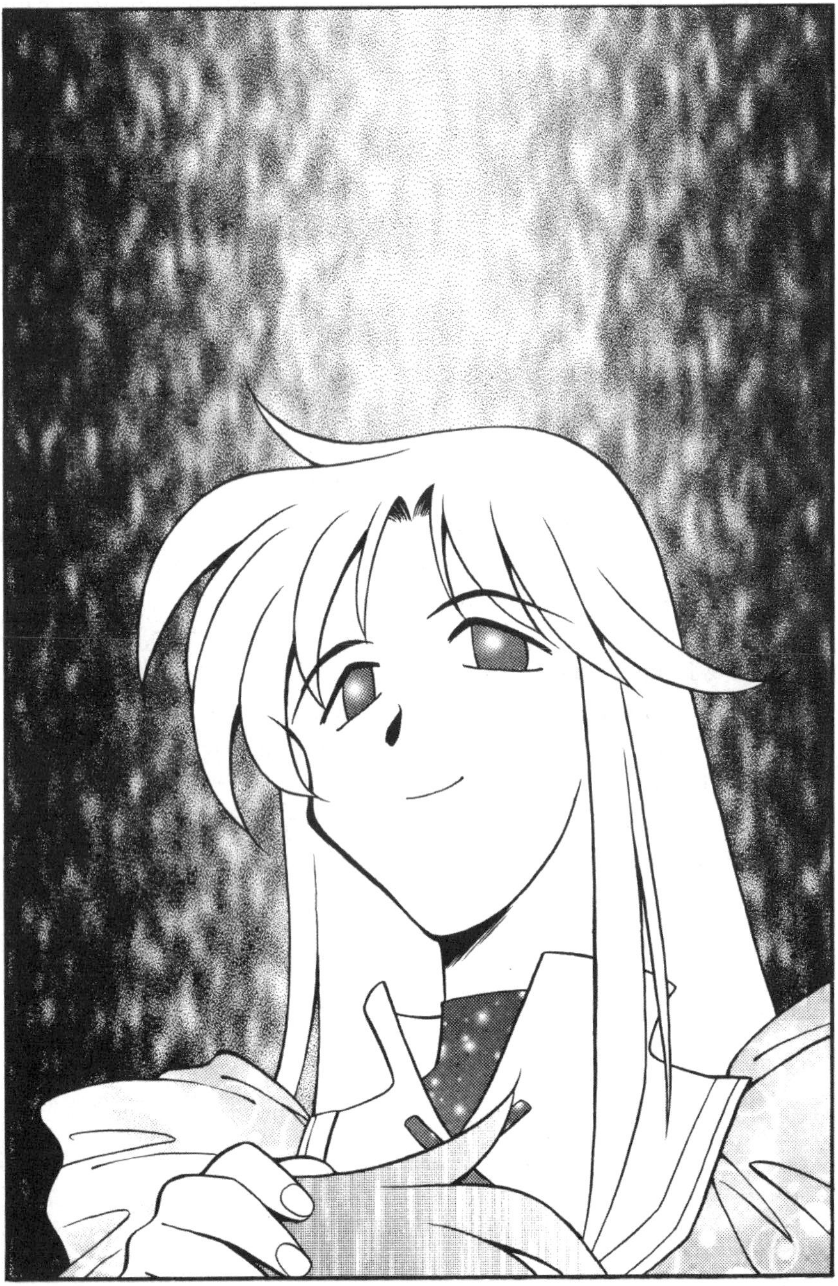

For a moment, none of us were sure what she meant by that.

"Sister?" Aria whispered hesitantly.

Bell simply continued to smile. At last, I saw it... the quiet madness dwelling in her eyes.

"What... are you talking about?" I asked hoarsely, but Bell didn't even spare me a glance.

"Kailus... He deserved it. To lose his honor, his life... branded a traitor. He brought it on himself... by stealing my love... and my happiness..."

"You mean... Kailus killed him after all?" Aria asked, shocked.

"Him"? Bell's first fiancé?

"He didn't say it in so many words... but... in my heart, I knew he did it. And so I changed Kailus... the others too... to make him start that insurrection... and to die in the disgrace he deserved."

"I... I don't know what you're talking about, Sister. What do you mean, *you* changed them?"

"Aria, I thought that I had given up. I thought that there was nothing left for me, that I had accepted my fate. But I was wrong. Despite all my resignation... hatred still began to amass in my heart. And so I changed everyone. I changed them all and incited insurrection in Kailus's name."

"You're lying!" Aria shook her head fiercely. "That can't be true! Because... if it was, it would mean *you're* the one we've been fighting!"

"I love you, Aria... my one and only sister. But..." Bell smiled sadly. "But... after my love died, Kailus asked me to marry him. I rebuffed him, of course. Until one day, he said to me, 'What if your little sister... if Aria... ends up like your fiancé?'"

Wordlessly, Aria began to tremble. I couldn't see her expression from where I was standing.

"That was when I became certain... that Kailus had killed the man I loved. Though looking back now, perhaps he simply wanted me to think that so I'd do as he wanted. Still, in that moment... I thought, 'I can't let Aria die... I just have to do as he tells me.'"

So the reason she married Kailus... was because he coerced her by threatening Aria? What a bastard...

"That... That can't be true..." Aria whispered shakily.

"It is, Aria," Bell responded quietly. "So... I love you... but at the same time..."

"I also hate you..."

Bell had sent her sister away because she loved her, so that she wouldn't get mixed up in the fighting. She also sent Aria away because she hated her, so that she would blame herself for leaving the city alone... and spread the word that Kailus was behind the insurrection. Perhaps Bell had sent Zonagein to keep watch over Aria too.

I couldn't deny that this explanation snapped a lot of pieces into place. If Bell's aim was to disgrace Kailus and get him killed, then after he was dead, she'd have no need of subordinates. On the contrary, having them put up too much of a fight against the imperial army would be contrary to her goals. That was why she'd programmed them to die.

But... how did she do it all?!

"It's not true!" Aria shouted, her voice trembling. "It can't be! Because... you aren't capable of any of the things you're describing! You don't even know anything about sorcery!"

"You're right... I don't know the first thing about it. Kailus made sure that I never learned, even after we married. I'm sure he was afraid... that I might take revenge on him if I did. And so... no matter how great the hatred inside of me grew... there was nothing I could do... until that person gave me power."

"'That person'?" I whispered, my brow knitted.

It didn't sound like she was referring to her dead fiancé, or to Kailus.

Still smiling at Aria, Bell answered me, "They never gave me their name... But they realized that I craved power and granted it to me. So I used it. It would have been easy to simply kill Kailus, but that wasn't enough for me. I wanted him to die a traitor. Thus I used my power to change everyone and exploit them."

"No! You couldn't do that!"

"But I did, Aria. And once we're dead, it will all finally be over."

"Aria!" Hearing those words, I made a beeline for the younger sister and grabbed her hand, tearing her away from Bell. I'd thought that she was going to kill Aria... But Bell just stood there, as still as could be, showing no sign of reaching for a hidden weapon.

"You're lying, Sister!" Aria screamed, tears in her eyes.

Bell looked from her to me and Gourry. "I'm sorry that you have to be dragged in this. But it will be over soon. No matter what kind of man Kailus was, it wasn't right for me to use innocent people for my revenge. That's why I'm going to kill myself too. But… it is necessary that Kailus's legacy remain that of a traitor… and so… you must die with me." She turned her gaze back to Aria and raised her right hand. "Behold, Aria… This is the power I have been given. Come to me… Dulgoffa."

What?!

Shadows appeared, coalescing in Bell's outstretched right hand. Then the darkness came into focus, forming a pure black blade.

"H-Hey! Lina! Isn't that—?!" Gourry shouted.

"Yeah," I responded with a calm that surprised even me.

I knew that name… and I'd seen that sword before. Dulgoffa was a demon that took the form of a blade wielded by a high-ranking demon General called Sherra. Gourry and I had crossed paths with her once before, and we'd seen the kind of grotesque monster the demon-sword could transform people into.

That explains how she "changed" everyone… It would've been easy with the sword's power.

"Sister! Stop this!"

"Let us… end this," Bell whispered as the magical sword began fusing with her hand.

"No!" Gourry screamed, speeding across the floor. The sword in his hand flashed. He was probably hoping to stop the fusion by slicing the demon sword out of her hand. But…

Zing! The blade in Bell's hand casually deflected his strike.

"What the…" Gourry whispered, confounded, as he leaped back.

Gourry's skill with a sword was masterful. To parry a serious blow from him would require equally masterful skill, if not multiple arms like Zonagein. It was hard to imagine Bell had that kind of fencing training, and yet…

"You're too late. The sword has been inside me all this time. Our fusion is nearly complete. I do not know how to fight… but… Dulgoffa does."

Dulgoffa's blade was drawing into Bell's right palm itself. Her hand was stained black, and the darkness continued to spread. Nobody could stop it now. Bell's whole body began to turn black until, at last, she was one with the magical sword.

"Sister!" Aria's scream echoed powerlessly around us.

When Gourry and I had witnessed Dulgoffa transform someone previously, it was against the victim's will. They'd become a true horror after the fusion—a writhing, hideous mass of flesh. But Bell had accepted Dulgoffa of her own free will. Not even I could say for sure if the being that stood before me now was Bell, Dulgoffa, or something else entirely.

Maybe this was what a true fusion with Dulgoffa looked like. In form, she looked quite a bit like Mycale. But whereas Mycale's body had been a clear, sparkling emerald color, this being's entire body was the shade of night, the black of void. Like a goddess carved out of pure ebony...

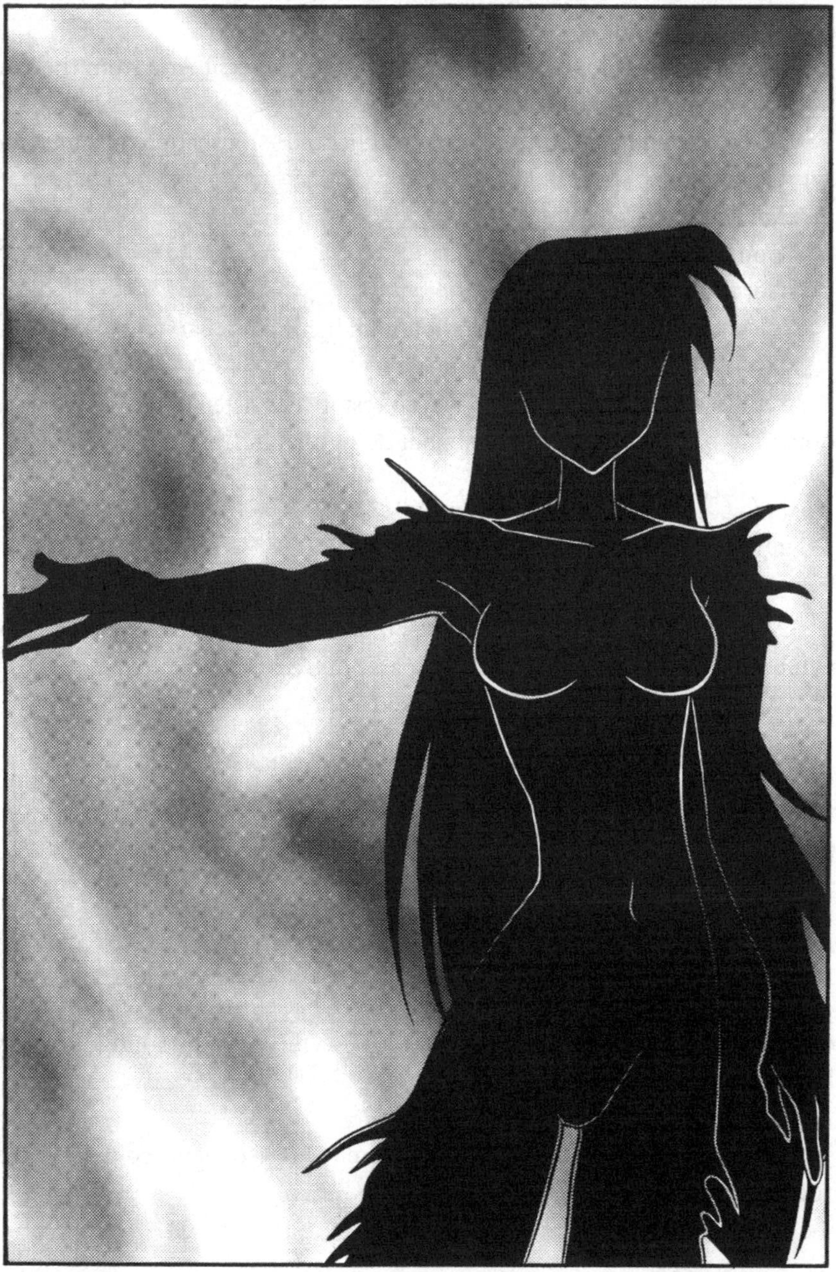

"Sister…" Aria tried to call to her, but in response, the being wordlessly raised her right hand.

"Move!" Gourry took off running. He flew straight at Aria from the side, sweeping her up in his arms without stopping.

Not a second later—*Crash!*—the wall behind Aria shattered from some invisible pressure.

Not good!

"Gourry! Skedaddle time!"

"Got it!"

I flew out into the hall. Gourry followed behind me, carrying Aria.

"Sister! Sister!" I heard her cry in agony.

Yet I knew there would be no way to restore her sister after this. We were going to have to… well, to kill her… but doing that in front of Aria would be cruel…

"Gourry! Let's get outside for now!"

"Right!"

We rushed down the stairs and kicked open the front door.

"Aria! Once we're in the city, go somewhere and hide!" I shouted. The lawn here at the estate was regretfully sparse of trees and other cover.

"What are you going to do?" she asked.

I responded with silence.

Aria fretfully looked away. "I… I suppose that is the only option. I understand. Please do it," she whispered, the words strained. "Master Gourry… I'm all right. I can run on my own…"

"Okay," Gourry said, then set her down.

"Let's go at least as far as the city together," I said.

"Certainly," Aria agreed.

I was afraid she might suddenly turn back, insisting on trying to convince her sister herself, but thankfully it seemed I had nothing to worry about. Except…

Huh?!

I felt a hostile presence incoming before we'd even managed to leave the property.

"Aria!" I cried.

We were running side by side, and no sooner had I pushed her away than something invisible passed between us, without sound or wind. And then…

Crack! A tree on the lawn far ahead of us snapped. I stopped and turned back to see the being slowly emerging from the front door. Guess getting Aria to safety was out of the question now… Aria seemed to be the main target, after all. It was likely Bell's conflicting love and hatred for her sister had snapped into a delusional fixation when she fused with Dulgoffa. Even if we hid Aria somewhere, Bell would probably ignore us and hunt her down first.

"Looks like we'll have to finish things here…" I muttered.

"Yes… it does," Gourry agreed.

We stopped our flight and turned to face the being that had formerly been Bell.

"Get back, Aria! But don't go too far!" I called.

"I won't!" she called back.

With that decided, I quickly began to chant a spell. The ebony being raised her right hand again. Her target this time was… me?! Right. She'd judged me an obstacle to her killing of Aria, and had thus decided to take me out first.

Keeping up my chant, I leaped to my right. An invisible presence then tore past me, and after unleashing it, the being charged straight for me. That was when I finished my incantation.

"Sight Frang!"

Bwoosh! Responding to my words of power, a thin mist rushed out to veil the area. This spell was usually used to make a quick escape, but I'd seen it used before against invisible projectiles. You could track their trajectory more easily by watching for ripples in the mist.

The being raised her hand once more. I felt a chill up my spine and jumped to the side again. I didn't see any movement in the mist, and yet…

Crack! I heard another tree split in the distance.

Wait, can she fire those things without even disturbing the air around her?! How is that fair?!

I counted the facts that she couldn't fire them off in rapid succession and that they were relatively easy to sense coming as wins, and kept on dodging them accordingly… but it wasn't exactly fun. We really needed to finish this ASAP.

As the being approached, Gourry interposed himself between us. I chanted a spell from behind him.

"Hyah!" With a cry, Gourry sliced at her!

Shing! Clank! I heard the din of metal on metal as she blocked each of Gourry's slashes.

At some point, she'd produced a black dagger in her right hand. It was longer than a normal one, but not long enough to be called a shortsword. She'd probably formed it from her own body instantaneously to parry Gourry's attack. But...

Clang! Cling! Clank! The metallic chorus continued as they traded blows. She seemed to be on par with Gourry in terms of skill, but as he was only human, she likely had an overwhelming advantage in terms of endurance.

She makes for one tough opponent...

Luckily, her invisible blasts seemed to require a degree of concentration to manifest, which meant they were off the table while she was locked in melee combat. With that in mind, I finished up my spell and... Seeming to realize what I was about to do, Gourry leaped back to put some distance between them.

Okay! Now!

I immediately fired! "Dynast Blas!"

Lightning struck the five points of a pentagram around her, then converged on her! But—*Vrm!*—her body trembled and a black mist enveloped her. It neutralized my magical lightning!

Not bad! In that case... I quickly began chanting my next spell.

Gourry moved to stop her again as she turned toward me once more. She blocked his sideways slash with her dagger yet again. Immediately, Gourry pulled his sword back and tried a thrust this time—but she produced another dagger in her left hand, using it in tandem with the one in her right to block his piercing attack. With her blades scissoring his, she lunged at Gourry!

"Guh!" Gourry quickly moved back.

While their deadly melee continued, I finished up my next spell! Gourry broke away from her again, probably anticipating my timing.

"Zellas Bullid!"

The ray of light I fired streaked straight toward her. She saw it coming and dodged it with a half step. As she did, Gourry attempted another charge, but...

Zing! She blocked his strike with the dagger in her left hand. Nevertheless, that held her in place for a brief moment!

Yes! Just what I was waiting for! The Zellas Bullid spell could be controlled by its caster mid-flight. Moreover, it channeled the power of one of the highest-tier demons, Greater Beast Zellas Metallium! Not even Dulgoffa could take that hit unscathed!

My ray of light had missed her once, but I willed it to change course midair, hooking it back around at her again from behind!

Got her! Just as I thought that, she artlessly raised her hand, brandishing her dagger. Then came a strange noise. *Wha—*

She'd cut through the incoming beam with her dagger! The slice had split it in two, dispersing the light on either side of her. The aftershocks of the scattering power hit Gourry, who lost his balance with a cry.

Not good! One second's opening could get him killed!

And indeed, she swiftly struck at him with her dagger after cutting through the light. Perhaps out of sheer desperation, Gourry ducked down low and swept at her leg with his foot.

Then, like it was nothing—*Whump*—she just collapsed.

"What the..." It had been so easy, Gourry couldn't help but pause.

He hadn't caught her by surprise or anything like that. It looked like she'd had a real amateur moment there.

Could it be...?

"Gourry! I don't think she can handle kicks!" I shouted.

Bell had said that Dulgoffa knew how to fight. But when I thought about it, why had she gone out of her way to produce daggers in both hands? If she'd wanted a longer reach, she could have extended her arms themselves... So what was the big idea?

Does Dulgoffa only know how to fight like a sword?

If my stupid theory was right, then beating her might not be so difficult after all.

"Well... let's find out!" Gourry said, sweeping her leg again as she started to right herself. Once again, she toppled helplessly. "Sorry! I really need to beat you!" After knocking her to the ground a second time, Gourry brought his sword down on her.

Ding! There was a hard metallic sound.

"What?!" All of us cried out at once.

She hadn't blocked Gourry's blade with her daggers. He'd plunged his sword right into her chest... without causing a single scratch to her ebony skin. Gourry swiftly and silently leaped away.

Of course... Should've seen this one coming.

If those daggers were physically a part of her—they'd just taken the form of daggers to capitalize on Dulgoffa's skill—then it stood to reason that her entire body was every bit as hard. Gourry's sword didn't have a name, but it was still a magical blade of considerable power. If even it couldn't pierce her hide, then...

"What do we do, Lina?!"

"How should I know?"

"Can't you use a spell to make my sword sharper?!"

"No way!" I responded firmly.

Sure, there were spells to temporarily enhance the power of ordinary weapons by imbuing them with magic. But there was no telling what they'd do to a sword that already had magical properties. If you got lucky and the magics played nicely together, you could very well end up with a souped-up slicer... but it was just as likely that nothing at all would happen, or worse, that you'd break the enchantment and end up with a useless hunk of metal. Worst of all, you might get a bad reaction that caused the magic to go haywire and blow! And this was no time to be taking a gamble like that.

The being quickly picked herself up, flipped away, and ran for the house.

"Is she trying to escape?!"

"Get her!"

If she'd truly lost her will to fight, then we had no reason to pursue... but given that she'd fused with Dulgoffa out of a delusional fixation on Aria, I was guessing she wasn't going to give up just because we'd bested her once. And if I'm being honest, I'd rather face a dozen brass demons than the prospect of something like her lurking out there with my number.

Besides, there was no guarantee she would limit her rage to us and Aria. Her fixation was specific at the moment, but what if she turned on the world at large? She'd already used Dulgoffa's power to transform the innocent people of the Crimson sorcerers' council, after all. We couldn't leave her out there unchecked.

"Could that dark blade do it?" Aria called from behind me. "The one you used to kill Kailus. Could you use it on her?"

"It would be tricky, and I'd have to outfence her..."

Even if her mastery was limited to bladed weapons, she was skilled enough in that regard to go toe to toe with Gourry. She'd probably run me through before I could get within kicking distance. More pressingly, that spell was a real drain on my magic... which was already pretty tapped from using it on Kailus earlier. I could cast it again, sure, but I wouldn't be able to keep it up for long. I'd probably get a few swings in at most, and I wasn't really confident I could land a solid blow in that short window.

As we pursued the being, she flew through the still-open front door and into the mansion. She stopped in a corner of the grand hall, beside the now-lifeless body of Zonagein. She reached for his corpse, and...

Skrrk! She stuck one of her daggers into him!

What in the world is she... Before I could even speculate, she withdrew the dagger and turned back to face us. *Wait, don't tell me...*

"Stop!"

At my warning, Gourry and Aria halted in the doorway behind me. We then watched as spider legs tore out from her back! *Kra-pash!*

Ahhh! Freakin' knew it!

"Retreat!"

"R-Right!"

"No objections here!"

We did a quick about-face to retreat. When we did...

"Freeze Arrow!" incanted a voice behind us. It was muffled, but it was clearly Bell's.

"Scatter!" The second we were out the door, we split up, letting the arrows of ice blow past us.

Aaagh! Seriously freakin' bad!

We reconvened and continued our retreat. I immediately felt a presence behind us. We turned to look... and she was right on our heels!

"What do we do, Lina?!" Gourry asked, sword at the ready.

"How am I supposed to know?" I responded in exhaustion.

"How could you *not* know?"

"I think she can absorb the power and knowledge of anyone she sticks with her daggers. So if she so much as scratches one of us, she'll master our fighting styles too!"

"Are you sure?!"

"Pretty darn sure!"

It was clear from her appearance that she could absorb physical properties. That she could also absorb knowledge was a guess, but I felt it was an educated one based on the way she was suddenly busting out Zonagein's greatest hits. Bell didn't know the first thing about magic, and Dulgoffa wouldn't have Freeze Arrow in its repertoire, so that knowledge must have come from the old sorcerer.

One way or the other, things were starting to look pretty grim for us. It would be impossible to beat someone with Gourry's mastery of a blade *and* arachnid appendages without taking a single scratch. The spider legs would also make her tough to outrun, and an aerial escape was equally off the table. If we took to the skies, she'd just absorb the winged doll in the garden and take flight after us. And once she could fly, we'd be truly helpless against her. We really had to put her down here and now.

"She absorbs knowledge... Does that mean she absorbs memories too?" Aria asked.

"Well... sure, probably," I responded, my eyes still locked on our enemy.

"Very well... I'll finish this."

"What?!" I couldn't help looking over at her.

A genuine smile appeared on her face. "Please, save my sister."

I...

For a minute, I couldn't figure out what Aria was getting at. But then she took off running—straight for the being.

"Aria?!" I reached out, but my hand just missed her.

I finally got it. I understood what Aria meant to do.

"Tch!" Gourry took off after her, but he, too, was too slow. The spider's legs were already reaching for her.

Aria thrust her hands forward like she sought an embrace. "Become one with me... Sister!"

And then—*Skrrk!*—the being's dagger pierced her chest. Without hesitation, I began chanting a spell. I couldn't afford to hesitate. I owed Aria this much.

Hail, Lords of the four worlds' darkness
I beseech your bond and beg you this boon

Aria's body fell limply to the ground with a soft thud. A spasm coursed through the spidery legs that bound her.

By your powers combined, entwined,
Bless me with magic mightier than mine

The talismans on my belt, my collar, and both wrists let out a faint glow. The being's body began to heave, as if crying. I started off slowly toward her while moving into my next incantation.

Blade forged of the freezing black void,
Be released under heaven's seal

"Hey! Lina!" Gourry called from behind me. He must have realized for himself that the violent rage had left her.

Become mine, become part of me
Let us mete destruction as one
Smash even the souls of the gods...

I stood before her, my spell finished. I quietly raised my right hand and recited the words of power. "Ragna Blade."

Darkness took shape in my right hand, and the blade of pure void sliced through her.

I stared silently out into the city beneath the moonlit night sky.

"Hey, are you crying?" Gourry asked.

"Yeah, right," I responded, looking back over my shoulder with a small smile.

We were on the street by the canal just outside of Kailus's mansion. No one else was around.

"I was just thinking, it feels so... heavy," I whispered, looking back over the city again.

"Hey, you mind if I ask?"

"About what?"

"Why'd she stop all of a sudden?"

"Aria stopped her... She used that being's ability to absorb the memories of others to let Bell know how much she loved her."

In that moment, Bell had probably heard her sister's thoughts and come to understand her feelings. When the hatred vanished from Bell's heart, it fractured the core delusion that had allowed her and Dulgoffa to attain a perfect fusion. That would've left Dulgoffa to absorb Bell against her will if unchecked, which was why I'd had to step in... To respect Aria's sacrifice, and save Bell's soul. Yet even so...

"C'mon, Lina." Gourry walked up to me and placed a hand on my head. "Cheer up... I'll carry half the weight for you."

"Gourry..." I reached for him slowly... and latched an arm tight around his neck! "Look at you, Mr. Obligatory Expressions of Support! I think you just know I'd throttle you if you tried to brush me off!"

"Urk! B-But you're throttling me anyway!"

"I've got to take my chances when I can, don't I?! You'd dodge or fight back otherwise!"

"Of course I would! But... it looks like you're okay, at least..."

"I guess I am... Just stewing in depression won't do anybody any good."

"True. Anyway... we stopped the insurrection, and the sword is gone," Gourry said with a smile. I smiled back, but halfheartedly.

He was right. After my dark sword hit her, her body had turned to ash and then vanished without a trace. That had probably done some damage to Dulgoffa, at least. But General Sherra was still out there, which meant Dulgoffa would be back. Why had Sherra given it to Bell? What were the demons plotting? I still didn't have the answer to those questions.

I silently kept staring at the moon in the eastern sky. The night had only just begun.

Afterword

Scene: Author + L

Au: Whew. Almost ate the big one there.

L: You survived?! Granted, I never put up a fight any of the other times you were killed in an afterword and then came back just fine... But reviving within the span of two simultaneously published novels still feels a little fast.

Au: What do you want from me? That's just how the world works. Anyway, this concludes the reprint of *Slayers: Delusion in Crimson*!

L: Even for the novels, which have a pretty high body count already, a lot of people sure do die in this story.

Au: True. I feel like the fundamental philosophy of part 2 is that people are going to die, but it inspires those they leave behind to appreciate life all the more.

L: Hang on. Do you think you said something cool just now? I used my laser beam to break you down to your constituent atoms, you come back one volume later all "whew, almost ate the big one there," and you expect to sound like a credible philosopher on death and sacrifice?

Au: Erk... You do have a point there. Damn. How do I get people to take me seriously again?

L: Let's pretend you *actually* died last time, and I'll handle all subsequent afterwords myself!

Au: No freakin' way! You'd just make them stupid!

L: Well, excuse me! Actually, wait... are you under the impression that the afterwords where you appear *aren't* stupid?

Au: Er, w-well... never mind that now. Ahem. But reviving so casually because I have to keep appearing in the afterwords does take some of the gravitas out of the deaths in the series... Ah! I know! Why don't we try it the other way? Everyone who previously died in the story will turn out to have been alive the whole time!

L: That's even more stupid! And it would completely undermine the drama! Think of volume 2, *The Sorcerers of Atlas*!

Halciform: To take back my lost love…!

Real Rubia: Whew. Almost ate the big one there. Oh, Halciform, long time no see!

Halciform: …Huh?

Rubia: Um, Master Halciform, is she…

Halciform: Wait, what? Rubia? You're… alive?

Real Rubia: Of course I am! You didn't really think that would kill me, did you, silly?

Rubia: (whispers) The real me is a very different person…

Then Lina and Gourry would have nothing to do but eat!

Au: Is that so wrong?

L: You bet it is! Even Talim, who's just a head, would come back saying "almost ate the big one there!"

Au: Yeah, okay. I guess that wouldn't work, would it?

L: See? Even my world food tour would be better than that!

Au: Yeah, I have to disagree. But, thinking about it, it's hard to decide who lives and who dies in these stories. A while back I was talking with a certain editor over lunch, and he said, "By the way, what happened to Randy from the short story? He's part of the royal family, isn't he?"

I replied, "Well, I wrote that he'd stopped moving at the end of the short story, so he's probably dead."

And then he said, "What are you saying, Kanzaka-san?! People can't die in *Special*!" He was so insistent, I thought *I* was going to die… but I took those words to heart.

L: I guess it's not so uncommon. Really, you have to wonder what happens to all those bandits Lina's always blasting away as a gag.

Au: I do usually gloss over that, yeah. Sometimes I leave it ambiguous, or I don't even decide for myself. That's to let the readers imagine things. Sometimes I talk about the games or the *Knight of Aqualord* comic or the anime as a parallel "part 3," largely because of that.

L: I see. So the reason you don't write about me is because you want to let the readers imagine my amazing adventures, and the infinite possibility they represent, for themselves!

Au: No, that's not what I—

L: If I just drop a title like "L vs. Beautiful Innkeepers Nationwide," then readers can enjoy imagining my exploits! That's your homework for next time, folks! Come up with my adventures based on that title and send in your letters before the next afterword comes out!

Au: Wait! The next afterword—

L: Well, see you in the next book!

Afterword: Over.

By Hajime Kanzaka
Illustrations by Rui Araizumi

CONTENTS

Chapter 1: Ah, the Demons One Meets on the Road

As darkness fell, so too did silence. A city of this size would normally still have bars open, leaving drunkards and other miscreants to roam the darkened streets... but this particular town was locked down tight. We were living in dangerous times, after all.

That meant I was the only soul out on the road. My cape flapped in the darkness, its color blending in with the night as I ran while trying to mask my footfalls as best I could. I was headed for—

"More bandit bullying?"

Grk! The sound of that unexpected voice from behind me sent a shudder through my body.

I whipped around. "Yeesh... don't startle me like that, Gourry."

Yep. The guy standing there in the faint moonlight with a wearied expression was my traveling companion, Gourry. He was tall, blond, handsome, and a master swordsman... which was all well and good. The fact that he had seaweed for brains? Not so much. He'd probably seen me slipping out of my room at the inn and tailed me.

"You're really the one complaining here?" he said. "Why do you always have to slip out on your own like this?"

"What, you wanted an invite?"

"Of course not."

Our conversation was held entirely in whispers. It was nighttime, after all, so we couldn't exactly cause a scene.

"C'moooon, man. I gotta go bully some bandits to replenish our travel funds. And to blow off steam," I said sulkily.

Gourry's expression remained exhausted. "Are you still annoyed about *that*?"

"'Course I am," I admitted bluntly.

He let out a soft sigh.

"Just to confirm... Is this report *entirely* accurate?" So the old sorcerer inquired, but his face and attitude were saying, *"This bitch is trying to play me."*

Ten days prior, I'd compiled the recent goings-on of Crimson Town into a report that I submitted to the Telmodd City sorcerers' council. I'd filled five scrolls with my account of what went down, but when this old council bigwig glanced through it, his initial response was skepticism.

"It is," I assured him confidently.

The old sorcerer just looked at me with a grimace. "Were there... any other witnesses?"

I was briefly stumped. Gourry had been there from start to finish, but where most people had their long-term memory, he had a bowl of mush. Even if I brought him in as a witness, he'd probably just say, "Did that all really happen?"—the final nail in the "she's lying" coffin.

So after a bit of thought, I ultimately replied, "My companion... isn't really credible. There are no other living witnesses to the report as written."

"Hmm... I see..." The sorcerer fell into uncomfortable silence. "I confess I find this difficult to believe. The involvement of the General of the Dynast's sword, the connection to the incident in Bezeld... It's all far too extraordinary."

Grr...

I could feel a vein bulging in my forehead under the sorcerer's dubious gaze. But, objectively speaking, he wasn't wrong to feel the way he did. While the world was full of entities that fell under the "demon" umbrella, the higher-ranking ones were few and far between. There were basically no formal records documenting their existence.

Dark Lord Shabranigdu, lord of all the world's demons, had five faithful lieutenants, each with their various Priest and General servants—that was basically the hierarchy of the upper echelons of (what passed for) demon society. But most sorcerers, in practice, regarded this as mere legend.

In all honesty, there was a time when I, too, found the stories of a dark lord in the mountains of Kataart pretty sketch. If past-Lina had read a report like the one I'd handed in, I also would've written it off as fame-grubbing nonsense. So on one hand, I couldn't really blame the old sorcerer for his reaction.

On the other… it still pissed me off!

"Well… I shall accept your report. But the council has a small request for you. If you really did what you claim to have done, you should find it simple enough." There was blatant sarcasm in the old sorcerer's voice.

The council ended up asking me to get to the bottom of some recent reports of mass lesser and brass demon spawnings. I was to head to the Kingdom of Dils, where there'd been a spate of them lately. But as with all council jobs, the payment I'd be getting for the job was well under what the work was worth, so I naturally didn't want to do it. There were no leads on the investigation, and there was no telling how long it would take just to interview the people involved. It was gross to expect someone to do such an annoying job for so little compensation. Refusing would have been easy…

Except if I'd simply said no, I knew exactly what that old sorcerer would've thought: *Ah, she's scared of demons. This confirms her report is a lie.* Thus I'd swallowed my pride and taken the crummy job.

Of course, I'd also requested a massive increase in remuneration. The piddly payment they were offering hardly covered such an open-ended task. It wouldn't have even covered room and board. In lieu of money, however, the council bigwig offered me payment in kind—a letter that I could show to any local sorcerers' council for free lodging and meals. Too bad not every city we stopped in had a branch, and even if it did, the quality of the food there wasn't exactly guaranteed.

The result? After just a little traveling and asking around, Gourry and I had already burned through the advance the council had given us. It was hardly the kind of situation that keeps you in high spirits. So if I vented my frustration by busting up a bandit gang and stealing—er, reappropriating—their cache to recoup my traveling expenses, who could blame me?

"Well… there's nothing wrong with beating up bandits, and I can't tell you to stop doing what's clearly in your nature…"

"My nature?" *I'm not a wild animal!* I was about to say something, but held off.

"Lina," Gourry called abruptly.

"I know." I nodded firmly in response.

The darkness around us had just grown deeper, and it wasn't a shadow passing over the moon. There was a presence mixed in with the darkness itself. Hatred, sorrow, jealousy, despair... All the negative emotions that plagued living things steeped the air in a melange.

Miasma. That can only mean...

"Say, Lina... would this be another fine mess we've gotten ourselves into?" Gourry muttered.

Before I could respond—*Thud!*—I heard an impact some distance away.

"Over there!" I called. Gourry and I took off at the same time. "It was somewhere around here..."

"Lina! Look!" Gourry stopped on a street corner and pointed. There were fragments of something scattered across the road. And beyond them lay...

A person?!

We ran up to the man on the ground. He looked a little over twenty years old. Dark fluid pooled around him, gleaming crimson in the moonlight. I lifted him into my arms, but it was clear he was already dead, bleeding from a gaping wound in his chest.

"What in the..." I started. But before I could finish the thought, I sensed a rush of malice headed our way.

Gourry sprang into action. The sharp clang of metal on metal rang out beside me as I jumped away. I looked over to see Gourry, sword in hand, squaring off with a dark figure.

And when I say "dark," I don't mean that it was hidden by the shadows. I mean that it was pitch-black from head to toe, including the light plate armor it wore and the sword it held. Curious white patterns scrawled all over its body stood out in the faint light of the moon. This dark figure looked a bit like a shaman from some weird religion, but its aura revealed its true nature...

Yup, we've got a demon on our hands!

It hadn't appeared out of thin air. I could see that the second-floor window of a nearby building (what looked like an inn) had been broken from the inside. I was guessing this thing had attacked a man staying there, then leaped out the window to confirm the kill.

"I have... business with... that man." The creature turned toward the fallen man, speaking in a halting, muffled tone.

"He's already dead," I told it.

My words caused the creature to fall silent for a time. Its face-not-face (which was really just a pattern on a black field) turned my way. "He is... dead?" It seemed to think for a moment before tilting its head. "I see... He is dead..." it whispered, cocking its head again and falling quiet once more.

Not one of our brighter demons, I guess...

After a period of silence, it looked back up at me. "You saw... me..."

Hang on a minute! Don't you dare—

Before I could even object, the "shaman" took off! It dashed to the side and got in close to me.

It's fast! I just barely managed to block its sweeping slash with my half-drawn shortsword. I then leaped in the opposite direction. *And strong!*

Truth be told, it was sheer luck that I was able to defend myself. If I'd moved a split second slower, the creature would've lopped my head off. And if I'd finished drawing my sword all the way, I wouldn't have been braced to resist the force of the blow completely. It would've cut my stomach open.

The shaman, realizing that its strike had been blocked, withdrew its sword... It then leaped back and, without even looking, took another slash at Gourry, who'd moved in on it! Had it tried a follow-up attack against me, Gourry most certainly would have run it through from behind. That had to be why it had changed targets.

Clang! When Gourry deflected the shaman's blow, it got around to his side. This time it was Gourry who leaped, getting a little distance from his opponent.

"Be careful, Lina! This guy's good!" he called.

Obviously, I'd pieced that together. I was already working on a spell chant.

Meanwhile, Gourry and the shaman sized each other up—and the shaman took the initiative! It raised its blade high and sliced down at Gourry. The big lug wavered over how to respond. With sword skills like his, he probably could have just eviscerated the thing... But would that be enough to finish a demon? His hesitation produced a moment's delay, and...

Cling! Gourry blocked the shaman's incoming sword. A second later, the shaman was on the move again! It used their swords' meeting point as a fulcrum as it leaped into the air—right over Gourry's head toward me! And then—

"Fireball!"

Bwoosh! My spell met the demon midair! Of course, a Fireball wouldn't hurt one of its kind, but the force of the explosion still sent it flying backward. The shaman landed some distance on the other side of Gourry and turned its face back toward us.

"Wait!" I shouted. The shaman was about to start up again, but it stopped at my call. "You're trying to kill us to eliminate witnesses, right?"

The shaman tilted its head and said nothing for a time. "That is correct. I must kill... all witnesses..."

"Then wouldn't it be better to run for now? That spell will have people swarming the scene any second now! Which means you're gonna have more witnesses than you can handle!"

I was afraid that it might just threaten to kill them all, but after a lengthy silence, the shaman leaped lightly off the ground and disappeared back through the busted second-story window.

"Did he give up?" Gourry whispered, his sword still drawn as he looked up at the shattered window. Just then...

Fwooom! There was a huge explosion from inside the room.

"So... what do we do?" Gourry asked the next afternoon over lunch at a restaurant.

"About what?"

"The thing yesterday when—"

"Hush!" I silenced him by shoving a fried chicken wing into his mouth, then cast a surreptitious glance at the tables around us. "Keep it down! Someone might hear you!"

He chewed on the chicken wing, swallowed, and lowered his voice. "So what? It's not like we did anything wrong... And the local authorities are searching for clues about what happened, so why can't we just tell them what we saw?"

Hahh... Gourry was being so shortsighted that I couldn't help but lament.

If you're smart, you've figured this one out already. That's right—after stumbling onto the attack, Gourry and I had fled the scene. My Fireball had attracted all kinds of attention, as expected, and it turned into a whole hullabaloo with the local guards running around questioning people since early this morning. Obviously, it would be easy to come forward and tell them what we'd seen. But...

"What do you think would happen if we did that, Gourry?"

"...They'd appreciate it?"

Haaaaaaaahhhhh... My lamentations grew deeper.

"Enlighten me here... Just what do you think that thing we fought yesterday was?" I had to ask.

"A demon, right? It felt like one."

"Right. I thought so too, though it seemed pretty dumb as demons go... and using an explosion for a cover-up isn't a very demon-like thing to do... But anyway, the victim was killed in his nightgown, and the room where he was staying got blown up—meaning the authorities don't really have a way to identify him. Now, let's assume we came clean to them about what we witnessed yesterday. They'd have an explosion at a local inn, an unidentified corpse, and a bloodstained sorcerer and her mercenary buddy at the scene crying, 'A demon did it.' Here's a question for you: What do you think the authorities would do with all that on their hands?"

"...Thank us for our cooperation?"

"Yeah, right! They'll look at the suspicious duo—that's us, just so we're clear—and say, 'A demon, huh? Likely story! I bet you did it yourselves!' Then they'll arrest us and won't listen to another word we say."

"Yeah? But once we explain the misunderstanding, I'm sure they'd let us go."

I clicked my tongue and waggled my finger. "Don't be naive. When a case is hard to crack, the authorities just want to arrest the first suspect they find so they can feel like they accomplished something. It's human nature. I did it all the time back in the day myself."

"You did?"

"Besides, even if we eventually clear things up, how much time gets wasted in the process? Remember how back in Solaria, despite all identities being known and the course of events being rather self-evident, we still had to spend a million years rehashing our story for everybody and their brother? Wait... I guess you wouldn't remember that, would you?"

"Um... actually..." Gourry slumped. "I don't remember the name of the city... but I do remember the questioning."

Huh. So it had been that bad even for him, had it?

"Good. Now, we're total strangers here and the identity of the victim is unknown. How long do you think it'd take the authorities to peg the deceased and then establish that we have no connection to him? Besides, say we *do* give our full testimony from yesterday. You think that'd really help things? If the authorities start looking into us, that's just going to waylay the real investigation—which isn't good for them *or* us. So I say our best move is to look the other way and skip town ASAP!"

"Is that really okay?"

"Of course it is!" It really wasn't. "So we're staying out of this. You follow, Gourry?"

The big lug just shrugged in response.

Still, I'm betting we haven't seen the last of that demon. We have a terrible track record when it comes to unfinished business... With that thought, I let out another internal sigh.

"A white... giant?" I couldn't help but scowl openly at the bizarre story I'd just heard.

Gourry and I had left the city behind a day ago to hear from witnesses in a small village that was recently attacked by a demidemon swarm. Given that status quo, I found it rather odd that the place seemed more or less untouched and that the villagers were going about their lives as normal. A bearded older gent had agreed to talk to us at the local tavern in exchange for the price of a meal.

"That's right. The handful of mercenaries we hired for protection started shouting and ran into town. We came out to see a mess of demons coming out of the forest to the south," he said, gesturing pointlessly as he spoke. "I've never seen a demon before... Looked like real bad news to me. I thought I was a goner, for sure."

"But didn't you hire the mercenaries to protect you?" Gourry asked.

The old man just shook his head. "Well, I think there were about a hundred of the things..."

"A hundred?!" I gasped.

"Yeah. And however strong the mercenaries might've been, there were only a handful of them. They didn't stand a chance, so they just raised the alarm about the demons coming, then scarpered. Can't say I blame them. We all thought we were done for, running around like chickens with our heads cut off…"

"And that's when the white giant appeared?"

"That's right. Oh, could I get more of the fried romarl?"

"Sure thing. Ma'am! Get this man another fried romarl fish plate! And I'll have three more fried sampler platters, lunch combo C, and a special salad on the side!"

"Oh, and I'll take one order each of the crown sausage, bacon, potatoes, and eggs, as well as lunch combos A through C!"

"Hey, Gourry, don't think I didn't notice you slipping in those orders! Two can play at that game! I'll take the roast lamb, the fish liver terrine, and the duck egg soup too! Anyhoo, now what's this about a white giant?"

"Th-That about-face gave me whiplash. Anyway… the demons were about to attack when suddenly the whole place lit up."

"It lit up?"

"Well, it's like… there was a flash. It blew the demons away in an instant."

"Huh?"

"I said it blew away the demons. There were plenty left, but something was burning nearby—not sure if it was the trees—and I could see the giant a little ways away."

I didn't quite know how to react to this information, but the old man kept talking nonetheless.

"It looked about the size of a big hill, I'd say, and it was white all over. While I watched, the giant released two or three more of those flashes and blew the rest of the demons away. The demons tried to fight back with their fiery arrows, but they didn't seem to hurt the giant. If you ask me, it's got to be a mountain god."

"I see…" I replied vaguely to the old man's story.

Even if the lesser and brass varieties were the lowest branch of the demon family tree, the idea of something blowing away a hundred of them with just a few blasts… It certainly didn't sound believable. Then again, plenty of what Gourry and I had been through would sound that way to a stranger too. Plus, when we'd first arrived in town, we'd seen the remnant scorch marks of a battle at the village entrance—huge trenches gouged out of the earth, their walls melted into smooth glass. I knew that no human could do that, so I'd been curious about their origin. Were they traces of the giant's attack?

But what the hell is this giant?

"Could you tell me more about how the demons or the giant behaved when they appeared?"

"I'm not sure what more I can say…" The old man screwed up his face thoughtfully. "The giant vanished right away, and the other villagers just watched from afar like I did. They don't know any more than me, I'd wager."

"Hmm… What about the mercenaries, then? I bet they'd know more about how the demons appeared, if not the giant."

"I told you, they made tracks before it all went down. We never saw them again, even after the demons were gone. Not that they were obligated to come back."

"Do you have any idea where they'd have gone, then? Well, I guess you wouldn't…"

"I don't. But I do wonder…"

"Wonder what?"

"I heard that Gyria City's been recruiting mercenaries in large numbers. Maybe that's where they went."

"Bugh!" I couldn't help but groan when I heard that name.

The afternoon sun gently bathed the landscape. Birdsong drifted from the forest to my right, and from my left came the sounds of flowing water—probably a small river just outside of view.

Hahh… I sighed wistfully, gazing glassy-eyed at the peaceful scene around us.

"What's wrong, Lina?" Gourry asked.

"What makes you think something's wrong?" I responded listlessly.

"You've been super down since we left that village. What's up?"

"Oh… that," I said with another small sigh. "It's what that villager said… about how Gyria City was recruiting mercenaries and we should check things out there…"

"What about it?"

"I've just got… bad memories of Gyria, you know?" I said with a melancholy air. I'd gotten mixed up in some… let's say… complicated trouble there once before.

Gourry, however, just smiled brightly at me. "Oh, is that all? That's not like you."

"'Is that all'?! Who would be happy about revisiting a city they have bad memories of?"

"Well, come on. Is there any city you have *good* memories of?"

"Grk!"

"See? If you let that get you down, you'll be depressed for the rest of your life. Just let it roll off your back!" he said cheerfully and patted me on the shoulder.

You know... whatever, man. You're not helping!

"Anyway. Just sighing won't—" Gourry began, then suddenly halted in place.

"Hmm? What's—" I turned back, about to ask what was wrong, when I realized it for myself. There was a faint presence lurking deep in the forest beside us.

This is...

Before I could even finish my thought, the presence was right on top of us! Gourry drew his sword and I began chanting a spell. A figure leaped out at us from the shadows of the underbrush. Gourry deflected a silent incoming slash with his blade. Our attacker then jumped away, out into the middle of the main road as if to block our path.

Oh, this thing again...

I didn't know the creature's name, so I'd taken to calling it "Shaman."

"Now... there will be... no more witnesses..." it said.

Then it dashed straight at Gourry! *Clang!* Just as their swords collided...

"Skree!" Shaman let out a cry like a raptor.

Two things happened at the same time: Gourry instinctively leaped back, and a dozen arrows of flame appeared where he'd been standing. They fired, streaking toward him! While continuing to rush back, he dodged some and knocked aside the others.

While this was unfolding, I released a spell of my own! "Zellas Bullid!" The beam of light it produced could change course midair to track its opponent, and it was powerful enough to take out most demons in one hit.

"Hraaagh!" Shaman let out another wail. A small, thin shield of light appeared beside it to block my spell.

Ha, silly demon! My beam of light shattered its shield! *I win!*

Or so I was thinking—but then Shaman effortlessly slipped out of the way to dodge by a hair.

Bwuh? My attack hooked back around for Shaman, but the thing once again summoned a shield of light and dodged when it shattered. By this point, Gourry had dealt with all the flaming arrows and was ready to get back in action, but he couldn't exactly jump in under the current circumstances. Shaman repeated the same shield-dodge play two, then three times, and...

Plink! My beam of light, at last sufficiently weakened, poofed out of existence as it pierced the last shield.

No way...

I couldn't help my astonishment. I'd seen demons tank my blasts and come out none the worse for wear. I'd even seen them evade them by shifting to the astral plane. But... this was my first time seeing one combine physical skill and minor defensive magic to neutralize a spell. Obviously, such a feat was much easier said than done. Shaman had dodged each of my beam's passes by the skin of its teeth. I'd underestimated the creature when we first met, taking it for a silly, third-rate demon... But it might be one tough cookie after all.

Shaman turned its face toward me.

"Hyah!" At the same time, Gourry stepped in with a cry and a slash.

Shaman deflected the blow and unleashed a counterattack, which Gourry blocked with his blade on the backswing. Perhaps realizing that another round of flaming arrows wouldn't be any more effective a second time, Shaman seemed intent to lock Gourry into a swordfight.

Obviously, I wasn't about to interfere. If I started chucking spells willy-nilly, I'd wind up nailing Gourry. I could charge in with my own sword to draw Shaman's attention, but at my level of skill, it was more likely that I'd just get in Gourry's way. I was basically stuck watching from the sidelines.

Still, it was clear that we wouldn't get anywhere like this. I needed a way to launch a spell into the fray without hurting my swordsman buddy...

Of course! I drew my sword and began a chant, then dashed at the two of them. Both noticed my approach and turned their attention to me.

"It's not safe, Lina! Stop!" Gourry cried.

I ignored him and pressed my charge. Just before I reached them, I changed course, got around behind Gourry, and grabbed him by the hair!

"What?!"

Then I incanted my words of power—"Lei Wing!"

Thanks to my amplified fast flight spell, we sped away from Shaman. I turned back and saw the creature first stare into space in confusion, then break into a dash.

"Ow, ow, ow! Are we running away, Lina?!"

"Heck no! That thing's already on our tail!"

Once we'd gotten sufficient distance, I set us down and dismissed my spell. Before Gourry could complain about me yanking his hair, I got behind him again and leaped up onto his back.

"H-Hey…"

Ignoring his attempt to protest, I began chanting another spell.

"Oh, I get it…" At last realizing what I was up to, Gourry turned to intercept Shaman's imminent approach.

That's right. I'd only fled in order to buy me time to chant a new spell. I was going to fire it from Gourry's back—meaning there was no way I'd hit him! I'd then jump down after I fired so that even if the spell missed, Gourry could immediately press the offensive. There was just one flaw with this plan: it looked awful silly!

I'd judged the distance perfectly, though. By the time Shaman entered Gourry's sword range, I'd already finished my spell. He blocked Shaman's strike with one of his own. I could only assume the demon was on guard for close-range magic. It could potentially dodge this no matter how abruptly I unleashed it, so I was biding my time for now.

Gourry and Shaman's swords clashed again.

Not yet…

Then a third time.

No, not y— I started to tell myself, but reevaluated.

"Bram Blazer!" I released the blue light at close range, and it consumed Shaman along with its sword!

"Graaaah!" Shaman's scream echoed through the surrounding area.

Yes!

The blue light was a shockwave that also dealt spiritual damage to an opponent. Normally it wouldn't do much against a demon, but I'd supercharged this one with my amplification chant. It wasn't going to be a one-hit takedown, though it should definitely smart!

Except, as I was thinking that, Shaman freaking *sliced the light in two*!

"What?!" I squeaked, so shocked I forgot to hop off of Gourry's back.

Shaman's sword had cut my spell right in half. It was likely that earlier howl wasn't one of pain, but an incantation. It had cast some kind of spell on its sword, allowing it to cut through mine. Perhaps Shaman had still taken some damage in the process... but if it had, it wasn't much. As if to attest to this, once it was done cleaving the blue light, it readied its sword again.

"Dam Blas!"

Clink! Just then, an attack spell struck Shaman's sword from the side and shattered it! Shaman leaped back.

"Tch... Missed," hissed a familiar voice from the patch of forest where the spell had originated.

"Looks like we just can't get enough of each other," I said breezily.

"Yeah, it's like a curse," Luke responded in a truly sour tone.

Three people emerged from the woods. First was the dour-eyed, raven-haired Luke in his swordsman's garb; second was the subdued, silver-haired Mileena. We'd been involved in incidents with these two twice before, but this time, they had a dark-haired man with them. He looked about twenty and was also dressed like a fighter, with a broadsword hanging from his hip.

Never seen this guy before. Although... Wait, nah. Bigger fish to fry here...

I looked back and saw Shaman looking carefully between its broken sword and the new trio on the scene. At least, I assumed that was what it was doing... I mean, it wasn't like the thing had eyes!

"I thought you were fighting an ordinary assassin, but I see I was mistaken," Mileena said calmly, her eyes on Shaman.

Luke nodded. "Yeah. This guy don't seem human to me." He then drew his sword and leveled it at the demon.

Shaman turned its face toward Luke and the others. "More... witnesses?" it whispered in an almost wondrous tone. It tilted its head for a while as if thinking something over, then... suddenly leaped away and disappeared into the forest. I could hear the tramping on grass grow more distant as I sensed its presence moving away.

"Huh…" I remarked.

"The damn thing ran away!" Luke shouted.

I wasn't sure if Shaman had realized it was at a disadvantage or if it had simply fled because it got confused and couldn't decide what else to do. I didn't know what to make of the disparity between its quick thinking in battle and its sluggishness otherwise… But for now, at least, it seemed safe to assume that the battle was over.

Luke apparently reached the same conclusion, sheathed his sword, and turned his gaze on me. "Looks like you got wrapped up in more weird crap, huh? Say, I gotta ask you somethin'…"

"How about I save the explanation for the nearest village?" I proposed.

But Luke clicked his tongue and wagged his finger at me. "That ain't what I meant."

"What is it, then?"

"I meant… how long are you two gonna play piggyback?"

"I told you, it was a strategy!"

"Okay, I get it. You got on his shoulders for strategic purposes and liked how it felt, so you stayed there. Mmhmm. I can just see how close you two are. It was perfect—like a spirit and the possessed."

We'd stopped at an eatery in the closest town and put in our orders. Luke had yet to shut up about my piggyback ride, and I could feel a vein throbbing in my forehead.

"Nnnngh… You need to drop this one, buddy."

"Tease 'em while the teasin's good. That's my motto."

"What's wrong with a piggyback ride? Shouldn't we talk about—"

"Shut up, Gourry. Well, Luke, that's quite a motto you've got! It sure explains why Mileena's so sick of you."

"Geh?! Wh-What're you talkin' about?! Mileena always says, 'That's what I love best about you—'"

"I never say that," Mileena interrupted, expression unchanged.

"Ha! See?"

"Hey, Lina…"

"I told you to stuff it, Gourry. I'm getting to the good part!"

"The good part?"

"Snerk! Luke's got a one-sided crush on Mileena and he follows her around everywhere against her will!"

"Y-You shut up! Get it straight, okay? Mileena's my—"

"Your what?" It was Mileena, not I, who cut him off cold. Luke went abashedly silent. Before he could say anything else, Mileena turned to me. "Now, who was that man you were fighting? His presence suggested a demon, but..." She sounded a bit doubtful.

There was a lot about Shaman that didn't seem demonic. The fact that it was wielding a sword that could be broken with a Dam Blas, its slow reactions... I could understand why Mileena had questions about its nature, but its aura definitely said "demon" to me. I'd met demon fusions—syntheses of human and demon—before, and this was totally different. Shaman actually had the kind of cold hostility that your brass demon-level creatures emit. I guess, at the very least, it couldn't be a very high-ranking demon...

"I don't know exactly what it is either. This shouldn't take too long to explain, but two nights ago— Ah!" I unconsciously cried out.

It had finally clicked. The man traveling with Luke and Mileena... I'd never met him before, but his face was naggingly familiar, and I'd just realized why. He looked like the man Shaman had killed that night. Not a dead ringer, just... similar. Brothers, maybe?

"What is it?" Mileena asked bluntly.

"Oh... nothing," I said hesitantly as I sipped at my qaran juice. The resemblance could just be a coincidence, after all, and I could always ask him about it after I heard his story. "Anyway, two nights ago, that creature... I don't know its name, so I'm just calling it Shaman. I happened upon it right after it had killed someone. Since then, it's been after us, claiming it has to kill witnesses. The guy it killed was in his nightgown and staying at an inn, and Shaman blew up his room right after... so I still don't know who he was, but..." With that, I cast a glance at the man accompanying Mileena and Luke.

"You want to know about him? He's our current employer," Mileena said, interpreting the gesture as the cue to introduce him. She then shared a look with Luke.

Luke nodded slightly. "Sorry for the late introduction. This is Jade, um…"

"Caudwell. Jade Caudwell," the man muttered in response to Luke's prompting.

There was something palpably somber in his voice and expression. He sounded like a man going through some *serious* stuff.

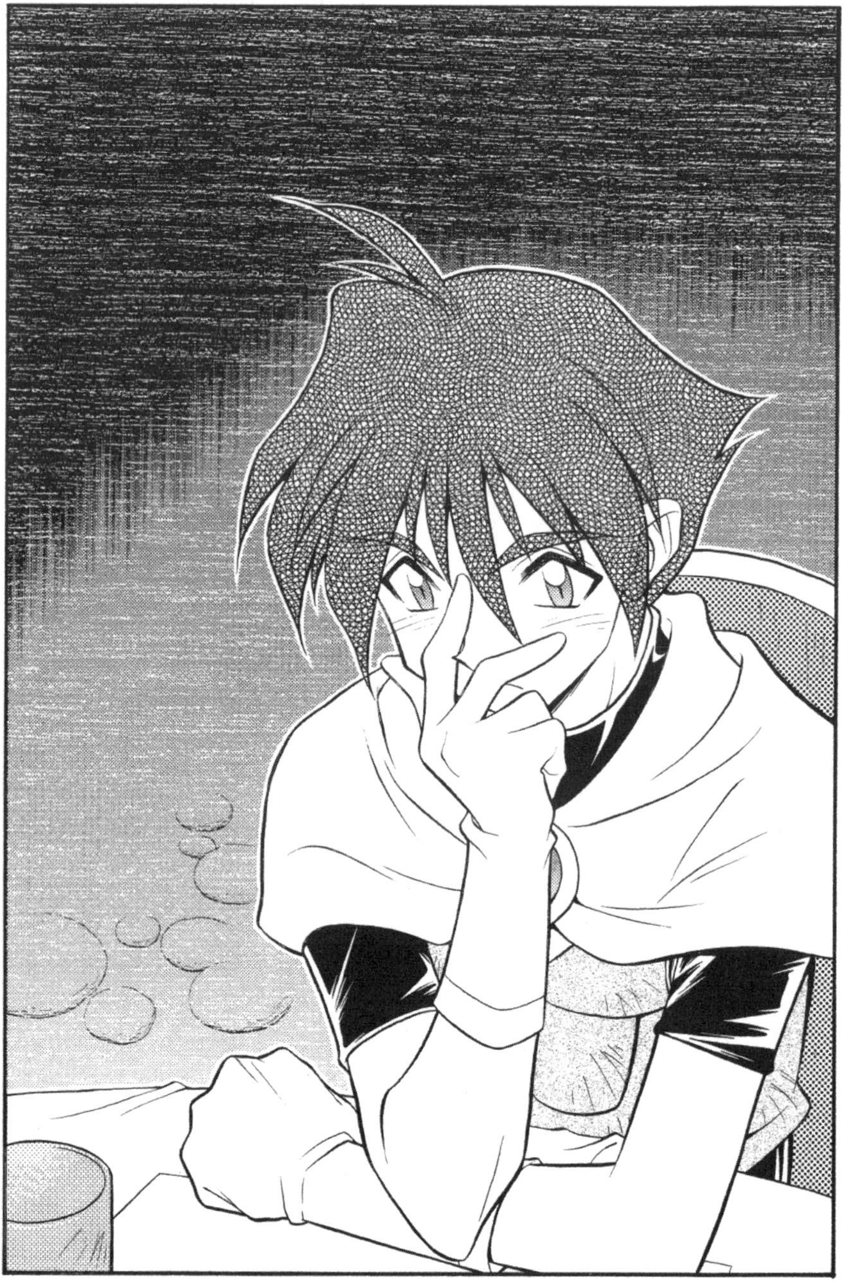

"Truth is, there's some pretty weird shit going down right now in Dils's capital, Gyria City. He went to inform the local lords, 'cept none of 'em would talk to him. But he ran into us and spilled the whole story," Luke explained without my asking.

"H-Hang on a minute here," I had to insist. "Are you sure you wanna tell us all this? You're not trying to drag us into it, are you?"

"Just hear me out. A while back... About a year now, I guess? I'm bettin' you've heard about it. There was this big, mysterious fire in Gyria. The whole place and its army ended up in ruins."

"Yeah, I'm aware..."

"The city's finally back on its feet... The army not so much. After all, even if you hire new recruits, it takes 'em a while to train into proper soldiers, right? So they've been recruitin' mercenaries to bolster up their forces quick."

"I do feel like I heard about that somewhere..." Gourry said, chewing on a baguette sandwich he'd ordered as an appetizer. It was like he'd forgotten he was a mercenary himself or something...

"Well, one of the mercenaries was head an' shoulders above the rest. The king decided he liked 'em and promoted 'em in a hurry, and now there ain't a thing that happens in the kingdom without their say-so. Things've been weird ever since."

"Yeah, you sometimes see ambitious types like that zooming up the ranks," I said as if it wasn't my problem in the slightest...

Which, I mean, it wasn't! This person was upending the kingdom's status quo, and Jade was probably asking the local lords to do something about it, but I could see why none of them would be willing to tackle the task. This is what the big brains like to call an "internal affair." No lord was going to poke their nose into an issue that thorny. I sure as hell wouldn't. So... while I didn't know whether it was Luke or Mileena who'd accepted the job, either way, it was kinda odd that they would.

As if Luke read my mind, he said, "If I'm honest, I didn't wanna get involved either at first. I changed my mind when he told me the new big-shot mercenary was a gal named Sherra."

"What?!" The name drew an involuntary shout from my throat.

Not so long ago, Gourry, Luke, Mileena, and I had thrown down with Sherra, the General in service to Dynast Graushera and wielder of the demonic sword Dulgoffa. I'd managed to improvise a way to get her off our backs at the time, but…

Mind you, it was possible that this was a completely different person with the same name. Given how we knew that General Sherra was already actively scheming in the vicinity, though, it seemed safe to assume it was her and that she was up to no good here as well. Speculatively speaking, she also might be the one behind the current demidemon spawnings. The timeline on that and her most recent mischief matched up too well. But what was her motive? And what was she up to in Gyria City now?

"No one knows what she's plannin', of course," Luke said gravely. He then indicated Jade with his eyes. "From what he's said about her, the name ain't just a coincidence. She's *that* Sherra for sure. Which means she's got more on her mind than a cushy castle post. Jade says his dad was a general in the royal army, an' he kept tellin' the king she was bad news, but he wouldn't freakin' listen. And then the chief retainers opposin' Sherra started disappearin' one after another. So his dad decided to get word out to the local lords…"

"And sent him as the messenger?" I asked.

Jade nodded. "I visited several local lords, but they all rejected my petition, saying it wasn't a matter they were fit to deal with. And… it's true. When I try to explain it, it really does sound like pure internal politics. Except… something about it feels… wrong."

"How so?" I prompted.

Jade frowned uncertainly. "That's… difficult to articulate. This feels like more than some mere power struggle. It just… smells different."

"Smells different, huh? Good instincts, bud," Luke put in.

"Er?" Jade asked, confused.

His mercenary companion waved his hand dismissively. "Ah, we'll explain later. Anyway, keep goin'."

"Right. I believe my brother was also sent out with my father's petition… but I suspect he fared no better than I did."

"Your brother?" I looked up. "You mean there was a messenger besides you?"

"Yes, there was. Why do you ask?"

Was I supposed to tell him, or not? It could have been a total coincidence, after all…

"I might be barking up the wrong tree here... Just stay calm and hear me out, okay? The man I mentioned earlier that was killed by Shaman... He looked a lot like you."

There was a considerable silence. Then, seeming to realize what I was getting at, Jade cast his eyes downward.

"Er, of course, it's possible that I'm imagining the resemblance and it was somebody else. It happened in a city one day's travel south of here... Want to go check?" I asked.

The man remained silent for a while, then shook his head slowly. "No... if it's not my brother, it would be a waste of time. And if it is... all the more reason for me to return to Gyria as quickly as possible with help."

"Okay. Got it." Unsure of what else to say, I just nodded my acceptance.

In the silence that followed, I felt someone tug on my cape. I looked over and found Gourry staring at me, clearly hoping for an explanation.

"So, it sounds like," I said, scratching my head, "there's real bad news going on in Gyria City, and we need to figure out if we should go there or not."

"Oh. You should've said that from the start," he replied cheerfully.

Hmm. Guess he wasn't following the convo at all...

"Er..." Jade started to look worried.

Luke waved his hand again. "Ah, don't worry. He's just that kind of guy."

"I see..."

"So, are we going to Gyria City, Lina?" Gourry asked.

"Yeah, we are," I answered confidently.

I couldn't look the other way after everything I'd heard.

The trip to Gyria City was eerily uneventful. Of course, this is the part where I add "so far."

We didn't forget to ask the people in the towns we stopped at along the way about any demon-swarming incidents they'd been party to. Of course, since we were trying to make good time, we were doing a pretty half-assed job of it. Every now and then we'd hear another story of the so-called "white giant," but nothing they could tell me really clarified what it was or what it had to do with anything. But even more worrying than that...

"It's weird he hasn't attacked us since then," Gourry muttered as we were enjoying a late dinner four days out from Gyria City.

We were in the kind of eatery-slash-bar you'd find in any little town. It was well past dinnertime, but plenty of people had come to drink, so the place was pretty packed.

"Who hasn't?" Luke asked insufferably, apparently blind to my careful ignoring of Gourry's comment.

"You know, the demon in black who attacked me and Lina before," the big lug continued.

"Do you mean the one you called Shaman?" Mileena chimed in.

Guh!

"It's true that we haven't seen it for some time. Is it possible it gave up?" Jade added.

You guys! Come on!

"What do you think, Lina?" Gourry inquired.

"Don't ask me, damn it!" I shouted without meaning to.

Everyone looked at me in surprise.

"Hey, Lina. Where'd that come from?"

"Aaargh! Don't you know how these things work?! When you say 'that demon hasn't attacked us in a while,' that's precisely when the demon attacks! It's a law of the universe!"

"I-Is it really?"

"Yes! That's why I'm decidedly attempting to avoid the subject!"

"Oh, don't be stupid. There's no way—"

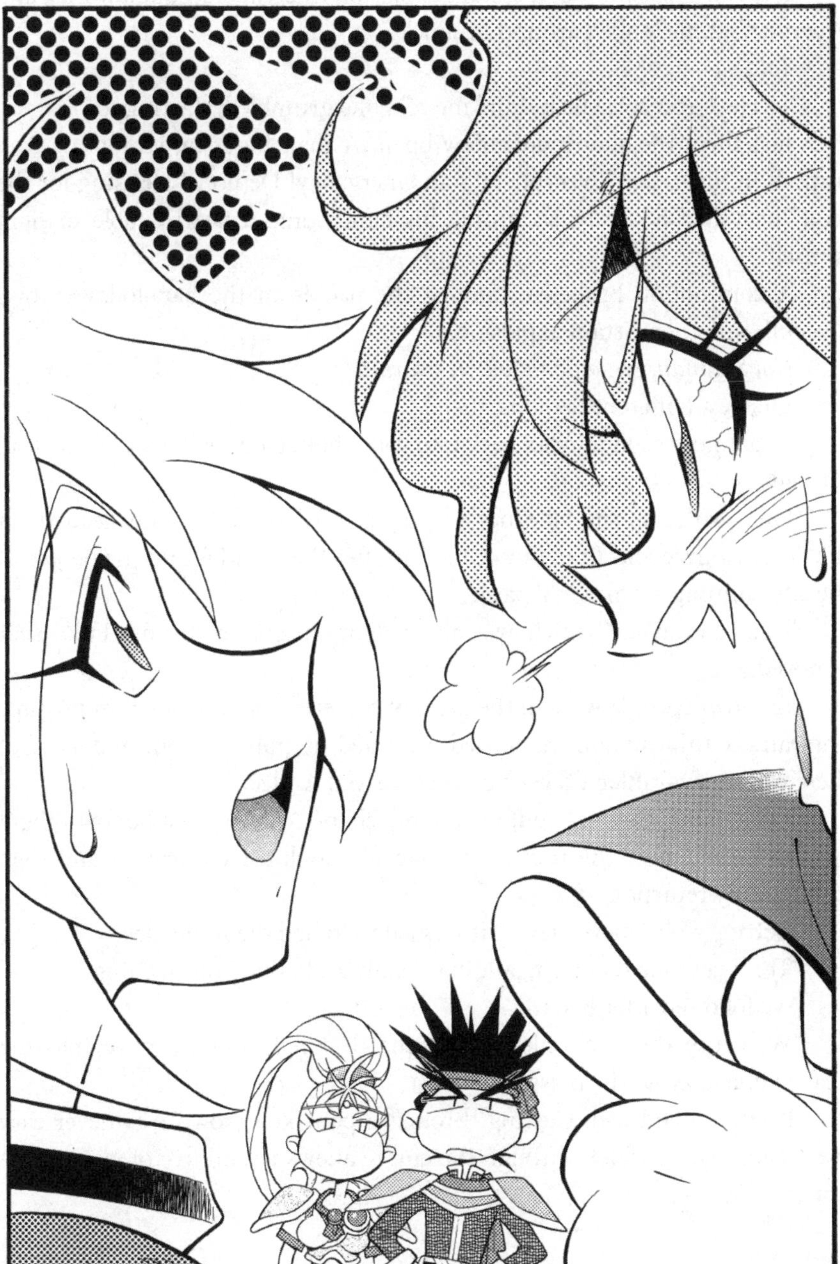

Fwoom! The sound of a distant explosion interrupted Luke's words, and everyone but me looked around in shock.

Told ya!

"H-Hey! You gotta be kiddin' me..." Luke grumbled, starting to rise.

Just then, the shop's door flew open. A man burst in, stumbling over himself in his haste. "Everyone, it's an emergency! Demons! Heading for the city!" he yelled hoarsely, slamming his hands onto a nearby table to right himself.

A commotion broke out among the people in the bar, followed by—*Fwoom!*—another distant explosion.

Not Shaman, but a demidemon swarm?!

"Oh, hey. Different demons, then."

"That's no reason to relax back into your chair, Gourry! It's still a big deal! C'mon!"

Luke, Mileena, and Jade, not needing my orders, had already headed out the door. Gourry and I ran out of the bar after them and found the people of the city running around in a panic.

"I can't even tell which way the demons're comin' from!" Luke spat, annoyed.

The townspeople were in the grips of hysteria, which made it impossible to glean the information we needed. I wanted to grab someone and ask, but there was no guarantee I'd get a correct answer. And so...

"Levitation!" Before I could begin my chant, Mileena cast her own flight spell to ascend over the roof of the bar. She took a look around and then immediately returned.

Getting a bird's-eye view... It seemed we'd had the same idea.

"This way," she reported, landing cleanly and taking off running.

We followed after her.

"We'll use the back alleys," Mileena declared, and we dove into the nearest one to avoid the masses.

It was a good call. Cutting through a panicked crowd was never easy. We turned right and left through the empty alleyways, all five of us in a line, until...

"?!"

When we came back out onto the main avenue, Mileena stopped. I ran out right behind her. And we saw... nobody at all. The street looked completely deserted.

"Are you sure this was the right way? We didn't take a wrong turn?" Jade asked.

"Don't be stupid. My Mileena's got a perfect sense of direction!" Luke protested in response, subtle self-interest and all. (Typical.)

"I'm not yours," Mileena objected, putting him in his place. (Also typical.)

"This is more than just going the wrong way," I murmured. "The noise is completely gone."

"Ah!" Jade cried out, apparently just now noticing that.

Indeed, the panicked voices we'd been hearing all this time had stopped entirely.

Jade looked around in a fluster, as perhaps this was his first experience with the phenomenon. "Wh-What's going on here?!"

"It's a barrier," I responded.

"Exactly," a new, deep voice replied.

Chapter 2:   The Shadows Lurking in Gyria

"What's that?" Jade whispered, turning his eyes to a narrow alley some distance away.

Yeah... Guess it's a pretty bizarre sight to someone who's never seen one of those *before.*

The figure, clad in a tattered black cape, was more or less humanoid... but anyone could tell that this thing *wasn't* human. The skin that covered its haggard—rather, abnormally wiry—body had the darkening of a necrotic corpse. Its face had no ears, nose, mouth, or hair—just two exceptionally large, wide-open eyes gazing glassily in our direction.

"That would be... a pure demon, yeah," I muttered in response.

Unlike demidemons—brass demons and lesser demons—which had to possess and transmogrify animals in order to manifest in our world, pure demons could manifest here entirely under their own power. Needless to say, that meant they were a heck of a lot stronger than demidemons.

"It's warped space itself to trap us here," I explained.

"Ohh. Very knowledgeable of you," the thing said, impressed with—or perhaps mocking—me.

"Well, I've been around the block a few times. But you didn't come here to make small talk, did you?"

"Certainly not. My business with you is even more trivial than that..." The bug-eyed demon began to walk down the avenue with a gliding gait. "I'd just like to ask you to die."

"Get back, Jade. Normal swords can't hurt this thing. And... be careful. It's probably not the only enemy here."

"Impressive insight. Come, you two!"

Two? As the bug-eyed demon called out, I felt a wave of hostility cast in my direction. *One's... above!*

Before I could even look up, Gourry had his sword out of its sheath. Talk about déjà vu!

Zing! I heard a hard ringing sound over my head. A moment later, the attacker landed on the street in front of me, then leaped back to put space between us.

Shaman... I knew it! Indeed, I'd expected that much, but... another hostile aura was now emerging from an alley opposite where Bug-Eyes had appeared. It was about as tall as a human and held swords in both hands. It was all black, like Shaman, but it had an entirely different upstairs situation going on. It wasn't that it had a different face—more that it didn't even have anything *resembling* a face. Where a head would normally be, it instead had a set of long, thin protrusions, almost like serpent heads, each about as thick as a child's wrist. It was like someone had transplanted a small hydra onto the thing's neck.

"Three of them?!" Mileena shouted out in a rare show of nerves.

Bug-Eyes let out a low laugh. "Well, three superior beings does seem a bit much to take out a mere five human rats... but orders are orders."

"Would those orders be from Sherra, then?" I asked calmly.

He narrowed his eyes. "Just who are you, scum?"

"Someone you prooobably shouldn't be calling scum..."

"I don't know how much you know... but it seems I really must dispose of you!" He swung his right hand as he spoke, producing spears of miasma midair—which he released in our direction! We all immediately scattered to dodge.

"Gourry, take Shaman! Luke, Mileena, you two get Hydra! I'll handle Bug-Eyes!"

"That ain't up to you!" Luke argued, albeit while following orders and dashing toward the demon I'd dubbed Hydra.

With a battle cry, Gourry slashed at Shaman. And then...

"My name is Rebifor!" raged the bug-eyed demon as I charged him, chanting under my breath. "I applaud your courage in facing me alone! But do not give me such a trivializing name!" His left hand flashed forward as he chastised me, sending a black blade my way!

I dodged to the side while unleashing my spell: "Elemekia Lance!"

"Fool!" Rebifor swept it away with his left hand. "You can't harm me like that!"

Looking slightly shaken, I drew the sword at my waist, then picked up chanting and resumed closing in on my foe. I dodged another miasma spear he fired and dove in close, thrusting as I did! The strike sunk deep into Rebifor's side. The demon's eyes narrowed in the suggestion of a smile.

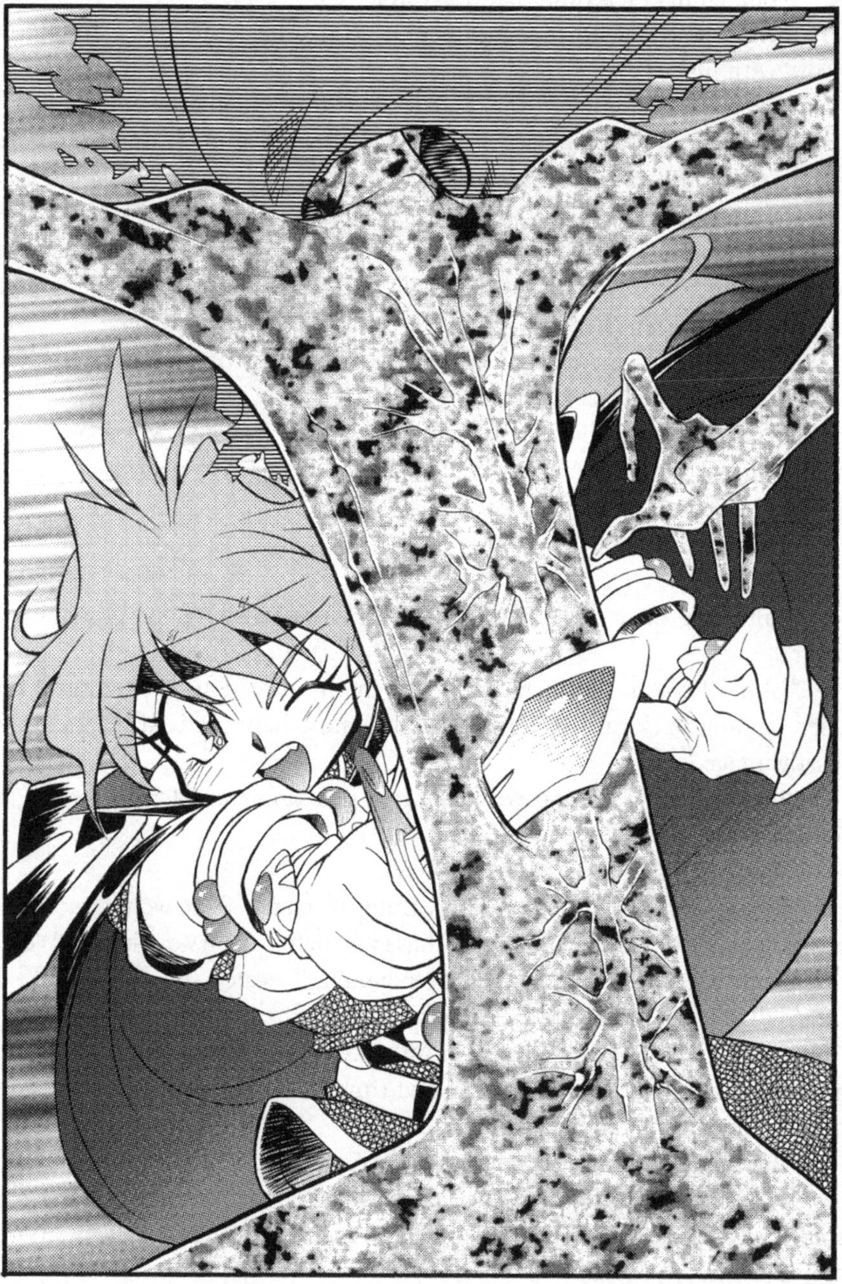

"Fool! Didn't I tell you? That won't wor—"

Before he could finish, I incanted, "Astral Vine!" The spell infused my sword with magic!

"Gaaaaah!" Rebifor screamed as he leaped back and away. I'd probably done some damage, but that wasn't enough to kill him. "Curse you!" He glowered at me after gaining his distance.

Seemed he'd finally put it together. My initial simplistic attack, combined with my rattled demeanor, was all a ploy to get his guard down. I locked eyes with Rebifor, whose gaze was now cautious. While gauging distance and positioning, I began chanting again.

"Elemekia Lance! Luke! Mileena!" With my eyes still locked on Rebifor, I unleashed my spell—at Hydra!

Fortunately, my shouting was enough to get Luke and Mileena diving out of the way. Despite being blindsided, Hydra managed to evade too, but the act left the demon off-balance...

"Bram Blazer!"

"Fell Zaleyd!"

...allowing Luke and Mileena to blow it away with a good ol' one-two combo!

"Gkh!" Rebifor shot a hostile glare in my direction. "Withdraw!" he cried, sliding backward into the alley. He must have realized he was at a disadvantage.

Shaman, still clashing with Gourry, also tumbled back in retreat at Rebifor's call.

"They're getting away!" Jade shouted.

"It's not safe to pursue," I said calmly in response. It would certainly save us trouble down the line to give chase and defeat them now, but... "We're still inside their barrier, so we'd never be able to catch them. More likely, they'd divide our forces and pick us off."

Rebifor and Shaman had been unlucky to lose Hydra out of the gate, but they wouldn't be so cavalier the next time we crossed paths. We'd be the unlucky ones if we underestimated them.

"But then how do we get out of this barrier, Lina?" Gourry asked.

"It'll probably dispel itself once Rebifor leaves it. The question is what comes after that. The next time we fight them, they'll probably be more prepar—"

I was interrupted by the abrupt return of the hustle and bustle of the city. The avenue, empty moments ago, was suddenly brimming with people. It looked like Rebifor's barrier had been lifted.

"Huh. Guess you were right," Luke remarked.

"But we still have work to do," Mileena added.

Though it should have looked like we'd appeared out of thin air to the people around us, nobody batted an eye. This stood to reason—they had bigger things to worry about. We'd driven Rebifor and his goons away, but there was still a whole demidemon horde to handle. We swiftly took off down the road, tearing through the crowd...

And then, all five of us came to a stop at once. We'd hit the plaza at the city's northern entrance, lined with empty stalls and shops and otherwise devoid of people. Beyond the gate, we could see a writhing mass of figures pouring down the road toward town.

"No way..."

"Those are all..." someone said hoarsely as we stood there.

They were far enough away that I couldn't say exactly how many there were, but it was definitely more than you could count on your fingers... and toes.

"Wh-What do we even do? I'm thinkin' this crowd might be more trouble than those pure demons..." Luke whispered, staring blankly.

As for me, however... "Hah! It might mess up the road, but I'll blast 'em all away before they even reach us!" I said, moving straight into a chant.

Thou who art darker than twilight

Thou who art redder than lifeblood

That's right, time to whip out the ol' Dragon Slave! Numbers were no object when it came to blowing up bottom-feeding demons with this puppy! Except...

"Hey, what's that white thing?" Gourry suddenly asked.

Just then, I saw a flash. And in that moment...

"What?!" I cried, so alarmed that I dropped my chant. There was a flash in the distance, and all the demons around it went flying.

"What was that?!" Luke shouted.

"What happened?!" Mileena followed.

Gourry, who had the best vision of us all, could apparently see what was going down, but the rest of us were in the dark.

"I'm going to try to get closer!" I said, dashing out before anyone could respond.

While I was running, the light pulsed a second time, then a third. Each flash mowed through more demons. And then...

I don't know how far I'd gotten before I finally stopped in my tracks, silent. By then, there was barely any of the demon swarm left to fight.

Kra-pash! Light audibly ripped through the air, and even more demons were blown away. The source of the blasts tearing up the ground and demons alike was...

"Is that... the white giant?" I muttered like a woman in a trance.

The villager we'd talked to earlier had described the white giant as a small mountain. That was clearly an exaggeration, but I couldn't fault the guy for using the word "giant" when it was definitely a good size bigger than the already hulking demidemons. Its white body glowed with a dazzling light. Its general shape was humanoid, but its head was half-sunk into its shoulders. It looked a little like an alabaster golem, if one sculpted with a lot of artistic license.

"Say, Lina... you ever seen anything like that before?" Gourry asked.

"Nope. Not as far as I can recall," I responded, still entranced.

The giant fired another blast of light from the palm of its outstretched right hand. More brass and lesser demons hit the ground. There was scarcely a sign of demon movement around us now. Without so much as a glance at its silently gawking audience (that is, us), the giant turned around and began to walk away.

"It's... It's leaving," Luke whispered.

Nobody responded. None of us knew how to react to what we'd just seen. If the giant was polishing off demons, it didn't appear to be an immediate threat. But that didn't mean it was safe to assume it was on our side either. At last, as we watched it go...

"Huh?"

The white giant literally vanished.

"What *was* that thing?!" Jade shouted, but no one knew what to tell him. If not for the demon corpses littering the ground around us, I would've said we were dreaming or hallucinating.

"Well, regardless… standing around here won't get us anywhere. Let's inform the townspeople that the danger has more or less passed," I proposed.

"True… Reassuring them comes first," Jade agreed.

"But I'm gonna say that *we* beat the demons and snag us a nice reward!"

"Hey, great idea!" Luke was on board. But…

"How dare you!" Jade objected. "That's fraud! We didn't do a thing!"

"Oh, but we did! We watched encouragingly as the giant did *its* thing!"

"Which provided no help whatsoever!"

"Grow up, man," Luke cut in. "Actions deserve rewards just as much as results do."

"But we didn't *act*! The fight was resolved entirely without us!"

"Sheesh… so argumentative."

"No, you are!"

Luke and I tried our best to persuade Jade, but either out of integrity or sheer bloody-mindedness, he refused to relent. He turned to Gourry and Mileena for backup. "Surely you agree with me! Please, say something!"

"Huh? Like what?" Gourry asked.

"Platitudes will only get you so far in this world," replied Mileena.

"Waaagh! Stop it!" Jade cried, cradling his head.

I could understand lamenting Mileena's reaction, but it was definitely his bad for counting on Gourry.

"B-But I'm still a noble knight of Dils… I can't be a party to such a sham," he muttered, and at last stood up decisively. "Very well! Do as you like! However, I'm going to tell the people what really ha—"

"Sleeping."

Thump! Zzzzz…

"Okay! With that settled, I'm gonna head back to town and spread the word!"

Leaving Jade in his magical slumber, I scurried off.

Cresting the hill brought into sight a metropolis surrounded by a wall—the capital of the Kingdom of Dils, Gyria.

"Home at last," Jade said wistfully as he looked down at the distant city. He'd been a little testy since the demon attack for some reason, but the sight of his hometown was apparently enough to put him back in good spirits.

"Sorry to ruin the moment, but this ain't the time to get nostalgic," Luke said in a far grimmer tone as he stepped up next to Jade. "Makin' it here means the real fight's about to start."

He was right. Rebifor and Shaman were undoubtedly acting on the orders of Sherra, who was here in this town. The fact that they hadn't made a move on us since our last encounter suggested they were focusing their forces here in the city, ready to attack once we arrived.

Sherra alone was already a hell of an opponent to face. And while we were lucky to have made it this far, there was still no guarantee we'd come out on top. To be honest, part of me was still considering hightailing it outta here and pretending we'd never heard about any of this... But I knew that wasn't a real option.

I couldn't say exactly what was afoot, but if a General-class demon had her fingers in the pie, it was probably a lot scarier than your average kingdom hijack. If we passed on our chance to do something about it, there was zero possibility that it would just resolve on its own. We had to strike before it was too late.

I'd have appreciated some help, but the sorcerers' council wouldn't believe us if we told them. Two former traveling companions came to mind as potential allies, but one of them was way off in Saillune and the other was who-knows-where. We probably didn't have time to track them down.

Well... guess we've just gotta do it, I thought to myself with a faint internal sigh as I and my four companions began heading down the hill... Down the road to Gyria City.

"I'm sorry, but we can't allow you in," the young soldier said awkwardly as he blocked our path with his halberd.

We'd just reached one of the gates set into the wall around Gyria.

"Wh-What are you talking about?" Jade asked, understandably stunned by this unwelcoming stance.

I probably don't need to tell you that the purpose of having a big wall around a castle town like this was to protect it from outside invaders—rival kingdoms waging war, hordes of rampaging monsters, that sort of thing. Generally speaking, ordinary folk coming and going from a city didn't undergo too much scrutiny. Enforcing excessive restrictions requires manpower, after all, and discourages trade and tourism, which creates stagnation in the economy. And indeed, even as the soldier blocked our way, we could see traveling minstrels, merchants, and others still pouring in.

Obviously, I'd expect blatantly suspicious characters and wanted criminals to be barred, but anyone who looked normal enough and had a plausible reason for entering the city should be good to go. Plus, at a time like this, I'd wager that even someone who *did* look kinda shady would still be allowed in as long as they claimed to be mercenaries responding to the call.

And yet we were denied entry, even with the local knight Jade in our company?

"This is absurd! I'm going to repeat myself... I am Jade Caudwell, knight of the second squadron of the Blue Knights of Gyria Palace, returning from a mission! I vouch for the four people traveling with me! Why is that not enough?!" Jade demanded, his voice rising.

But the soldier responded awkwardly, "Actually... I know who you are. That's why I can't let you in."

"What's that supposed to mean?"

"Those... were my orders."

"Orders?"

"Yes... Regarding you and your brother Grya..."

"What are they?! Stop stammering and tell me!"

"Ah... well... you were stripped of your titles for going AWOL..."

"What?!"

"So... we were told not to let you in... even if you returned."

Stripped of their titles and exiled?! That seemed excessively harsh, even to third parties like us, and the news was clearly an incredible shock to the man himself.

"Who... Who decreed that?!" he inquired.

"Well... it was..." The young soldier broke into a sweat under the gaze of the other soldiers around him. "General Allus..."

"General Allus?!" Jade sputtered angrily.

The soldier continued defensively, "Well, he said our liege authorized it... so I couldn't exactly argue..." He was referring to the king, of course.

"Fine, then. It's not your fault. If we can't get in, we can't get in... but could I ask you for a favor? Would you please pass on a message to my father, General Grancis Caudwell?"

"Well… actually…" The soldier fell into awkward silence again.

"What? Don't tell me you were ordered not even to pass along messages on my behalf…"

"No, it's just that General Grancis… He passed away… of illness."

It was now Jade's turn to fall into silence. He simply stood there, stunned.

The tavern that night was boisterous. The smell of alcohol filled the room, as did the bragging of drunkards, occasionally punctuated by raucous laughter. Our table was the only quiet one.

We were in the bar on the first floor of an inn in a small town next to Gyria. Its size was surprising given its proximity to the capital, but perhaps travelers rarely stopped in, instead choosing to make the last leg to the big city.

"So, I gotta ask…" Luke piped up around the time we finished eating our dinner, as if something had just occurred to him. "Just who is this General Allus guy? When his name came up this afternoon, you acted like you had a history…"

Jade took a sip of his radda wine, then responded, "He's the leader of the Red Knights. I know it's poor character to gossip, but I've never heard much good about him. They say he didn't exactly come by his current position honestly, and he frequently locked horns with my proper-to-a-fault father. He's also the one who first promoted Sherra and introduced her to our liege. Father believed he was trying to curry favor with the king."

"Hmm… So a bad guy, is what you're saying," Luke summarized, taking a bite of fried pork. "What's the plan now, Master Jade?"

"What do you mean?" Jade asked, his brow furrowing.

"You know. Dad gone, title gone, and now you're locked out. Sounds like you don't owe this kingdom nothin' no more."

Sheesh, dude! Have a little heart!

"All things bein' equal, you still feel like you need to stop Sherra and fix things here? Even if it puts you in danger? I gotta be honest. Seems like it'd be easier to move somewhere else an' find someone new to serve. How 'bout Zephilia? I hear good things about the queen there."

Jade remained silent for a while, then downed the rest of his cup. "No… I still love my kingdom."

"Gotcha," Luke said, then poured Jade his next round.

"Moreover... I have my doubts," Jade confessed after taking another drink. "For my father to die of illness at a time like this... That's a little too convenient, don't you think?"

"You suspect murder?" Mileena muttered. Jade nodded.

He had a point. General Allus was Jade's father's rival, and he'd also sponsored Sherra. General Grancis, suspicious, had sent his sons to seek the aid of local lords... and then kicked the bucket while they were gone. It was natural to suspect that either Allus or Sherra might resort to drastic measures to get him out of the way. And since the guy I pegged for Jade's brother had been killed by Shaman, who was also presumably working for Sherra, I wouldn't be surprised if his father had met a similar fate.

"If it's true... then at the very least, I want to find out who did it."

"All righty... Then our next step's obvious. We gotta cook up a plan," Luke announced.

"Yeah. We're up against a pretty tough opponent, after all," I said in agreement.

Of course, having a plan wouldn't guarantee our victory. Silly name or not, Sherra was Dynast's personal General. Now, when it comes to demons, sometimes there's a wild disparity in strength between individuals sharing similar titles—like the Priest of the Beast having power equivalent to the General and Priest of the Dragon combined—but we're still dealing with a totally different league than your average grunt-level demons. I'm talking "mountains to pebbles" different. Charging in with no plan at all would be suicide.

"First, let's take stock of what we got. Three of us can use black or shamanistic magic. As for the other two..." Luke looked at Gourry first. "You guys said you were lookin' for magic swords, right? Seemed like you found a pretty decent one in Solaria... Found a better one since?"

"No, he's still using that one," I responded for him. "It's sharp, it's durable, and it can deflect most spells. It also seems like it can do some damage to demons—but only *some*, so don't expect any sure kills against a powerful foe."

"Gotcha." Luke thought for a minute. "Mine's only on the upper end of decent, blade-wise, but it can absorb a single spell."

"It can absorb a spell?!"

"Yeah. When I'm fightin' normally, it'll employ an effect similar to the spell it's absorbed. So if you hit it with an Elemekia Lance in advance, that gives it the power to cut through demons."

"That's totally awesome!"

"I can also fire the stored spell. No need for a chant—I just will the sword to do it and it does. Pretty good for catchin' someone off guard, but then it's a normal sword again until it gets a new spell cast on it. That said, in either case, the spell's less powerful than it would be straight from the caster's mouth. The main problem is, I don't have a great idea of how strong a spell the sword can really stand. So if I get desperate an' cast somethin' too powerful on it, it might just break altogether."

"Hmm…"

"So, how about we split up the magic swords between the two non-casters?"

"Good idea."

In other words, distribute our resources wisely. Without a blade capable of fighting demons, Jade had been sidelined during our fight against Rebifor. If we had to face greater numbers in the future, a helpless Jade would seriously weigh us down.

"Then how about if Jade takes Gourry's sword, and Gourry takes Luke's?" I proposed.

Mileena nodded in silent response.

"Er… you're all making it sound like demons are all we're going to fight," Jade cut in.

Luke paused our sword-swapping discussion in realization. "Oh… right, we ain't told him." He thought for a minute, then scratched at his cheek. "Let's see, how to put this… It's kind of a long story, but, uh… I'll be blunt. Sherra's a demon."

There was a moment of silence.

"Excuse me?" Jade asked, dumbstruck by this totally un-sugarcoated reveal.

"Like I said, she's a demon. Follows that she'd be surrounded by demons, right?"

"But… she just looks like an ordinary woman…"

"The stronger they get, the more human they appear. They also get better at concealing their demonic presences."

"Ah… is that how it works?" Jade asked vaguely, as if he didn't entirely believe us.

"Anyway, our first task is to get into the city… which I guess means we're hidin' out at your place, Master Jade," Luke proposed.

Jade looked unhappy about the idea. "But… my mother passed when I was young. If my father's dead and I'm exiled, then it's possible they've confiscated all my assets…"

"Oh, c'mon, it ain't like they'd tear the place down overnight. Anyway, step one is gettin' inside the city. We'll spend tonight restin' to build up our stamina, then really get rollin' on the plan tomorrow. You with me?" Luke asked.

We all nodded in agreement.

The ruckus in the bar had died down some time ago. The hours crept by in the stagnant darkness.

"Ah! I can't sleep!" I shouted as I leaped out of bed, probably sometime around midnight.

At times like these, a warm meal would send me right to dreamland. I doubted the bar-slash-restaurant downstairs was still open, but I nevertheless got dressed, left my room, and headed for the first-floor eatery. Despite my expectations of disappointment, I found the lights on as well as a certain compatriot…

"Mileena?"

Yup. The silver-haired mercenary was seated at a corner table, nursing her way through a bottle of wine.

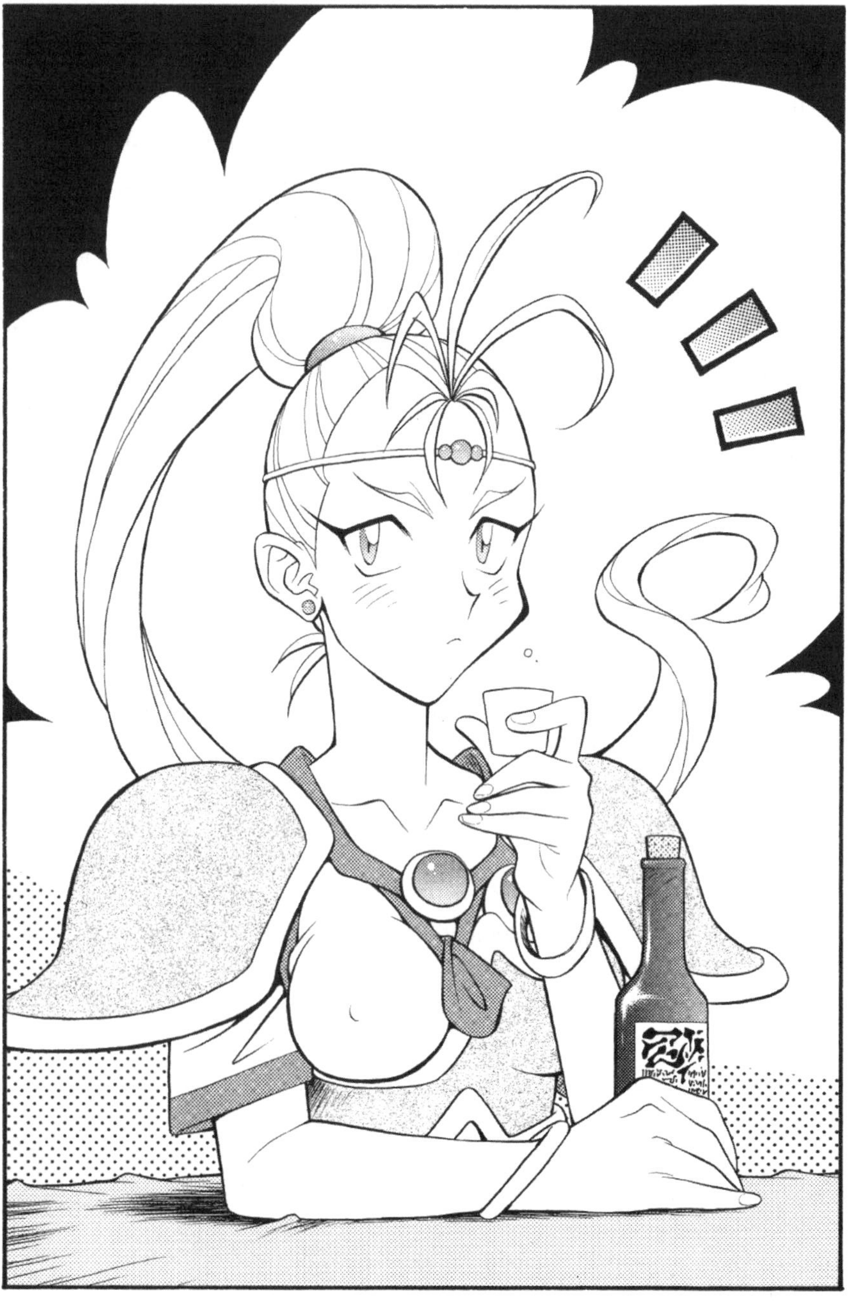

"What are you doing here by yourself?" I asked. "Oh, hey, innkeep. Got anything hot to eat?"

"I could warm up what's left of the stew."

"Sure, sounds great." I put in my order and sat down across from the bar's only other patron. "Couldn't sleep either?"

"I suppose not…" she responded listlessly, taking another sip of her drink.

I couldn't blame her. We'd be heading into Gyria City the following night, and since time was of the essence, we might end up going straight to the palace for a showdown with Sherra. Knowing we were about to pick a fight with the General of the Dynast, a serious business demon, wasn't exactly conducive to R & R.

"Come to think of it… I don't find myself in situations like this very often," I admitted.

"Situations like what?" she asked.

"You know. Just us girls talking. Luke's always with you, after all."

"And Master Gourry is always with you."

I scratched at the tip of my nose. "Well… he *does* call himself my guardian. That said, I'm the one who makes most of the money, so he's more a gigolo than anything. You mind if I ask, Mileena, why you travel with Luke?"

Mileena was silent for a while, a smile hanging on the corners of her mouth. "Because I'm very awkward," she replied enigmatically.

Um…

"You mean—" I started, then found myself turning around.

The dim restaurant interior, the lamp swaying from the ceiling, the dingy walls—everything looked exactly as it had before. I thought I'd felt a strange presence for a moment, though… Was it just my imagination?

"You didn't imagine that," Mileena interjected as if she'd read my mind. She then rose to her feet and put a hand on her sword. "The innkeeper has disappeared."

I whipped around and saw she was right. The man who'd previously been visible beyond the counter in the kitchen was now nowhere to be seen. "Then do you think…"

She nodded in response. "We're back inside a barrier."

"Heh heh. You've certainly let your guard down. Or are you simply that confident?" A deep voice echoed through the dark room.

Where is he?! I looked all around and couldn't see any sign of the intruder. I could sense his presence for sure, though.

"Heh heh heh... You can't see me, can you? Humans are so pathetic. I wonder why Lady Sherra fears you so..."

Fwshhh... Accompanying the disembodied voice, I heard a sound like sand pouring in from somewhere.

Where is that coming from?! The center of the room...?

"The lamp!" I shouted.

Mileena looked up. The faint light cast by the lamp had begun to fall to the floor in a thin stream, like a ray of sun beaming down between clouds. As I watched, it started to expand and take a roughly humanoid silhouette. Two dark, empty eyes sat inside a head that seemed to be made of calcified luminescent moss.

"Do you see me now, humans? Remember my name. I am Gubagg, servant to General Sherra."

So it *was* a demon working for Sherra! Still, knowing this guy's employer didn't change our top priority—and by that, I mean beating his ass!

I had no intention of waiting until the moss-man finished assembling himself, so I released my spell immediately. "Dynast Blas!"

With a furious crackle, my magical lightning blasted the luminous figure away! *Nice!*

"It's not over yet!" Mileena cried.

For a minute, I didn't understand what she meant. I looked back at the pale figure and...

I was stunned into silence. I watched as my raging magical lightning was sucked into moss-man's gaping black eyes. Before long, the bolt was completely gone and Gubagg turned his gaze back at us.

"That won't work." There was a smile in his voice. "The eyes of Gubagg lead all things to void. As long as they work, you cannot defeat me... Do you see now?"

L-Lead things to void? Sounds like a certain golden-haired dark lord I know... But if Gubagg was on that level, he wouldn't be running errands for Sherra. He had to be using some kind of dimension-warping trick to send the power that hit him somewhere else. Either way, though, this was going to be a tough fight.

"We've sent assassins after your friends as well, granting you the mercy of killing you all together. Now, let me show you… my other power."

As Gubagg spoke—*Rustle*—something moved on the floor at his feet.

I looked in the direction of the sound and found myself at a loss for words. Gubagg's moss-like body was spreading out from his legs, eating away at whatever it touched. *Corrosion?!*

"Soon I will expand until I devour this entire barrier… including the filthy humans within!" Gubagg pronounced triumphantly.

All the while, the corrosion continued to spread, blocking the staircase to the second floor and the way to the front door. Not that going up the stairs or out the door would do much good inside a barrier space anyway…

Corrosion plus spell nullification, huh? It was true that most humans wouldn't stand a chance against this guy. Too bad I wasn't most humans! I began to chant a spell. But—*Whoosh!*—before I could finish it, Mileena took off! She drew her sword and charged Gubagg.

What the heck is she doing?!

I didn't have time to stop her. She thrust her sword into the white moss eating through the floor!

"Fool! That won't work!"

Gubagg was right. The white moss wasn't inhibited at all. Rather, it began to creep up Mileena's blade. She quickly pulled her sword out and lifted it into the air, but sticky trails of the moss clung to it tenaciously.

Bad move, Mileena… Yet just as I thought that, Mileena made her next play! This time she jumped and rammed her sword into Gubagg's eye.

That won't work…

Gubagg was probably thinking the same thing. But before he could say it…

"Elemekia Flame!" A strike from close range enveloped his entire body!

Aha!

"Geh!" Gubagg let out a short scream.

Crick. There was a soft snapping noise at Mileena's feet as she landed. *Crick. Crackapop. Crickle.* It continued intermittently, until at last—*Ziiing!*—with a sound like crystal shattering, Gubagg's luminescent body collapsed in pieces.

Huh… nice one, Mileena.

She'd intentionally gotten part of Gubagg to cling to her sword, then shoved it into the demon's eye. Hitting him with an attack spell then meant that if he absorbed it into his eye, he'd be sucking his own body into the void at the same time, allowing the spell to hit him that way. In other words, Mileena had set Gubagg up to take the spell no matter how he responded.

Guess Gubagg's decision to intimidate us by monologuing about his abilities had been his undoing. Granted, I hadn't done much myself...

Mileena turned to face me. "What's wrong? You look disappointed."

I mean... I was hoping to hit him with my Ragna Blade and go, "Well? How do you like the taste of real void?" But, you know, whatever...

"Ah... It's nothing. Nothing at all," I said, feeling a little deflated nonetheless. I shook it off and looked around. "Is the barrier still active?" I whispered, and Mileena followed my eyes. The kitchen beyond the counter was still deserted.

"Does that mean someone else put it up?" she asked.

I nodded. "He said assassins were after the others too, right? Let's go, Mileena!"

We both nodded and made a beeline for the stairs, when...

"Excuse me! Ma'ams!" the innkeeper shouted from behind us.

Huh? We turned to see him emerging from the kitchen, holding a bowl of stew.

"It's ready," he called.

"Oh... um..." Mileena and I shared a glance. Did that mean... the barrier was down?

"Mileena!" Suddenly, we heard Luke shouting from the top of the stairs.

Ah, guess he made it out... But what about the others? Before I could put words to my thoughts, Luke tore down the stairs and seized Mileena in his arms. *Uh...*

"Er... Luke..." she mumbled.

"I'm so glad you're safe, Mileena," he sighed.

"Um, listen..."

"Were you hurt?"

"No, but... um..."

"Ahh, it's lovely to be young. But keep it in your rooms, all right?" the old innkeep chimed in.

That finally snapped Luke out of it, and he released Mileena. "Ah! Sorry, couldn't help myself…"

"Yes, you could. Now, where are the other two?"

"Oh, right… Yeah, they're fine."

"Hey, Lina." As if waiting for that cue, Gourry and Jade peeked over at us from the railing atop the stairs. "Figured you'd be okay."

He figured, huh? *Well, I guess that's a sign he's got faith in me… But you could still show a little concern, Mr. Self-Proclaimed Guardian!* At least there was no need to worry about him sweeping me into his arms.

"They sent a demon after us. It wasn't that Rebifor guy, though. What about you guys?" I asked.

"Two of them. Master Gourry and Master Luke defeated one, and the other disappeared. Rebifor wasn't among them," Jade responded.

I wondered if Rebifor's absence was because he'd yet to recover from the blow I'd dealt him. Or perhaps…

"Hmm… Then it's possible they might attack again right away," I mused.

"Right away? You mean tonight?" Luke asked.

I nodded. "Yeah. We've skated by so far because they keep underestimating us, but the minute they decide to take us seriously, they might just start sending waves of opponents to wear us down. I mean, it's kinda weird that Rebifor wasn't here for this little shindig, right? Makes me wonder if there's a second, more powerful force waiting in the wings. If so, our best bet right now is to get moving."

"Get moving? You're suggesting—"

"That's right," I nodded, not letting Mileena finish. In other words, we were heading straight for Gyria.

Mileena looked at me for a long moment and at last nodded.

"I completely agree!" Jade said from over the railing.

"Okay! It's decided! Let's get going—"

"Wait a minute!" came a sudden interruption.

I turned to the source… and remembered the innkeep was still there.

"I'm sorry to repeat myself, but your stew is ready."

"Hurry up, you guys!" I called encouragingly.

"You don't get to say that!" Luke grumped.

After I'd eaten my stew, we'd packed our things, paid our tab, and departed the inn down the night road to Gyria City.

"How could you have stopped to eat stew?!"

"C'mon! I couldn't just leave food on the table!"

"Still, is it safe to be taking the main road? If the enemies are en route for a follow-up attack, we might run into them," Jade said, interrupting my argument with Luke.

"I wouldn't worry about that. Pure demons wouldn't exactly be walking the road to our inn. They just pop outta nowhere unexpectedly. The one that split earlier probably popped over to wherever Sherra is... I guess not-so-unexpectedly. But if a second wave is coming, they'll also pop up unexpectedly at the inn. Which means the road to the city is probably safe for now," I explained as we walked along in the faint moonlight.

I continued on, my voice carrying on the chilly night breeze, "These demons seem to be pretty confident in their skills, and they don't regard humans as much of a threat. That's their weak point in general, and it applies here too. Even if they can teleport, catching people who are on the move will take them as long as it would anyone else."

"Teleport?" Jade breathed in near disbelief. I could understand how surreal the idea sounded to anyone who'd never seen it with their own eyes. "But teleportation suggests very fast movement. I wonder why there's been such a delay between their attacks..."

"Hmm..." Dude had a point. From the time Shaman had first attacked us on the road to Rebifor's ambush in the city, and from then to tonight's raid... There'd been multiple days between each skirmish. Given that they knew we were heading for Gyria City, they could've been a lot more aggressive in their pursuit. "Well, I'm sure they've got their reasons. For now, let's hurry on to Gyria City!"

"I told you, you don't get to say that!"

Fortunately, we managed to reach Gyria before dawn. (I was still pretty sleepy though.) I took advantage of the dark to Levitate us over the wall and enter the city with the guards none the wiser. (I was still *really* sleepy though.)

The plan was to sneak into Jade's house, catch some Zs, then find a home base come dawn, but…

"It's… gone," Luke whispered.

"Indeed… it is," Jade said emptily, just standing and staring.

Where the house should have been sat a pile of rubble. It must have been a mighty fine mansion before its untimely toppling, though. The grounds were vast, and though they were hard to see from here, the gardens appeared to be well tended. There just… wasn't a house anymore.

Sheesh… Jade said something about them seizing his assets, but I didn't think that would include destroying the house itself…

"So… what's the plan?" Gourry asked with a yawn.

I snapped out of my thoughts. "Oh, good question! We can't just sit around gawking, now can we? I guess it's time to…"

"Time to what?" Luke prompted me.

I just stood there in silence for a while. The truth was… I hadn't actually thought of anything.

Guh! My lack of sleep is giving me brain fog!

"Anyway, let's… get moving! Jade, is there anywhere else around here we can lie low?"

"W-Well, I wouldn't know much about places like that…"

"Then… we'll have to walk around until we find something," I said, starting off in a random direction. The others followed behind me.

Guh! When you're looking forward to hitting the hay, missing it feels all the worse!

"How about an inn in the slums?" Luke suggested.

"Sounds good. Which way're the slums?" I asked Jade.

"I'm sorry… I don't really know," he replied.

Such mind-numbing conversations continued as we traipsed around and the eastern sky began to lighten.

Haaahh… Dawn already?

More and more people started to appear out on the streets as we went. Merchants off to sell their wares, children up early, soldiers on their patrols…

Wait, soldiers?!

"Hey! You there!" Before I could follow that train of thought to its appropriate reaction, a small group of soldiers was already coming after us. One pointed and said, "You're Jade Caudwell!"

"I am," Jade responded, puffing out his chest.

Ahhh! He's not thinking!

"I knew it! For entering the city in defiance of your exile—"

I wasn't about to let him finish this time! "Let's beat it, guys!" I said, taking off in a dash. Everyone else quickly followed suit.

"Hey! Wait, you!" The soldiers gave chase.

We zig-zagged down streets and alleyways until...

"Diem Wind!"

Whoosh!

"Gwuh!"

"Ack!"

The wind spell Luke, our rearguard, let fly stopped the heavily armored soldiers in their tracks. We continued to speed off, leaving our pursuers in the dust.

Okay! We're in the clear! Yet no sooner had I thought that than— *Fweeeee!*—a high-pitched squeal rang through the area. One of the soldiers was blowing the whistle on us!

Not good! He's gonna draw a crowd!

If we were dealing with demons, we could blow them away and no one would complain. But these were just ordinary folk following orders. We couldn't off 'em like that. Which meant our only recourse was to run, but... where? That was the question.

"This way!" I heard a voice call from behind a building.

Huh? It kinda sounded familiar. We turned to look and saw a young man beckoning.

"Sir Jade, over here!" he called again.

"You're—"

"Hurry!"

"Understood! Come on, everyone!"

On Jade's urging, we followed after the young man. He took us through the back alleys, up a fire escape and...

"Here we are."

Eventually, he brought us to a room on the second floor of a rather new-looking building. It was a bit cramped for six people, but beggars can't be choosers.

Once we'd caught our breath, I indicated the young man with my eyes and asked Jade, "You know this guy?"

The young man answered for himself with a wince. "Well... we met yesterday, actually. At the gate."

At the gate? Wait... Oh!

"You're Gatekeeper No. 1!" I exclaimed.

"Um... I have a name. It's Maias," he said, wincing further.

"Who?" Gourry asked.

"You know! That guy! The unremarkable little toady who wouldn't let us through yesterday!" I told him.

"Well... I wish you'd put it another way..." Maias grumbled.

"But why did you save us? I've been exiled, haven't I?" Jade inquired.

At this, Maias lowered his voice. "Those were my orders and I'm still a soldier, so I didn't really have a choice in front of the others. But if I'm honest... I don't trust General Allus at all." He let out a sigh. "The promotion of that mercenary woman, her getting the run of the place, and the report of General Grancis's passing... It all felt, um..."

"You think he was murdered?" Jade asked.

Maias nodded. "I do. Rumor is spreading all across town. And if it's true... the kingdom is finished! So, Sir Jade... I want you to find out the truth!"

"Why don'cha just do it yourse— Mmgh!" Luke began before Mileena clamped a hand over his mouth.

As reliant on us as our little toady was, the simple fact that he'd given us a place to hide out was a million times better than the alternative.

I wasn't sure if he'd heard Luke or not, but Jade replied, "Listen... are you sure this won't cause trouble for your family?"

"Don't worry. I came from another city to become a knight here. And no sacrifice is too great if it means making our kingdom a better place!"

"Very well! I shall honor that dedication. We'll expose the intrigues of General Allus and Sherra the mercenary to protect the people! Even if I've been stripped of my rank, I still have my pride as a knight! I'd gladly lay my life on the line to save the kingdom!"

"Sir Jade! You are truly the epitome of knighthood!"

"No, far from it. A true knight must—"

Yeah, I did not have the energy to deal with this chivalric rabbit hole.

"Anyhoo… let's get some shut-eye," I said.

"Good idea."

"I'm just gonna lie down wherever."

Ignoring Jade and Maias as they got lost in their own little world, the rest of us settled in.

We got a move on much later that day, sometime after nightfall. We'd awoken while it was still light out and discussed our strategy some, but there wasn't a lot to say about the basic strokes of what we had to do: infiltrate the castle, find Sherra, and beat her.

Jade knew the castle's basic layout, but understandably, not where Sherra herself would be or what the defenses were like. Our safest course of action thus would've been to gather intel first, but there was no guarantee we'd learn what we wanted to know. Moreover, reconnaissance was time-consuming. Every minute we wasted in town was another minute Sherra might be using to muster her forces or track us down, putting us in even hotter water than before. That left us with only one option—strike first, ask questions later! Yeah, it might've been absurdly reckless, but it was the only hope we had of catching the enemy flat-footed.

And so we left Maias to guard the fort, while Gourry, Luke, Mileena, Jade, and I made for the night-cloaked castle. The sliver of moon in the sky illuminated its dim stone walls.

"Welp, guess we'd better do this," Luke said.

The group nodded in response. Our three casters then started chanting spells. I grabbed Gourry and Luke lifted Jade over the wall with a Levitation spell. Our destination was the guest lodging house on the castle grounds, which Jade claimed to know well enough. We flew along, letting him point the way.

Obviously, it was no sure bet that Sherra would be there, but it was as good an educated guess as any. If it turned out to be wrong, we could always tie up some guards there and get them to spill the beans on her whereabouts.

Soon enough, we touched down on the roof of the lodging house.

"So… how do we sneak in?" Luke asked.

"No need," replied a voice that didn't come from any of us.

In surprise, we all looked to see who it was. The source was a floating shadow, backed by the sliver of moon…

A demon!

Chapter 3: The Castle at Night, Consumed in Flames

The creature looked kind of like a black kite. It was about the size of a person, but its body was flat, triangular, and translucent enough that we could see the vague outline of the moon through it. It had no arms or legs, but its head(?) contained a single unnervingly realistic eye. It was a cartoonish design by many measures... although I doubted there'd be anything fun or whimsical about what this guy could do.

On top of that, we had a couple of factors working against us right now. One was our footing. The other was the soldiers visible in the courtyard below, which signaled that the demon hadn't locked us in a barrier. Its intent was clear—it wanted to force us to use flashy spells that would bring people running.

But... hang on a minute...

"Lady Sherra told me... not to underestimate you..." The demon's lone eye rolled in my direction. "Lina Inverse... the woman who terminated Lord Hellmaster Fibrizo."

"Huh?!" Luke, Mileena, and Jade were understandably shocked.

I mean, if you wanna get technical, Hellmaster terminated himself. But on a brass tacks level, I might've been the cause, sure...

Nevertheless, the demon kite continued gravely, "I find it difficult to believe... but I see no reason why Lady Sherra would lie. And so I must not let my own guard down."

Dang, you guys are stupid! See, while it was blabbing on, I was finishing an amplified chant. "Dam Blas!"

For claiming it wouldn't let its guard down, running off at the mouth while I was whipping up a spell was proof of the contrary. Or maybe this thing was banking on my spell not being able to hurt it... Which was totally true! But I wasn't aiming for the monster!

Crash! Instead, the destructive fallout unfolded at my feet. My actual target, see, was directly below us—the roof we were standing on!

The monster's eye opened wide. It looked stunned. It must not have expected me to blow in the roof. If it voiced any kind of surprise, though, I couldn't hear it over the explosion. Of course, the rest of us would've been hurt pretty bad if we fell straight through. Thankfully...

"Levitation!" Luke and Mileena activated their spells simultaneously, so our descent to the building's top floor, down onto my freshly created pile of rubble, was a leisurely one. I wasn't sure if they'd anticipated my maneuver or if they'd had other plans in mind when they started their chants, but it all worked out either way.

"Let's go, everyone!" I said and took off down the corridor. "Jade! Cover your face with a rag or something!"

"But why?"

"Just do it!"

As we ran, shouting back and forth, a door up ahead opened and a pudgy old man poked his nose out in surprise. He had a rather seedy look to him, but if he was staying in the castle guest lodgings, he had to be some kind of bigwig from another kingdom. I could work with that!

"What in the—" he started.

But before he could finish, I yelled, "Intruders! We must flee!" I grabbed his hand and began pulling him toward the stairway.

"What?! Intruders? Who are you people?" he clamored.

"Your fellow countrymen!" I assured him. "His Majesty ordered us to keep an eye on you in case something like this happened! Now hurry!"

"R-Right!" The flustered old coot seemed to take me at my word.

We thus proceeded first down the hall and stairs using the old man as cover. To no one's surprise, we encountered a group of guards along the way.

"Intruders on the top floor! Hurry!" I called to them before they could question us.

The patrolmen immediately looked confused. They probably recognized the old man... but seeing him on the run, escorted by a group of total strangers? Naturally they wanted to know who we were!

"Identify yourselves," they demanded, zeroing in on us.

The old man replied with gusto, "No need to worry! My kingdom sent them! Now hurry!"

"Right!"

Deferring to the old man's claim, the soldiers took off again. Maybe they'd just gotten used to seeing mercenaries around lately, or maybe we just didn't look that suspicious.

"Wait!" I shouted after the guards. "Where's Lady Sherra? We must inform her!"

"The northern tower, I believe…"

"Got it! We'll report in!"

Don't ask me what my "report" was going to contain. I was flying by the seat of my pants here!

Ha. It's so easy to trick people in a chaotic situation…

The moment that demon had spotted us on the roof, I'd decided to follow the great laws of infiltration. Namely, when sneaking into a place, to do it as unobtrusively as possible. And the best way to blend in right now was if the whole castle was thrown into chaos. That was also why I'd asked Jade, the most recognizable member of our group, to hide his face.

We went through the same song and dance with the guards a few more times before making it out of the building. "Let's get away from here! And fast!" Spurring on the old man with us, we all headed for the northern tower while Jade quietly pointed the way. We only made it a short distance before…

"You!" A figure appeared to block our path. Do I have to say who it was? You guessed it—the demon we'd met on the roof. "How dare you deceive—"

But I didn't even have to chant a spell to take care of this dunce. I just pointed at the demon before us and shouted at the top of my lungs… "The invader!"

"What?!"

"Where?!"

"This way! This way!"

"Fiend!"

The castle guard immediately gathered around me.

"Get your bows!"

"No! It's a demon! Call the palace sorcerers!"

"What... Wait!" The demon didn't know what to do as all the soldiers turned on it. And in its hesitation...

"Fell Zaleyd!" Luke and Mileena fired off a joint spell.

"Guh!" the demon cried, destroyed on the spot.

Whew. What a hack...

"There's one more on top of the guesthouse! Hurry!" I called.

"Got it!" Having bought completely into my bullshit, the soldiers went running.

"All righty, now we're going *this* way!" At my urging, our party continued northward. After making sure the soldiers no longer had eyes on us...

"Hyah!"

"Ack!"

I delivered a chop to the back of the old man's head and laid him out. "To the northern tower! Hurry!"

"Hey... that was pretty harsh," Gourry scolded. I ignored him!

Running full tilt, we closed in on the tower. Despite being called a tower, it wasn't a freestanding structure. A long, straight corridor stretched from the castle to a wide, rectangular building with a round turret sprouting from it. Most of the castle guard was headed for the guest lodgings, so there didn't seem to be any security on the place. Once we'd gotten close enough...

"What?! What's going on?!" a bearded man in early old age asked as he poked his head out of an open door.

"Invader!" I explained in brief. "In the guesthouse!"

"An invader?! Who?!" he questioned further.

Before I could answer, Jade got out ahead of me, leaped at the man, and knocked him to the ground!

"What?! What are you—"

"It's me," Jade said fiercely, stripping off the mask covering half of his face. "I've come, General Allus."

"Jade?!" the man on the ground gasped in surprise.

Was this the notorious General Allus who'd put Sherra in power?!

"I have many questions for you," Jade said, then fell silent a moment.

I could only imagine. He needed answers from Allus... About Sherra. About his father's death. About what was going on in the kingdom.

"But right now, only one matters. Where is that woman... Where is Sherra?"

Allus let out a small sigh. "That woman, eh?" He sounded exhausted. Yet the split second Jade let his guard down...

"Hah!" Allus knocked the younger knight aside and got to his feet. "If you care to find out..." He drew the sword smoothly from his belt. "Fight and defeat me!"

"I shall!" Jade replied, returning the gesture. "Stay out of this, all of you!" he shouted to the rest of us as he charged off swinging.

Clang! Their blades collided with red sparks. Allus blocked Jade's slash, took a step back, then let fly a wide horizontal slice of his own. Jade blocked it and responded in kind. It was a proper duel—strength against strength, steel against steel. They traded blows two, three times. Both men swung their swords in wide, high slashes. And at last...

"Ngh!" It was General Allus who fell to one knee. Jade's last slice had left a shallow cut straight down from his right shoulder.

It wasn't that Allus was a poor swordsman. He wasn't particularly exceptional either, but Jade was clearly his better.

"You truly are General Grancis's son... I never stood a chance," he conceded.

"You dare speak my father's name? After you killed him?!" Jade accused.

Allus shook his head. "I didn't..." he began, then shook his head again and swallowed. "No, perhaps you're right to say that. It was I, after all, who introduced that woman to our liege... and who sent our kingdom down the path to ruin."

"You make it sound like you had nothing to do with my father's death."

"I won't ask you to believe me. It's natural for you to be wary, given the difficult relationship your father and I had. But I am truly devoted to King Wells. That is one thing I will not allow you to call into question. I don't think it's wrong to try to bring joy to the object of one's esteem," Allus said.

He was referring, of course, to the reigning monarch of Dils, Wells Xeno Gyria.

"But it's also true that such loyalty can be viewed as sycophancy... That's how General Grancis saw it. I brought Sherra to meet our liege because I thought he'd be pleased to acquire such a retainer. That should have been all it was... yet it wasn't so. I don't know how she got so close to the king after that either, but the next thing I knew, the two were inseparable. Still, I thought it was fine as long as my liege was satisfied. That day, too, your father called me to the castle to speak about Sherra's ambitions... And some days later, I received news of his passing..."

Jade kept silent as he listened, sword still in hand.

"That was when I began to think, for the first time, that I might have been misguided..."

Just then...

"General!"

"General Allus!"

A group of soldiers flooded into the building, interrupting Allus's story. *Of course! Was he just buying time until his forces arrived?!*

"You..." The soldiers turned their blades on us all at once.

"Wait!" General Allus stopped them. "The invaders... are outside. They left through another door. Don't worry about me. Go..."

We were all shocked—the soldiers included. The general's unexpected statement left everyone dumbfounded for a second.

"B-But General...!" the soldiers hesitated.

"Go!" Allus barked at them.

Still, they couldn't just blindly accept what he was asking them to do. Some of them had to have recognized Jade. Jade, an exile, who was standing over the wounded general while holding a bloody sword... It would have been crazier for them *not* to question the situation.

"That's an order!"

Hearing that word, the soldiers grudgingly looked at each other. "V-Very well. But you're wounded, General..."

"I told you not to worry about me. I have more to say to these people. Now go."

The soldiers fell silent, then... "Understood. Please... take care." They must not have known what else to say. And so, with those rather foolish final words, the soldiers turned around and headed in the direction Allus had indicated.

"Why did you..." Jade pressed once they were gone.

"As I said... there's more I have to say," General Allus responded with a self-reproaching smile. "It was around that time that I began to regret what I'd done. I thought that the only thing that mattered was pleasing our liege... but I found myself wondering if there were times I should have told him no anyway."

Jade quietly sheathed his sword and glanced at us. "Would one of you... someone who knows healing magic... please heal this wound for him?"

"Sheesh, what a soft touch. Yeah, sure, just believe everything he says..." Luke muttered in disgust. Mileena, meanwhile, stepped away from him and cast a Recovery spell on Allus. Seeing this, Luke awkwardly added, "Uh... but I guess it ain't bad to trust people sometimes."

The cut on Allus's arm slowly but surely began to close. "Thank you," he said to no one in particular, then went on. "Several days later... the king summoned me and told me... that he'd put out the order, in my name, to have you and your brother exiled. And inevitably, by his side stood that woman... Sherra. That's when I realized she's the one running the kingdom now. A kingdom of fools—myself included. If only I had realized it earlier..." Allus let out a small sigh. "Sir Jade, you don't have to believe me. You can even kill me if you wish. But... I'd like to ask you one favor. That woman is still with our liege. I won't ask what you seek to do with her, but please... do not harm His Majesty."

"I am devoted," Jade said with a firm nod, "as I have always been, to King Wells. Aside from that, right now, I have no way of judging the truthfulness of your tale. And so... I have no grounds to punish you here and now."

"I see..." The general sighed again.

Mileena watched silently from where she was crouched at his side. Allus's wound hadn't been especially serious to begin with, and it was now mostly healed. Nature would take care of the rest.

"I've kept you for too long... That woman, Sherra, is likely with the king in his office in the northern palace."

"All right."

"I don't know who or what she is... but please be careful."

"I'll be back soon." Jade gave Allus a knight's salute, then turned around and ran down the hall.

The four of us followed after him. I looked back and saw General Allus, still slumped where he was, watching us run off...

Owing to the commotion outside, there were scarcely any soldiers in the castle complex itself. We passed the obligatory patrolman here and there, but either Gourry tackled them to the ground, or Mileena or I chucked a Sleeping spell to put them out like a light. All in all, we didn't hit any major obstacles as we ran the breezeway across the lawn to the central palace. If Sherra was with the king, then the royal guard in general was probably sticking close by despite the ruckus outside. I anticipated we'd run into quite a few guards en route, but...

The minute we stepped inside the palace, we all stopped at the same time.

We found ourselves in a small meeting hall. It wasn't the main hall, obviously. Probably one meant for small groups of soldiers and servants to gather. The place was a ghost town at the moment, yet it was filled with a particular presence... Miasma.

"Another of those barriers?" Jade asked.

"Correct," a familiar voice answered.

"Rebifor?!" I called the name of the bug-eyed demon who'd attacked us with Shaman once before. I looked around but couldn't see him anywhere.

"I thought I could leave you to the castle's human soldiers and simply watch from afar... But you've forced my hand."

"Guess I'm better at reading and manipulating people than you guys are."

"Yes, it does appear so..." Rebifor seemed unfazed by my taunt. "Which means all the humans scampering about are in both of our ways, wouldn't you say? So I've taken them off the board entirely." With that, the door across the lobby suddenly opened with a bang as if to say *come right this way*.

"Ha! Don't make me laugh!" I puffed up as I responded to the still seemingly absent Rebifor. "We're only after Sherra! No way are we stepping into some trap obviously intended for us to waste time on cannon fodder!" I proclaimed.

"Er, Mistress Lina..." Jade whispered in response. "We have to go that way to get to the king's office."

Um...

"But I suppose we should get you off our backs before we fight Sherra, so we accept your challenge!"

"Are you only saying that because we don't have a choice?"

"Shut up, Gourry. Anyhoo, don't anyone let their guard down!"

And so we strode toward the door across the hall... to the battlefield where demons awaited.

We were ready for a fight. We'd infused Gourry's Magic-Sucker Sword (named by yours truly) with a Dark Claw spell so it would pack a good wallop against demons. Every time we came to a fork in the hallway, Rebifor's voice told us which way to go.

"We appear to be heading for the audience chamber," Jade whispered as we followed the demon's instructions.

"Where's this office Sherra's supposed to be in?" I asked.

"I've never been there myself... but my father mentioned you have to go through the audience chamber to get there."

"Figures," I grumbled before falling silent.

Rebifor and his buddies were probably waiting in the audience chamber. After some walking, we arrived at an entryway.

"This is it..." Jade said, reaching for the door.

I grabbed his shoulder to stop him and cast a glance at Gourry. The big lug nodded, then drew his sword.

"I'll open it!" he declared, and then...

There came a blast of hostility from the other side. Gourry's sword flashed. The door, cut into several pieces, clattered to the ground. Beyond it were countless skulking shadows... and countless beams of light heading straight for us!

"Vuum Aeon!" Luke and Mileena incanted. Their anti-magic barrier surrounded us instantly!

Vsshahshahshahshah! The innumerable rays burst against the field, dispersing into particles. The moment the wave passed, I stepped out of the barrier and released the spell I'd been chanting!

"Bram Blazer!" The amplified strike tore through several of the shadows.

"Hraaaaah!" Meanwhile, Gourry and Jade came running in from either side, slashing and shouting. Luke and Mileena dropped their barrier, then rushed through the door too while chanting their next spells.

The audience chamber was a large hall with a high ceiling. A line of red carpet flanked by marble pillars led to an unoccupied throne. I estimated about twenty or thirty of the dark figures in the room, all reminiscent of Shaman and Hydra. Black from head to toe, bodies decorated in strange, mystical patterns... They had a variety of head and limb shapes. Some were even carrying weapons.

The place was swarming with them—but just them. There was no sign of Rebifor as far as I could see. Shaman might have been mixed in with the crowd, but I didn't have time to search him out now. If I let my guard down for a second, I'd get pounded with lances of fire and ice from all directions.

I desperately dodged through the incoming attacks, chanted a spell, and let 'er rip. "Blast Ash!"

Whm! The spell I released enveloped several of the dark figures, rendering them dust. I didn't really have time to get a look around, but it sounded like everyone else was in the thick of the fight now too. That said, for pure demons, these things weren't particularly tough... In fact, they seemed pretty darn weak. More on the level of lesser or brass demons.

Hang on... Have we got this in the bag?!

Yet no sooner had that thought crossed my mind than I detected a presence behind me. Startled, I didn't waste time turning around. I instantly dove to the side—just in time for a beam of light to streak by me, tearing through my cape.

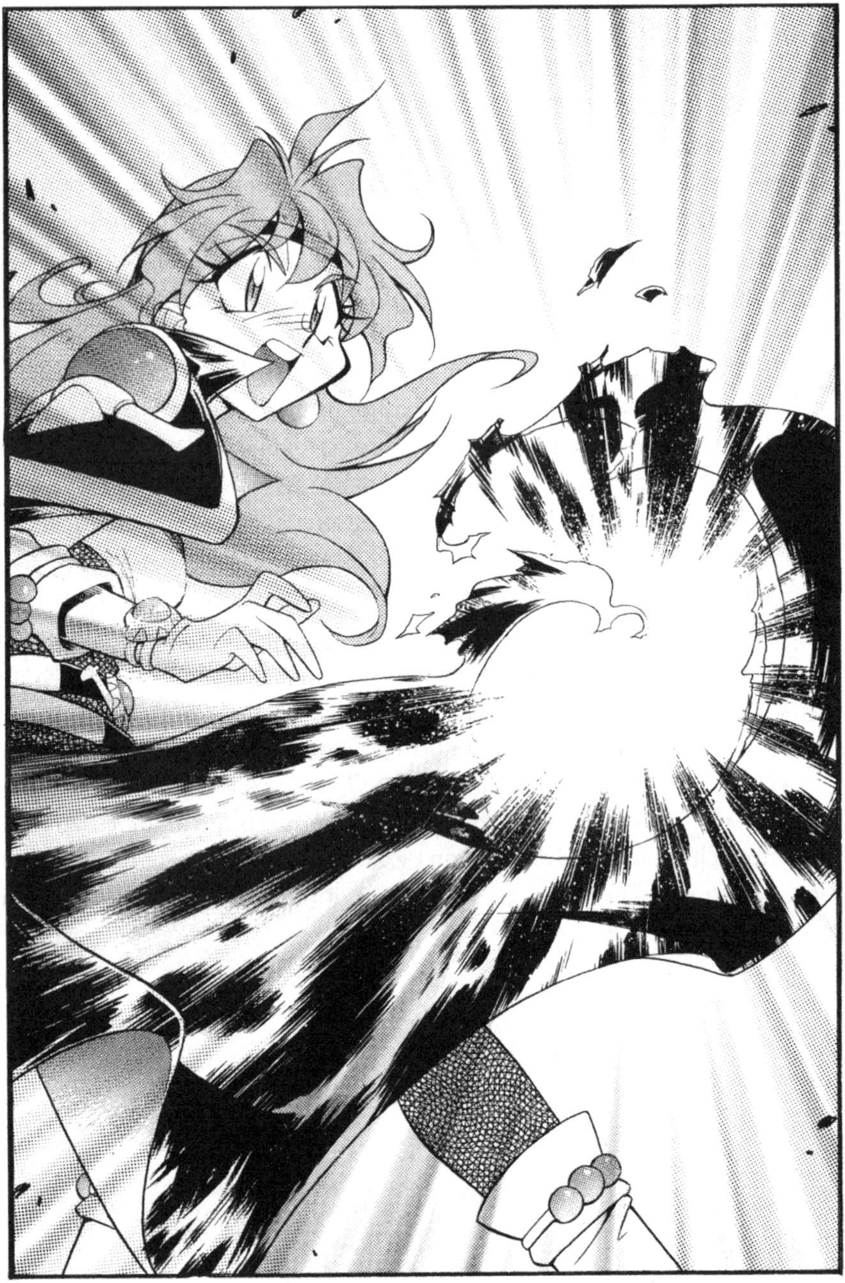

"Excellent instincts..." Upon hearing this new voice, the demons in black all stopped in place.

I turned to see four figures standing there. It was Rebifor, Shaman, and two more demons I'd never laid eyes on before. One of the newcomers looked like a large, translucent man with no face. The other was moss green, with two tentacles dangling from each shoulder and a face made up of a single eyeball.

Rebifor scanned our party and said, "I didn't expect these to finish you, but to see you clearing through them this quickly..."

That much was true. We'd wiped out... not quite half, but a third of the black demons in short order.

"I suppose the raw material makes all the difference... So they're useless, then," he muttered incomprehensibly, then turned his gaze on us. "It has been a while. I didn't realize the last time we met that you were Lina Inverse, so I let my guard down. It's time for me to repay the favor..."

"Oh, don't trouble yourself. Some people are just too polite," I replied blithely to Rebifor's words and slowly began to move.

The rest of the gang was also slowly moving into more strategic positions while keeping an eye on the black demons and Rebifor's party. Rebifor's squad showed no signs of movement on their part, either because they didn't notice or didn't care about our own.

"I owe a debt to the men as well," the moss-colored demon announced.

"Wait, who's that guy again?" Gourry whispered to Luke.

"You know who! He attacked us in the inn before!" Luke barked back.

Of course. This was the surviving half of the demon pair who'd attacked Gourry and Luke back in town.

"Well, all he did was give a hotshot introduction then run away cryin' after we beat his buddy, so it's no wonder you don't remember him! What's your name, anyway?" Luke taunted.

"Rikakizu," the demon replied, seemingly unfazed by the provocation.

"You say something too, Baiz," Rebifor prodded.

The faceless giant gave no reply. Of course, I was watching the whole time for an opportunity to whack him with a spell... but even as Rebifor talked, his party's attention remained undividedly on us.

"Hmm... no introduction, then? That reminds me..." As if suddenly remembering, Rebifor turned toward Shaman with a pregnant tone. "Did *you* ever introduce yourself to them?"

"Introduce... myself... to them?" Shaman asked, tilting its head.

"Yes. Did you ever tell them who you are?"

"There was... no need... to..."

Rebifor's eyes narrowed in amusement. "Never mind that. Tell them your name."

"My... name..." Shaman said, then continued haltingly, "My name is... Grancis... Caudwell..."

A chill seized the room. *Grancis... Caudwell?! That means...*

"Absurd!" Jade's cry broke the silence. "That's... my father's name!"

"Yes, I know," Rebifor said mockingly. "And indeed... He is Grancis Caudwell, one and the same!"

"Liar! That thing's nothing like my father! Besides, my father is—"

"Dead? But have you seen his corpse? Saying someone has passed away from illness is a common cover story for assassinations... but it also works for disappearances."

"That proves nothing!"

"Are you familiar with lesser demons?" Rebifor continued, interrupting Jade. "They're the product of a lower-ranking demon on the astral plane inhabiting a small animal or similar creature with low mental defenses, transforming its body in the process."

"What are you talking about?!"

"Lady Sherra has the most amusing blade, you see..."

Ah!

"The demonic sword Dulgoffa... It's both sword and demon. It possesses a person and eats away at their soul, then transmogrifies them into what we call a greater demon. But what if Dulgoffa were to possess a person just long enough to annihilate their will, leaving us a human shell with no mental defenses whatsoever? And then, what would happen if we summoned a lower-ranking demon from the astral plane to possess that shell? This is the answer—a quite unusual form of low-rank demon."

"What... are you talking about?!" Jade cried, his voice shaky.

If you hadn't witnessed Dulgoffa's power for yourself before, Rebifor's story would have sounded like some tall tale… But for me, I couldn't deny it reeked of the truth.

If Shaman wasn't a pure demon and had to walk everywhere he went, that would explain the long downtime between attacks since he'd have had to return to the palace every time he needed new orders. That also explained the discrepancy between the way he fought and the way he talked, and why the other figures here weren't much stronger than lesser or brass demons.

This new revelation meant that General Allus really was merely a stepping stone, just as he'd claimed. Sherra didn't need his help at all once she'd established herself.

"…But there are a few problems with this method. Their magic power is roughly uniform, but their physical strength varies greatly based on the human host's potential. You don't find the others in the audience chamber much of a challenge, do you?"

"You mean…" I cast my eyes around the horde of dark figures filling the room.

"Indeed. They're various nobles and officials of the kingdom who tried to stop our plans. Quite a few were also said to have passed from illness… But it seems most of them weren't particularly athletic to begin with."

"You're lying!" Jade shouted.

"I'm not," Rebifor responded coldly. "But you're welcome to see for yourself if you doubt me. You've crossed swords with your father in practice before, surely. You must remember his fighting style. Grancis, fight him. But go easy on him."

At this, Shaman took a smooth step forward. He raised the sword in his hand…

"Graaah!" Jade roared as he ran straight for Shaman.

Clink! Shaman easily parried Jade's opening strike like he'd seen it coming.

"You… Damn you! Damn you!"

Jade lashed out again and again. Shaman dodged or deflected each strike until—*Zing!*—he saw an opening and attacked for himself. Jade parried the blow and leaped back.

"It can't be…" he whispered quietly. His voice was quaking. "It can't be!"

"Are you so certain?" Rebifor pressed.

Jade fell silent for a moment, at a loss for words. "You're lying! So… So why—?!"

"Why is his sword technique the same? You know the answer, don't you? Grancis knows how you fight. You practiced together so often, after all."

"Ngh…" Jade went silent, his fists trembling. Then he turned his glare to Rebifor. "Turn my father back into a human!" he spat.

"I'm afraid I can't do that," Rebifor replied, unfazed. "Even if I removed his demon host, he'd be nothing more than a drooling vegetable now."

"Liar!"

"It's true. If any part of Grancis's will still remained, do you think he would have killed your brother, his very flesh and blood, with his own hands?"

This time, Rebifor's words had Jade frozen completely.

He's right. I saw Shaman—no, Grancis—kill the man who was probably Jade's brother…

"You can't argue with that, can you? Heh heh heh…" Rebifor let out a quiet laugh, as if enjoying himself tremendously.

He's feeding off of Jade's despair…

Indeed, demons thrived on the negative emotions of the living.

"So?" I spoke up in Jade's silence. "What exactly are you people planning? Infiltrating a kingdom, seizing power, turning people into monsters… Chaos Dragon Gaav did something similar not too long ago. His plan was to pick a fight with the demons of Kataart, but what about you? Trying to start an all-out war with the humans?"

"I don't really owe you an explanation, do I?" Rebifor responded with a smile in his voice. "We're only here for one thing—to try to kill each other. So we should really get started promptly, shouldn't we?"

"Promptly," my ass! After you took all that time to mess with Jade…

"You're right…" But it was Jade who agreed with Rebifor's statement. "That's the only way to save my father, isn't it?" With that, he leveled his blade at Grancis. "Then… let us begin."

And with that, we did.

Jade charged. Grancis did likewise at the same moment. The three pure demons fanned out, and the remaining black figures—the humans effectively turned into demidemons—took battle-ready positions.

"Fell Zaleyd!"

"Assher Dist!"

Luke and Mileena, having already recited incantations, fired spells that mowed through the shadowy throng.

"Graaah!"

Clink! Grancis deflected Jade's opening strike, then counterattacked. Jade parried and dodged. Grancis looked perfectly at ease, while Jade was the furthest thing from it—both in terms of technique and emotion. There was a palpable reserve in his blows. There was no way he could win like this.

Their swords met again, and again. Jade showed a moment's vulnerability, and Grancis didn't hesitate to exploit it! Then... *Clink!* Just before his blade reached Jade's body, Gourry's sword intercepted it. Grancis hopped back to take some distance.

"I don't need your help!" Jade cried.

"Look, man..." Gourry kept his sword between himself and Grancis, speaking to Jade with an awkward expression. "You're fighting like you're trying to get yourself killed. I understand how you feel, but I can't just stay back and watch a guy do that, even if you ask me to."

Gourry knew it. Jade did too—he couldn't beat Grancis. Jade was skilled, to be sure, but in an everyday sort of way. The skills Gourry and this version of Grancis possessed defied all logic.

"Right now, the only way to save my father... is to kill him," Jade whispered. He clenched his trembling fists. "I want... to save my father. It's my duty as his son... but... I know I'm not strong enough to beat him." It sounded like it killed him to say the words, but he nodded to Gourry. "Please... save my father."

"Yeah... I will. So now..." Gourry readied his sword again, facing Grancis. "Looks like I'm your opponent. Let's go."

Then came the clash of blades, Gourry's against Grancis's.

"Elemekia Lance!" I unleashed a spear of light, which Rebifor readily dodged. But when he did... "Break!"

I snapped my fingers, and... *Crash!* The light burst as it sailed by Rebifor! I'd altered the spell a bit to accommodate a delayed torrent.

"Tch!"

It wouldn't do much damage, but it should still feel like an ice-cold shower, forcing the demon to flinch. In that moment, I drew my sword and charged at him, chanting.

"That same trick again?!" he shouted.

I thrust out the sword in my right hand.

"I won't let you hit me!" Rebifor leaped back, just dodging the tip of my blade.

I took another step in, then raised my left hand... toward Rebifor's head! I'd finished my spell!

"Not good enough!" he hissed as he dipped low.

Trying to avoid my attack and counter, was he?! Too bad...

"Elemekia Flame!" Magic doesn't always have to manifest in the palm of your hand! I used a slightly altered chant to make it blast out from my abdomen—right on the level where Rebifor's head now was!

In his surprise, the light hit him dead-on!

Fweee! Moss-colored tentacles whistled through the air at Luke from four directions in slightly delayed succession. The barrage forced him to leap back to avoid the whips or swipe them aside with his sword, but he did manage to thwart them all. When he did...

"Blast Ash!"

Whm! Responding to Luke's voice, darkness consumed the body of the moss-colored demon. Then... *Snap!* With a sound like a wet balloon popping, it broke out of the enveloping shadow! Rikakizu had overwhelmed the Blast Ash through sheer magical force!

"What?!" Luke exclaimed in surprise.

Rikakizu closed in. Luke drew back while chanting his next spell. Waiting for that moment of vulnerability, the demidemons showered him with an indiscriminate hail of flaming arrows!

"Tch!" He just managed to dodge them, but it left him completely off-balance.

Rikakizu's moss-colored tentacles howled through the air. One was aimed right at Luke's neck!

Magical arrows fired by the demidemons sailed at Mileena. She evaded them by the skin of her teeth, but the demons were already taking aim again… A split second later, one of them collapsed with a scream. Jade had run in from the side and cut it down.

The demidemons' attention now shifted from Mileena to Jade, but that didn't mean Mileena was completely off the hook. An exceedingly powerful, massive arm swung through the air toward her.

Whoosh! With a rush of wind, the translucent giant Baiz took a sweep at Mileena. She effortlessly evaded it with a leap backward—or at least, that was the plan. She landed, then dodged in a panic. The oversized arm passed literally right in front of her nose!

Did she misjudge the distance?!

I said Baiz was "translucent" before, but that was a little imprecise. To clarify, his body was sorta like that of a jellyfish. That had to make his moves kinda hard to read…

Mileena jumped back to get even more distance, then took a step to the side and released a spell she'd chanted at Baiz.

"Fell Zaleyd!"

But with swift strides belied by his monstrous size, Baiz easily avoided it. Mileena's spell kept flying and hit one of the demidemons beyond him. Then once again, Mileena and Baiz faced off.

Cling! Clank! Clang! The clash of sword against sword rang out incessantly. Grancis parried a strike from Gourry, and then Gourry deflected one from Grancis. Sparks flew again and again until both fighters jumped back simultaneously to get their distance. Then Grancis charged!

He was stooped low, as if he were crawling along the ground. He struck with an upward slash, which Gourry met with a downward one. If the blows were equal in terms of power, Gourry had the advantage!

Clink! Sparks flew through the air once more, and just then… Grancis released his left hand from his sword to pincer Gourry's blade between his fingers.

"What?!" the big lug cried.

After securing Gourry's sword with one hand, Grancis used his other to take a sideways slash at Gourry's legs! The blond swordsman managed to dodge with a vertical leap. If he could land on top of Grancis now, he could probably beat him.

Yet just as Gourry jumped, Grancis twisted his left hand—including Gourry's sword and Gourry along with it. A move like that must require inhuman strength, but then again, Grancis was no longer human.

Normally, Gourry would have been cast to the floor, but...

"Hng!" He managed to right himself in the air and maintain balance enough to land feetfirst. This maneuver, too, was frankly inhuman.

Before Gourry could straighten up, though, Grancis was upright again. His left hand was still holding Gourry's sword. And then... the now free sword in Grancis's right hand swung straight for Gourry!

Rebifor's head was shorn clean off. *That's one down!* At least, that's what I thought, but an unsettling feeling suddenly raced up my spine. I turned around just in time to see...

Whoosh!

A beam of light passed by me. The caster was... Rebifor! *He's still alive?!*

"Know when to quit already!" I screamed.

"Actually, you didn't even hit me," the headless demon declared. The area around his shoulders then began transforming to regenerate the missing appendage!

Wait, that's not right... Rebifor said that I hadn't hit him, and that could mean only one thing. He'd transformed to remove his own head before the spell made contact in order to dodge it.

What a freakin' creep...

When we'd fought before, I'd caught him off guard and forced him to retreat... But knowing he had a skill like this made him one tough cookie. To defeat him, I'd have to take him by surprise again. Could I do it? One way or another...

"Astral Vine!" I infused my drawn sword with magic.

"It's no use." Rebifor's eyes were smiling.

Severed by Rikakizu's tentacles, a head went flying... followed by several more, all belonging to demidemons.

"Stay out of my way, small fry!" Rikakizu scolded, leaving them quaking.

Meanwhile, Luke had managed to regain his balance. He interrupted his chant to say, "Huh, I dunno what your game is, but I oughta thank you."

"It's nothing… After running away once, I don't want anyone to think I won due to the aid of trash like them. I want to kill you myself. I'd like to kill you all, in fact… but you're the one person I *need* to kill."

"Cool. Go ahead and try it!" Luke invited, picking up his chant again.

"I will!" Rikakizu roared as he leaped forward.

Luke leaped back in turn, still chanting, but Rikakizu was faster! The demon got within grabbing distance, sending all four tentacles snaking toward him at once. Midair, they split apart and became a swarm of a dozen much narrower tendrils—all racing to entangle Luke!

The battle between Mileena and Baiz seemed to have reached an impasse as they swapped blows, all easily dodged. Mileena wasn't misjudging the distance of Baiz's punches anymore. Once you knew the trick, it was easy to deal with. Baiz's translucent arms grew a little longer every time he swung. If you managed to evade his first punch mistakenly thinking his translucency just made his attacks difficult to gauge, you'd be in for a nasty surprise with the second.

But Mileena dodged him, chanting another spell. Baiz's punch attack came with a magical projectile, which Mileena avoided as well. Then…

"Elemekia Lance!"

Baiz dodged Mileena's spell, but it speared through another demidemon.

For most warriors, an opponent taking control of their weapon would be the death of them. But like Grancis, Gourry wasn't most warriors.

Bam! A blow from Gourry's fist to the flat of Grancis's blade sent it off course. He simultaneously planted a kick in Grancis's stomach. Grancis immediately released Gourry's sword and withdrew. Gourry pursued.

Grancis screeched as he flew back, conjuring a storm of magical arrows to hurl at Gourry. The big lug didn't have time to dodge them all!

"Sword!" Gourry shouted as he thrust his blade toward the incoming shafts of light. This triggered the Dark Claw spell cast into it, negating Grancis's light as the two magics collided! And then…

Thrrrk! Following through on his strike, Gourry ran Grancis through.

"Elemekia Lance!" Rebifor didn't seem bothered by my umpteenth casting of the spell. He simply opened a hole in his stomach to let it pass through. Too bad this one was a little different!

"Break!" As the spear of light was moving through him, I used the command to shatter it! He couldn't dodge this one! Except...

"Heh..." A small smile appeared on Rebifor's face. "I expected you to do that... but unless I let my guard down, a weakened spell like that won't hurt me in the slightest!" As Rebifor spoke, the hole in his stomach filled in.

Grr! He saw it coming! I'd thought of other ways to surprise him, but the timing would be tricky. If I tried something right now, there was a good chance I'd fail. That meant I needed to buy some time.

I chanted a spell under my breath...

"It's no use!" Rebifor approached, his tone brimming with confidence. "Nothing you do will—"

"Fell Zaleyd!" Mileena incanted from behind Rebifor. She'd fired a stream of magical bullets this way while tangling with Baiz. They were headed straight for Rebifor.

The surprised demon just managed to transform himself in time, opening a hole in his chest to let the projectiles pass through.

Now! I moved, thrusting my left hand out at Rebifor's face! He turned toward me again.

"Did you really think that would—"

"Elemekia—"

"—catch me off guard?!"

The hole in the demon's chest closed. When it did...

"Gaaaah!" Rebifor screamed.

In the moment Mileena's magic had distracted him, I'd thrown the sword in my right hand at exactly the right time. Rebifor had looked down at the hole that he'd opened in his own chest, then turned his attention to me—or rather, the spell I was about to fire. He'd then started filling the hole in his chest almost unconsciously... right around the sword I'd just thrown into it. A sword enchanted with an Astral Vine spell.

And just as Rebifor screamed, I finished incanting my words of power. "—Lance!"

Bwoosh! This time, distracted by the pain in his chest, Rebifor really did get his head blown off.

Luke suddenly stopped in the middle of his backward retreat. He tossed his blade aside… and rushed at Rikakizu! The demon, confused by the sudden change, was momentarily stunned.

"Ruby-Eye Blade!" Luke's voice rang out.

The next instant… Luke vertically bisected Rikakizu, a ruby-red blade glimmering in his hands.

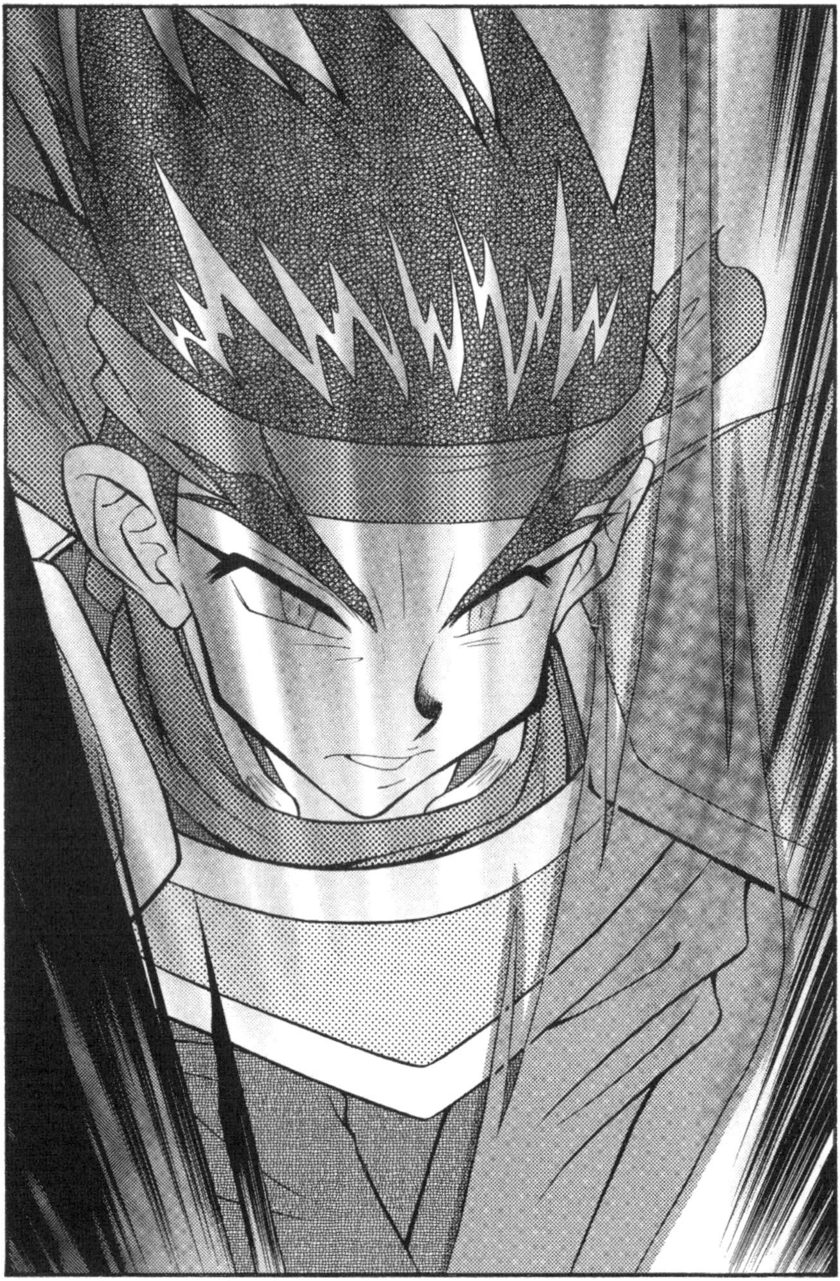

Baiz's arm swept through the air.

Has he realized it?

Mileena readily dodged the magical blast Baiz silently released with the swing.

Guess not...

Mileena wasn't trying to defeat him, but to hold his attention while aiding her allies. She was only firing off spells when there was another opponent behind Baiz. Sometimes it was a demidemon, and sometimes it was Rebifor.

Baiz failed to realize he was the only demon left in the room—right up until I shot a spell dead into his back.

Chapter 4: The Ancient Dragon Knows the Dynast Army's Plans

"I think… it's over," Luke whispered.

"Here, at least," Mileena replied.

As for Jade… Jade just stood there, still and silent, gazing at the fallen Grancis. If his nature were really more similar to a lesser or brass demon than a pure one, a normal sword would be enough to do him in. And sure enough, Grancis had been felled by Gourry's blade even after he'd expended the magic within. As we watched, his body crumbled in the manner of demons both demi and pure, leaving no trace behind.

"Ah… er…" Gourry stammered, clearly at a loss over what to say.

Jade turned to him and bowed. "Thank you for what you've done."

Still unsure of how to respond, Gourry stood there in silence, scratching his head.

Jade straightened up, then looked around and said, "Let's proceed." His voice was firm and his face resolute. "To the office. To Sherra."

Waaaaaaaaaaaah… aaaaaaaah…

"Is that… screaming?" Mileena asked quietly as we ran down the hall en route to the office.

We'd reached an area of the palace where only the king and his closest aides were normally allowed, and I gotta say… it was *way* drearier than I expected. The place was mainly unadorned stone walls punctuated only by the occasional sconce. A persistent howling echoed down the dimly lit corridor, its source unclear. Frankly speaking, it was eerie as hell.

"All I hear's the wind," Luke said indifferently.

"But it really does sound like a voice…" Gourry added, equally indifferent despite the inherent creepiness of what he was suggesting.

"The wailing of King Dils..." Jade whispered.

"What's that?" My ears pricked up.

"Oh! It's an old ghost story," Jade replied, quickly waving me off. "People like to say that the former king is still alive, locked away somewhere, the victim of a demon's curse..."

I'd heard that story myself. Twenty years ago, King Dils II had gone to slay the Kataart demons and returned to the castle afflicted by a curse known as Raugnut Rushavna. The curse had transformed him into a writhing mass of flesh, immortal yet eternally in pain. To this day, he supposedly remained shut away in the depths of the castle, howling ceaselessly, unable to die...

"But I think the tale is really just a way to account for the sound of the wind blowing through the halls," Jade concluded.

That would be a fitting explanation, but the rumor seemed plausible to me. Everyone knew that the old king had gone to slay demons and was never seen again. And I personally knew that demons were real—Raugnut Rushavna too. If I'm being honest, part of me wanted to go find out if there was any truth to the myth... but this was no time for a side quest.

"Oh, right. Gourry, draw your sword again. Everyone else step back," I said and chanted a spell. "Blast Ash!"

Bwoosh! Darkness enveloped the sword, coalescing on its steel and spreading across it briefly before the blade returned to its silver sheen.

Okay, now his magic sword's all charged up! Not that I expect Blast Ash to do much against the likes of Sherra...

"This'll affect a decently wide area... probably a little larger than an adult's arm span, so don't unleash it on an enemy if any of us are too close by. Got that?"

"Yeah, got it," the big lug responded casually, sheathing his sword.

Do you, though? If he accidentally hit one of us with that spell, his usual offhand apologies weren't gonna cut it...

"Say, do you really know where this office is?" Luke asked as we continued forth.

Jade replied hesitantly, "I think so..."

"You think so, huh?"

"Well, as we left the audience chamber, I saw placards marking the antechambers and such. Now, I was just a low-ranked knight and I never visited his office myself, but I've never heard of anyone getting lost looking for it."

Not that anyone who did *get lost would be eager to cop to it…*

Fortunately, the hall ahead was a straight shot for the most part. We hit a branching path here and there, but none of them were particularly long, suggesting it would be harder to get lost than not. I also couldn't really imagine that our destination would be deliberately secreted away.

"Oh, right, Jade. Let's get this squared away in advance," I said while running. "That Allus guy said Sherra was with the king, right?"

"Yes, I recall that."

"So when we get into the room, the first thing I want you to do is grab him and make tracks."

"Huh?!" Jade stopped in place, incredulous. "W-Wait a minute! I want to fight with you! I won't be a burden, I swear!"

"It's not about that," I said, hurriedly waving my hands. I mean, yeah, I did think Sherra was a bit out of Jade's league… But for that matter, I wasn't confident that the rest of us stood a chance against her either. "All I'm saying is that if we're gonna throw down, *someone* has to get the king to safety. We can't just be chucking spells willy-nilly while he's in the room, right? Sherra might even use him as a hostage! Someone needs to get him out of the danger zone, but the four of us have neither the desire nor the duty to do the deed in a pleasant manner. We're here to beat Sherra, not save the king. So the task falls to you."

"B-But…" Jade argued, redoubling his pace to catch up to us.

"What? You'd rather fight, even if it means the king dies?"

"No! Obviously, I can't let that happen…"

"Right? That's why this is on you. Of course, the king trusts Sherra, so I doubt he'll be inclined to just do what we tell him… If you really want to get him to safety, you'll probably have to knock him out and drag him away."

Jade fell silent at my words. "Very well. I'll get him to safety, then return as fast as I can to join the battle. Is that acceptable?"

"That's not what I'm saying, man…"

He wants to fight that bad, huh? Sherra was far more powerful than Jade imagined… possibly even more than Luke and Mileena imagined. She wasn't gonna go down with one good stab from some piddly magic sword.

I sighed. "If you want to make sure the king is secured, you have to get him out of the castle. Out of the city, even. If we catch Sherra in a *destroying* mood rather than a *fighting* one, nowhere within the outer walls is safe."

"Surely you exaggerate…"

"Hardly. And think about it. Those demons we fought in the audience chamber… You really think that's all the goons they have?"

"You mean there are more?"

"Entirely possible. These guys want this nation in their control for some reason, which means they won't let the king go without a fight. Who's to say they won't send a goon squad after him once you drop him off somewhere and come running back?"

"That's… a good point."

"And it's like you told that guy… What was his name again? The dude who took us in. Gatekeeper No. 1."

"Maias?"

"Yeah, him. It's like you told Gatekeeper No. 1. Even stripped of rank, you still have the heart of a knight. And a knight's job is to defend his king, right?" I shot Jade a wink.

"Ah…" he breathed, then smiled slightly. "Yes, that's true. Very well! I, Jade Caudwell, hereby reswear my sacred oath to protect His Majesty Wells Xeno Gyria with my life!"

Attaboy.

"You'd better be ready to follow through on that sacred oath of yours," said Luke, coming to a stop and looking back. There was now a door in view at the end of the long hallway with light streaming through its cracks. "Looks like we're here."

The plaque on the door declared it an office, so we knew we were in the right place.

Knowing what I did, we couldn't risk this dragging on for too long. Sherra wasn't called the General of the Dynast for nothing. She was hellaciously strong. So much so that a single blow from her would kill any of us on the spot. And once one of us fell, the rest would follow like dominoes.

In other words, the outcome of the fight ahead boiled down to a solitary question: Would Sherra obliterate one of us before our teamwork could best her? Either way, it would be a short match. The only uncertainty was who would be left standing when it was over.

We all exchanged a silent nod, and then... *Wham!* Gourry kicked in the door, his sword at the ready.

The room beyond was far bigger than I was expecting. Just ahead of us sat a large dark oak desk stacked with papers, beyond which were a man and a woman. The man was presumably King Wells. He looked to be in his mid-thirties, with long black hair and a solid build. I had to admit, he had the aura of a leader... He didn't strike me as the kind of guy who'd succumb to Sherra's feminine wiles or magical influence, but as they say, it's the ones you don't suspect that are the most dangerous.

Kneeling not far behind him was a figure clad in a blue dress uniform with silver embroidery. Her long hair was done in a braid, and she carried a black longsword. The two seemed the spitting image of a king and his loyal knight. But this knight's true master wasn't the lord of this kingdom... it was the lord of darkness!

"Who are you people?" the man boomed, seemingly uncowed as he stood from his chair.

Jade immediately went down on one knee. "Jade Caudwell, formerly of the Blue Knights. I came here against your wishes... Please forgive my impudence."

"Jade... Caudwell? Ah, yes. One of General Grancis's sons, aren't you? I believe I ordered you exiled, did I not?"

"Indeed, my liege. But the clear corruption in our kingdom behooved me—"

"Silence, traitor!" the knight—Sherra—interrupted. Slowly, she rose to her feet, her eyes fixed sharply in his direction. "Are you the one stirring chaos in the castle? What are you after? My liege's life?!" she barked.

Smart little demon... Sowing the idea that we were here to kill the king all but guaranteed he wouldn't listen to a word we said.

"My liege, you must believe—" Jade pressed.

"Silence!" Sherra shouted, interrupting him. "Do not dirty your ears with their lies, my lord. I beg of you, take your leave. I shall dispose of them posthaste."

"Please do. I'm counting on you," King Wells agreed placidly without any sign of misgivings.

She took a knee again and kissed the back of his hand. "I swear it upon the sword that serves you."

And as she rose once more, Wells turned around and manipulated something on the wall. *Thunk.* With a low sound, a partition in the back opened.

Of course... Every good palace has a couple secret escape routes.

"Majesty!" Jade tried to follow after his king, but Gourry stopped him. "What?!"

"Don't be stupid! You'll be killed if you go now!"

Dude was right. Sherra was standing at the opening. *Rrrumble...* And with another heavy sound, the wall closed behind King Wells. I doubted there was any way to reopen it from here. But that didn't mean we should just give up on tracking him.

"Jade! Find General Allus! Work with him to get the king to safety!" I shouted.

"I shall!" Jade spun around and rushed out of the room.

A man of Allus's rank surely had to know all the castle's hidden passageways. If Jade apprised him of the situation, I was betting he'd be willing to lend us a hand.

"All righty." I turned my eyes back to our opponent. "Now it's just us and you... General Sherra."

Slowly, she returned my gaze. "I see... So Allus sided with you, did he?"

"He did. But boy, you sure are selling this whole loyal knight schtick... Kissing the king's hand and everything. Ever thought about quitting the demon business and taking up acting?"

"Is that all you have to say to me after all this time? What poor manners. You've been a fly in the ointment of my plans, Lina Inverse."

"Maybe your plans just kinda suck? You're the servant of Graushera and your name is Sherra, so if your schemes have a gimmick half as cheap as your name—"

"Silence!" Sherra roared angrily enough to quiet me. "Do not comment on my name!"

Ah, whoops. That one really ticked her off! I'd meant to talk trash, but that might have backfired. Maybe she'd asked Dynast about her name after all and gotten an answer like *"I just didn't care, teehee!"*

"That aside, you said I was a fly in the ointment of your plans..." I quickly changed the subject. "But what exactly *are* your plans? I know you've been lending Dulgoffa out here and there... Are you behind the demon hordes spawning across the region too?"

"I don't owe you an answer!" she said bluntly, then drew the black sword, Dulgoffa, smoothly from her belt.

Wuh, that was fast! She's got even less chill than the last time we tangled!

"This is... my last chance!" she said. I didn't know what she meant by that... but I didn't have time to wonder! Her aura of hostility was swelling!

She's coming!

Dulgoffa sliced through the air—*Vrum!*—producing a black shockwave on a beeline for us! We immediately scattered. The black wave tore through the room and destroyed the sturdy door on the other side.

"Fell Zaleyd!" Luke must have been cooking up a spell in advance, but the moment he unleashed it, Sherra dispersed it with a flick of her left hand.

"What?!" he shouted, stunned by the power of a top-class demon.

Mileena was right on his heels with a follow-up attack. "Elemekia Flame!" The blast, which could terminate a brass demon in one hit, was dispelled by an effortless swing of Sherra's sword. And then...

"Graaah!" Gourry dove in from the side while her arms were spread wide from blocking both spells. He wasn't about to let this opportunity slip by!

Slash! He sliced right through Sherra's torso, then swiftly leaped away... but Sherra's expression didn't change in the slightest. She just hurled a series of small magical projectiles after him. The big lug managed to evade them.

Figures... Gourry's slash didn't do a thing. The power of a Blast Ash couldn't put a scratch on her.

"This is freakin' ridiculous!" Luke complained.

"Yeah, just like Lina's been saying!" Gourry responded. "In which case..."

Whomm! Gourry swung his sword at Sherra again. She was well outside of its range, but for a moment, a darkness enveloped her and then disappeared. Gourry had unleashed the Blast Ash from his sword... and Sherra had completely no-sold it.

What did you think that was gonna accomplish, big guy?

Sherra didn't even spare the others a glance, just unleashed a shockwave at me as I chanted! I began a dash to the side. Sherra tore across the floor, keeping pace with me.

So she's after me first!

But she'd have the advantage at close range! The shortsword in my hand couldn't block the magical sword-slash-demon Dulgoffa! Gourry ran in from the side, thrust out his sword, and parried Sherra's shockwave with his blade!

Of course! He wants to absorb some of Sherra's power!

But could the sword take it?! The shockwave twined around the blade, and—*Crick!*—the metal screamed!

Is it hopeless after all? I lamented. But as I did, Gourry drew the sword back. Letting what remained of the shockwave's power slip past him, he put himself between Sherra and me.

"Keh!" Sherra breathed, withdrawing as she realized the property of Gourry's sword. And then...

"Dynast Blas!"

Krickakrack! I unleashed a magical thunderclap, amplified for good measure!

Sherra let out a silent cry as the lightning wreathed her body, and then... *Pop!* With a bursting sound, it dispersed.

"Hyahhh!" In that moment, Gourry slashed at her.

Clink! Dulgoffa rose to intercept his sword. The keening collision echoed through the room when the two blades met. But Gourry had the upper hand in terms of skill! After a few clashes, it was Sherra who leaped back.

"Hrah!" Gourry swung when she did, sending the shockwave she'd released moments ago flying back at her.

"Trivial!" Sherra mocked, dispersing it midair. She then produced more magical projectiles around her and—

"Ra Tilt!"

Bwooooosh! Mileena conjured a blue pillar of flame to engulf Sherra. Gourry sprinted forward, thrusting his sword into the silhouette within the fiery column.

"Did we do it?!" Mileena cried.

But the show wasn't over yet! All Gourry's sword pierced was a shadow—the old demonic lizard's tail trick! She'd left a fragment of her spirit form as bait while retreating into the astral plane. And then she reappeared...

Behind me?! I thought at first, but she was behind Mileena instead!

"Look out!" Gourry cried.

Sherra let fly her volley of magic projectiles. Mileena twisted in an attempt to dodge them, but...

Crash!

While she avoided the worst of the damage, one of her pauldrons was blown to pieces as the shockwave sent her flying back! Sherra pursued, and...

"Ruby-Eye Blade!" Luke produced a crimson magical blade and charged in to stop her!

Twice in one day?! That's gonna be pretty damned draining!

Magical shockwaves went flying as Dulgoffa clashed with Luke. His Ruby-Eye Blade would be the sharper of the two swords, but Dulgoffa could regenerate itself indefinitely so long as Sherra was around. In other words, Luke would run out of energy first!

That meant I had to make my move now, while Sherra was locked in place. I began reciting the incantation for my void sword, the Ragna Blade.

Will I make it in time?! As I watched Luke's magic sword wane with wicked speed, I figured the answer was *probably not.* I hadn't finished my spell yet.

At last, his crimson blade was extinguished. Dulgoffa swung down, and...

Slash! There was a flash of steel. Sherra's body pitched forward.

Gourry!

His earlier thrust hadn't been for nothing. He'd absorbed the Ra Tilt's power into his emptied blade. *Look at you, using your head for once, my man!* Even for a top-rank demon like Sherra, a blow like that had to smart.

Dulgoffa spilled out of her hand... and into Luke's freed one! *Hang on, wait a—*

"What?!" Sherra cried out in shock, just as...

Thunk! Luke pierced her with Dulgoffa!

"Ah..." A faint moan escaped her throat.

Luke quickly released the black blade and leaped back.

"...Ah..." Unsteadily, her own sword protruding from her stomach, Sherra began to lurch toward him. As she approached...

"Hahh!" The Ra Tilt Gourry unleashed from his sword tore into her.

Sherra was still standing... but not for long!

"Ragna..." She turned to face me. A shadow of doubt flashed through my mind, but I didn't have time to entertain it! "...Blade!"

The sword of void I summoned sliced straight through the General of the Dynast.

Plink... With a low, clear sound, the demonic blade snapped. As each piece hit the floor, it crumbled like parched earth. Dulgoffa was dying, having lost the source of its power—its master, Sherra.

"Well, we worked it out... I think," Luke whispered.

"Even so," Mileena scoffed, "grabbing that sword the way you did was reckless."

"Aw, Mileena! You really do care!"

"It might have possessed you, and then we would have had another enemy on our hands," she countered heartlessly.

"Aw..." Luke whimpered.

Mileena was right, though. If, in that moment, Sherra had ordered Dulgoffa to possess Luke, we would've been screwed for sure. I mean, not that she'd ever expected someone to swipe her sword and turn the damn thing against her...

Still, as a gal who'd pulled off more than her fair share of seat-of-the-pants nonsense, I really had to hand it to Luke.

"Well, at least that's over," Gourry said cheerfully.

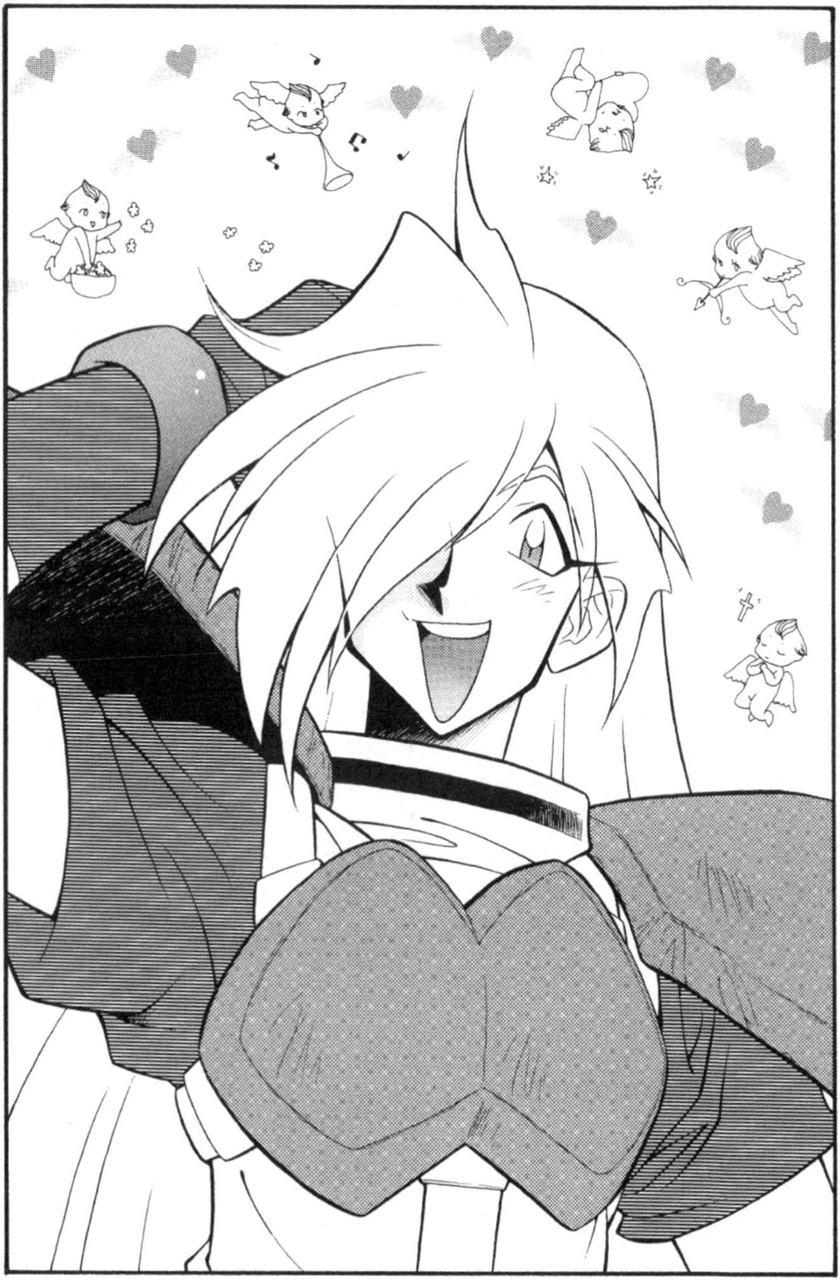

Except…

"What are you talking about? Now we have to straighten out all the political crap around the castle, and that ain't gonna be easy!" I reminded him.

"Right…" Luke and Mileena muttered in agreement.

But Gourry replied with his indefatigable smile, "Hahaha… Silly Lina. Thinky stuff is above my pay grade, so as far as *I'm* concerned, it's over!"

"That's not something to brag about!" I shouted as I gave Gourry a glorious sock to the face.

"So… what was the point of all that, anyway?" Luke whispered as if that question had only just occurred to him. "Sherra was tryin' to take over the kingdom and all, an' we stopped her by killing her. I get that much. But what was her endgame?"

Dude had a point.

It was now a few days later, after we'd departed Gyria City. The immediate danger was behind us. General Allus had gotten Sherra branded a spy from a hostile kingdom (though I was skeptical anyone really believed it), and he'd intervened to have Jade reinstated as a knight. The guy whose name I forgot—Gatekeeper No. 1 who'd sheltered us—netted himself a sizable reward, and we also bagged a little compensation for our work. (Not exactly *fair* compensation considering we'd slain the freakin' General of the Dynast… but whatever. I'm over it.) Once that was all worked out, General Allus had resigned from his post, and the Kingdom of Dils turned back to reconstruction. But…

Seriously, what was Sherra planning? We'd never uncovered what she was really up to, and that didn't sit right with me. It just felt like there *had* to be more to her scheme.

Moreover, I couldn't stop wondering… Had Sherra really given her all against us? I wasn't exaggerating when I'd told Jade that nowhere in the city would be safe if she got serious. Yet she'd only used a fraction of her power. Granted, we might've just managed to finish her off before she had the chance to flex. Had she thought she could beat us without using all her strength? Or was she so desperate to get the king under her thumb that she'd willingly restrained herself? Either way, the thing nagging at me the most was when I'd used the Ragna Blade to kill her…

Was it just my imagination... or was she smiling at me then?

Of course, I hadn't mentioned that part to anyone. Could've just been my eyes playing tricks on me, after all.

"Welp, we're not gonna think our way to an answer in this case," Gourry chimed in.

"When have you ever thought your way to an answer in *any* case?" I teased him. Nevertheless, the big lug was right.

"Not to change the subject, but we seem to be goin' in the same direction... Where are you guys headed next?" Luke asked idly, then clicked his tongue and wagged his finger at me. "Ah, but don't you dare say, 'Wherever you're going.' I don't need you hornin' in on me an' Mileena's honeymoon."

"This is not a honeym—" Mileena began, then stopped short.

We followed suit. We were currently walking east down the city road, a wide highway packed with pedestrians and carriages. It was flanked by forest, and from the woods came a sudden war cry...

"Hraaaagh!"

Kra-booooosh! A flying ball of fire took out a covered wagon up ahead. A cacophony of screams erupted around us.

"Rrrrrgh..." A growling lesser demon burst out of the brush—no, not just one! There was a second, then a third, and then... I could sense their presences among the trees all around us.

Another demidemon swarm? Was Sherra not behind them after all?! I didn't have time to dwell on the answer. The demons were tearing into the people on the road!

"Elemekia Lance!" The spell I chucked killed a lesser demon heading for a woman paralyzed by fear.

"Hyah!" With a cry, Gourry ran out, swinging his sword at the demons. Luke joined in, and so did Mileena.

We made it rain attack spells, but there were just too many targets! I also had no idea how many more demons were lingering in the woods... If they'd all been clustered up some distance away, I could blast the whole forest away with a Dragon Slave, but we were already in the thick of the onslaught.

To be honest, it was getting frickin' annoying! Demon charge, attack spell. Demon charge, attack spell. We were certainly chewing through the suckers, but they just kept a-comin'!

"Dynast Breath!" *Crack!* I blasted another demon as it lunged from the brush.

"H-Help me!" As I was chanting my next spell, a middle-aged traveler suddenly grabbed hold of my cape.

Hey! I get that you want help, but you gotta let me move, man! I thought to myself, but just as I was about to wrest my cape free... a brass demon roared out of the underbrush!

Ack! Not good! My spell wasn't ready yet! And I also had a dude clinging to me!

The brass demon locked eyes on me. Then... it was mowed down by a beam of light. *Kra-paaash!* The light's movement was lagged by a roar as it sent trees and demons alike flying.

That light...

Then came a second beam.

Is that... the white giant?! I realized, turning my eyes toward the origin of the light. When I did, there was another flash behind me. *Huh?!* I whipped back around, but the trees inhibited my view.

"Waaaaagh!" The man crawled away from me, clearly confused beyond comprehension.

It did seem like the giant was after the demons, but one hit from that thing was liable to roast us on the spot.

"What *is* that?!" Gourry shouted at me.

"I think it's the white giant!" I shouted back over the din.

"But there are two of them!"

"Yeah!"

"What do you mean, 'yeah'?!"

While we were discussing that... "Hey! Anyone think we maybe oughta get outta here?!" Luke called.

"I do!" Mileena agreed as they ran up to us.

"But there are still people around!" I objected.

"No there ain't!" Luke insisted.

I looked around and saw that we were, in fact, the only ones left. *Huh?! When did you little bastards...* The man who'd grabbed my cape, previously cowering helplessly on the ground, as well as the petrified woman were now booking it down the road like champion sprinters.

You just leave us holding the bag?! At least there was no reason to stick around now!

"Got it! Let's make tracks!"

"But Lina—"

"But what, Gourry?! FYI, if you say something dumb, I'll smack you down right here!"

"It's just... I think the attacks have stopped."

"...Huh?" Come to think of it, I couldn't hear any more smashy-roary around me. No further signs of demons in sight either. "Is it... over?"

"It is. For now," said a man from deep in the underbrush.

Huh?! Wait... I know that voice. I turned to see him just as he emerged from the flora. Indeed, it was exactly who I was thinking of—a handsome, blond middle-aged man in loose-fitting blue clothing.

"Master Milgazia?!" I was so shocked to see him that I couldn't help crying out.

A while back, in the midst of a different kerfuffle, I'd paid a visit to the towering Dragons' Peak in the north and met Milgazia, a golden dragon elder. He was a legit dragon, but he could also take on human form, and when he did, this was how he appeared.

Aha... I assumed that last blast of light was from the white giant, but it was actually a golden dragon's laser breath.

Still, what was Milgazia doing off Dragons' Peak?

"I heard familiar voices and names," he said. "And indeed, here you are. It's been a while, human girl. You too, human man."

"Long time no see," Gourry replied, scratching the back of his head.

"Don't tell me you don't remember him," I said.

Gourry looked hurt. "Come on, of course I remember! He's that big lizard guy."

"Please do not call me a big lizard." Milgazia leaned in and stared straight into the big lug's face, his expression terribly serious.

"Ahhh, sorry, sorry!" Gourry apologized hastily.

"But I must say," Milgazia turned his eyes to Luke and Mileena, "your other two companions have changed their appearances a great deal."

"You got it all wrong!" exclaimed Gourry, waving his hands.

"Totally different people!" I followed suit.

"I am aware. It was a joke," Milgazia said, still stone-faced.

Guys... I so do not get dragon humor, okay?

"But if you're alive and well, then you must have conquered your previous trial," he continued.

"Yes, I'd say so," I replied, looking around. "But, uh, what's going on here? First it's demidemon swarms, and now a guy who's never left Dragons' Peak before is out in the world. I figure it's gotta be something serious, but..."

"Indeed," Milgazia muttered in assent, then cast a glance back at Luke and Mileena.

"Oh, don't worry about them," I assured him. "They're trustworthy. They helped us beat General Sherra."

"What?!" Milgazia looked understandably shocked. "You defeated... No, I suppose this isn't your first time surviving such an encounter, is it? Hmm," he said, then sank into thought.

"Hey... someone wanna fill us in here?" Luke asked.

"It's a long story. I'll catch you up later," I responded.

Soon after, Milgazia looked up again. "Yes, I see... If you promise to keep it among yourselves, I believe there is something I should share with you."

"Surely there's no need for *that*, Uncle Milgazia," came a piercing voice, this time from behind me. I turned to see a beautiful woman step out of the brush, moving so smoothly that she didn't even rustle the leaves. She looked about twenty years old, had long golden hair, and was wearing curiously designed white plate mail over loose-fitting blue clothing.

Now, I said she *looked* around twenty because she was undoubtedly much older. Those pointed ears and that skin like porcelain? Yeah, totally pegged her as an elf. Elves lived five or six times longer than humans and possessed magic many times more powerful, but they rarely showed themselves before our kind. If I had to guesstimate, I'd say she was probably a century old.

She continued to address Milgazia without even sparing us a glance. "Mere humans will be of no assistance whatsoever. They'll just spread more chaos, at best."

"*Mere* humans?" A vein bulged on Luke's brow, but she unsurprisingly paid him no mind.

"No more of that, Mephy," chided Milgazia. "As fellow inhabitants of these lands, they have a right to know. And they may very well be useful."

"But..."

"I've made my decision. I'm going to tell them," he declared simply.

"Very well..." this so-called Mephy agreed grudgingly.

"Pardon the interruption. She has little fondness for humans."

"I can tell," I said with a shrug.

Once upon a time, humans had persecuted elves. That was ages ago in human terms, but to someone much longer-lived, the wounds still probably felt fresh.

"Now, where to start... I needn't tell you of the recent rash of lesser and other low-tier demon spawnings. They seem to be acting primarily as an arm of Dynast Graushera's army, and I've seen a similar pattern once before."

"A similar pattern?"

"Yes. Demidemons spawning, fear running rampant among the populace... Said fear seeds war, which in turn seeds further chaos. Dynast wasn't responsible last time, but given the similarity of the circumstances, I imagine the goal is the same."

"What goal?" I asked.

Milgazia was silent for just a moment. He then said gravely, "Another Incarnation War."

Afterword

Scene: Author + L

Au: Another reprint in the can! That's *The Dynast Plot*!

L: It seems the readers spent a lot of time between publications imagining my awesome adventures! I received forty thousand letters describing their ideas!

Au: Yeah, right! This was a simultaneous reprint—three volumes at once! There's literally no time for that to have happened! You're lying your ass off!

L: Erk! You got me!

Au: I sure did! Besides, what was the title? "L vs. the Beautiful Innkeepers Nationwide: Kansai Chapter"? That sounds like it would just be about you complaining about the innkeepers at various destinations and picking fights with them.

L: Ye of little imagination! As an example, let's integrate battle manga elements! My master is killed, so I set out on a quest to find the culprit! I fight tofu in Kyoto, then spend three days training at Mt. Rokko to hunt the nefarious Kobe beef. And at last in Osaka, there's a violent clash over whether it's okay to eat okonomiyaki with rice! An ally comes to save me in my time of need! I drive them away without hesitation!

Au: You drive them away?!

L: There could be some romance too! I travel alone to Kyoto, where I happen to meet some fine tofu and we share a steamy encounter—

Au: Wait a minute here. You can describe it like a battle or like a porno, but all you're doing is eating tofu! The beautiful innkeeper never actually appears!

L: Who cares?

Au: Who cares?! It's in the freaking title!

L: Those don't have to be totally accurate as long as it comes around in the end. Maybe after all that, I return to my inn where I meet the beautiful innkeeper, and we have a fight about our difficult life experiences.

Au: What kind of book is that?! It'll just depress your readers! Moreover, is it really okay for that to be the only place the book's namesake matters?

L: Oh, chill out. You called this book "The Dynast Plot," and that only becomes relevant when the stupid dad-joke dragon comes along at the end to say Dynast might be up to something. We'll only find out in later volumes if he's right or not!

Au: Erk! Well, it's pretty common for me to get close to finishing my manuscript and still not know the subtitle. It's also pretty common for me to choose a random title for something and end up with a story that doesn't really match. That may be why, when I'm choosing stories for the short story collections, I'm just looking at a list of titles and going, "Wait, what happened in these?"

L: So it's okay if the beautiful innkeeper only makes a cameo, right?

Au: Erk! Okay... fine, you're right.

L: I could also make it a mystery! Strange serial murders occur wherever I go!

Au: That's pretty cliche... but it might be more interesting than your other proposals.

L: I never learn the culprit!

Au: Hang on a minute! Aren't you supposed to solve the mystery?!

L: Huh? Why should I? Crimes are for the police to solve, yeesh.

Au: Okay, that's totally valid! But it's still supposed to be a mystery, yeah?

L: So? Mysteries are *about* the mystery. In other words, mystery is all you need. Who said you have to solve anything?

Au: Argh! There was that old *X-Files* show that was a mystery series, but the culprits always ended up being aliens or other strange creatures. But wait! If there are murders everywhere you go, doesn't that suggest *you're* the killer?

L: Oh, please. By that logic, the culprit in every detective series would be the detective. It's all just a coincidence. But if you insist on finding out who the murderer is, maybe I'll catch a news report at the next inn revealing that they caught the culprit. They'll even reveal the motive!

Au: That's not very exciting.

L: Well, I've given you plenty of material to work with. The readers can run with that to imagine more of my adventures!

Au: You call that material? Guys, don't fall for this. It'll just make her more insufferable.

L: I'm counting on you, everyone!

Afterword: Over.

J-Novel Club Lineup

Latest Ebook Releases Series List

The Apothecary Diaries
An Archdemon's Dilemma:
    How to Love Your Elf Bride*
Ascendance of a Bookworm*
Backstabbed in a Backwater
    Dungeon
Bibliophile Princess*
Black Summoner*
BLADE & BASTARD: Warm ash,
    Dusky dungeon
By the Grace of the Gods
Campfire Cooking in Another
    World with My Absurd Skill*
A Cave King's Road to Paradise:
    Climbing to the Top with My
    Almighty Mining Skills!*
The Conqueror from a Dying
    Kingdom
Cooking with Wild Game*
The Coppersmith's Bride**
D-Genesis: Three Years after the
    Dungeons Appeared
Dahlia in Bloom: Crafting a Fresh
    Start with Magical Tools
Death's Daughter and the Ebony
    Blade
Did I Seriously Just Get
    Reincarnated as My Gag
    Character?!*
The Disowned Queen's Consulting
    Detective Agency
Doll-Kara**
Dragon Daddy Diaries: A Girl
    Grows to Greatness
Endo and Kobayashi Live! The
    Latest on Tsundere Villainess
    Lieselotte*
Enough with This Slow Life! I Was
    Reincarnated as a High Elf and
    Now I'm Bored
The Faraway Paladin*
Forget Being the Villainess, I Want
    to Be an Adventurer!
Full Metal Panic!
Full Clearing Another World under
    a Goddess with Zero Believers*
Fushi no Kami: Rebuilding
    Civilization Starts With a Village*
Grand Sumo Villainess
The Great Cleric
Gushing over Magical Girls**
Haibara's Teenage New Game+

Hell Mode
Holmes of Kyoto
Housekeeping Mage from Another
    World: Making Your Adventures
    Feel Like Home!*
How a Realist Hero Rebuilt the
    Kingdom*
I Parry Everything: What Do You
    Mean I'm the Strongest? I'm Not
    Even an Adventurer Yet!*
I Shall Survive Using Potions!*
I'm Capped at Level 1?! Thus
    Begins My Journey to Become
    the World's Strongest Badass!*
The Ideal Sponger Life
In Another World With My
    Smartphone
Infinite Dendrogram*
Invaders of the Rokujouma!?
The Invincible Little Lady
Isekai Tensei: Recruited to Another
    World*
Karate Master Isekai**
Lady Rose Just Wants to Be a
    Commoner!
A Late-Start Tamer's Laid-Back Life
Let This Grieving Soul Retire
The Magician Who Rose From
    Failure
Making Magic: The Sweet Life of
    a Witch Who Knows an Infinite
    MP Loophole
Min-Maxing My TRPG Build in
    Another World
The Misfit of Demon King Academy
My Daughter Left the Nest and
    Returned an S-Rank Adventurer
My Friend's Little Sister Has It
    In for Me!
My Quiet Blacksmith Life in
    Another World
My Instant Death Ability is So
    Overpowered, No One in This
    Other World Stands a Chance
    Against Me!*
My Next Life as a Villainess: All
    Routes Lead to Doom!
Now I'm a Demon Lord! Happily
    Ever After with Monster Girls in
    My Dungeon*
Oversummoned, Overpowered,
    and Over It!*

A Pale Moon Reverie
Peddler in Another World: I Can
    Go Back to My World Wheneᵥ
    I Want!*
Perry Rhodan NEO
Re:RE — Reincarnator Executionᵉ
Reborn to Master the Blade: Froɪ
    Hero-King to Extraordinary
    Squire ♀*
Rebuild World*
Record of Wortenia War*
Reincarnated as an Apple: This
    Forbidden Fruit Is Forever
    Unblemished!
A Royal Rebound: Forget My
    Ex-Fiancé, I'm Being Pampereᵈ
    by the Prince!
Seirei Gensouki: Spirit Chroniclesᵢ
Seventh
The Skull Dragon's Precious
    Daughter**
Slayers
Sometimes Even Reality Is a Lie!*
Survival Strategies of a Corrupt
    Aristocrat
Sweet Reincarnation**
The Tales of Marielle Clarac*
Tearmoon Empire*
To Another World... with Land
    Mines!
The Unwanted Undead
    Adventurer*
VTuber Legend: How I Went Viral
    after Forgetting to Turn Off Mᵧ
    Stream
Welcome to Japan, Ms. Elf!*
When Supernatural Battles Becaɾ
    Commonplace
The World's Least Interesting
    Master Swordsman
Young Lady Albert Is Courting
    Disaster*
Yuri Tama: From Third Wheel to
    Trifecta

...and more!
* Novel and Manga Editions
** Manga Only
Keep an eye out at j-novel.club
    for further new title
    announcements!